THE SOCIAL PSYCHOLOGY OF HUMOR

This important new book provides a comprehensive analysis of humor from a social-psychological perspective, addressing questions about the use of humor and its effects in daily life. It examines the social psychology of humor on micro-level phenomena, such as attitudes, persuasion, and social perception, as well as exploring its use and effect on macro-level phenomena like conformity, group processes, cohesion, and intergroup relations.

Humor is inherently a social experience, shared among people, essential to nearly every type of interpersonal relationship. In this accessible volume, Strick and Ford review current research and new theoretical advancements to identify pressing open questions and propose new directions for future research in the social psychology of humor. The book explores fascinating topics such as humor in advertising, political satire, and the importance of a sense of humor in maintaining romantic relationships. It also examines how racist or sexist humor can affect personal and intergroup relations and discusses how to confront inappropriate jokes.

Offering new, precise, and operational conceptions of humor in social processes, this book will be an essential reading for students and academics in social psychology, media, and communication studies.

Madelijn Strick is an Associate Professor of Social Psychology at Utrecht University in the Netherlands. She teaches courses on social influence and communication. She has published extensively on the psychology of advertising, focusing (among other subjects) on the impact of humor, being moved, and narrative transportation.

Thomas E. Ford is a Professor of Psychology at Western Carolina University, USA. He is a former Editor-in-Chief of HUMOR: *International Journal of Humor Research*. His research interests include the role of disparagement humor in promoting expressions of prejudice and the relationship between humor and subjective well-being.

Current Issues in Social Psychology
Series Editor: Johan Karemmans

Current Issues in Social Psychology is a series of edited books that reflect the state of current and emerging topics of interest in social psychology.

Each volume is tightly focused on a particular topic and consists of seven to ten chapters contributed by international experts. The editors of individual volumes are leading figures in their areas and provide an introductory overview.

The series is useful reading for students, academics, and researchers of social psychology and related disciplines. Example topics include: self-esteem, mindfulness, evolutionary social psychology, minority groups, social neuroscience, cyberbullying and social stigma.

Current Directions in Ostracism, Social Exclusion and Rejection Research
Edited by Selma Rudert, Rainer Greifeneder & Kipling Williams

New Directions in the Psychology of Close Relationships
Edited by Dominik Schoebi & Belinda Campos

The Psychology of Food Marketing and Overeating
Edited by Frans Folkvord

Psychological Perspectives on Praise
Edited by Eddie Brummelman

The Psychology of Political Polarization
Edited by Jan-Willem van Prooijen

The Social Psychology of Humor
Edited by Madelijn Strick and Thomas E. Ford

THE SOCIAL PSYCHOLOGY OF HUMOR

Edited by Madelijn Strick and Thomas E. Ford

LONDON AND NEW YORK

First published 2021
by Routledge
2 Park Square, Milton Park, Abingdon, Oxon OX14 4RN

and by Routledge
52 Vanderbilt Avenue, New York, NY 10017

Routledge is an imprint of the Taylor & Francis Group, an informa business

© 2021 selection and editorial matter, Madelijn Strick and Thomas E. Ford; individual chapters, the contributors

The right of Madelijn Strick and Thomas E. Ford to be identified as the authors of the editorial material, and of the authors for their individual chapters, has been asserted in accordance with sections 77 and 78 of the Copyright, Designs and Patents Act 1988.

All rights reserved. No part of this book may be reprinted or reproduced or utilised in any form or by any electronic, mechanical, or other means, now known or hereafter invented, including photocopying and recording, or in any information storage or retrieval system, without permission in writing from the publishers.

Trademark notice: Product or corporate names may be trademarks or registered trademarks and are used only for identification and explanation without intent to infringe.

British Library Cataloguing-in-Publication Data
A catalogue record for this book is available from the British Library

Library of Congress Cataloging-in-Publication Data
Names: Strick, Madelijn, 1979- editor.
Title: The social psychology of humor / edited by Madelijn Strick and Thomas E. Ford.
Description: Abingdon, Oxon; New York, NY : Routledge, 2021. | Series: Current issues in social psychology | Includes bibliographical references and index. |
Identifiers: LCCN 2020048033 (print) | LCCN 2020048034 (ebook) | ISBN 9780367487195 (hbk) | ISBN 9780367487188 (pbk) | ISBN 9781003042440 (ebk)
Subjects: LCSH: Wit and humor--Psychological aspects. | Wit and humor--Social aspects. | Social psychology.
Classification: LCC BF575.L3 S655 2021 (print) | LCC BF575.L3 (ebook) | DDC 152.4/3--dc23

LC record available at https://lccn.loc.gov/2020048033
LC ebook record available at https://lccn.loc.gov/2020048034

ISBN: 978-0-367-48719-5 (hbk)
ISBN: 978-0-367-48718-8 (pbk)
ISBN: 978-1-003-04244-0 (ebk)

Typeset in Bembo
by MPS Limited, Dehradun

CONTENTS

List of Figures	*vii*
List of Contributors	*viii*
Preface	*ix*
Madelijn Strick and Thomas E Ford	

PART I
Individual social psychological processes   **1**

1 How humor can promote central-route persuasion:
  The role of ambivalence   3
  Madelijn Strick

2 Political humor   20
  Jody C. Baumgartner

3 Paradoxical thinking as a paradigm of attitude change:
  Comparison to satire and the role of humor (or lack thereof)   39
  Boaz Hameiri

PART II
Interpersonal relationships   **55**

4 Uniting and dividing in personal interactions: Four key
  functions of humor in communication   57
  John Meyer

vi Contents

5　Humor and long-term romantic relationships　　　　　　74
　　Jeffrey Hall

6　Humor and figurative language: Good for a laugh,
　　and more　　　　　　　　　　　　　　　　　　　　92
　　Herbert L. Colston

PART III
Group processes　　　　　　　　　　　　　　　　　　**109**

7　Workplace humor: The good, the bad, and the
　　non-existent　　　　　　　　　　　　　　　　　　　111
　　Barbara Plester

8　Humor competence in the classroom　　　　　　　　　130
　　Ann B. Frymier and Melissa B. Wanzer

PART IV
Intergroup relations　　　　　　　　　　　　　　　　**149**

9　Disparagement humor and prejudice: Advances in theory
　　and research　　　　　　　　　　　　　　　　　　　151
　　Thomas E. Ford and Andrew R. Olah

10　Cavalier humor beliefs: Dismissing jokes as 'just jokes'
　　facilitates prejudice and internalizes negativity among
　　targets　　　　　　　　　　　　　　　　　　　　　170
　　Gordon Hodson and Elvira Prusaczyk

11　Addressing the challenges of confronting disparagement
　　humor　　　　　　　　　　　　　　　　　　　　　189
　　Julie A. Woodzicka and Robyn K. Mallett

Index　　　　　　　　　　　　　　　　　　　　　　*206*

FIGURES

1.1	Illustration of the pairing of a brand with humor and non-humor in the 'magazine paradigm' used in Strick et al. (2009, Experiment 3)	8
1.2	Illustration of the proposed theoretical model	13
1.3	Graphic illustration of the mediating effect of heightened elaboration between emotional ambivalence and persuasion on high-involvement topics in Strick and Weijers (2017). $\star p < .05$, $\star\star p < .01$, $\star\star\star p < .001$	15
5.1	Three Dimensional Model of humor in romantic relationships	79
8.1	Instructional humor processing theory	139
9.1	Prejudiced norm theory: The effect of disparagement humor for people high in prejudice against the targeted group	153
9.2	Disparagement humor expands the bounds of acceptable behaviour to include responses that would otherwise be considered wrong or inappropriate	155
10.1	The Group-Dominance Model of Humor Appreciation, depicting how Cavalier Humor Beliefs facilitate 'favorable' reactions to outgroup-disparaging humor, which in turn exacerbate outgroup prejudice. Thicker paths through inoffensiveness/harmlessness indicate primary theoretical mechanism. Reproduced with permission from Hodson and MacInnis (2016)	176
10.2	A visual depiction several strategies to delegitimize others. Reproduced with permission from Hodson and MacInnis (2016)	182

CONTRIBUTORS

Jody C. Baumgartner, East Carolina University, USA
Herbert L. Colston, University of Alberta, Canada
Thomas E. Ford, Western Carolina University, USA
Ann B. Frymier, Ohio University, USA
Jeffrey Hall, The University of Kansas, USA
Boaz Hameiri, University of Pennsylvania, USA
Gordon Hodson, Brock University, Canada
Robyn K. Mallett, Loyola University Chicago, USA
John Meyer, University of Southern Mississippi, USA
Andrew R. Olah, Western Carolina University, USA
Barbara Plester, The University of Auckland, New Zealand
Elvira Prusaczyk, Brock University, Canada
Madelijn Strick, Utrecht University, The Netherlands
Melissa B. Wanzer, Canisius College, USA
Julie A. Woodzicka, Washington and Lee University, USA

PREFACE

Madelijn Strick and Thomas E. Ford

Dr. [Martin Luther] King was a human being. He had a sense of humor which was wonderful.

As the quote above suggests, humor is a fundamental human experience. It is, however, a concept that historically has eluded a precise and widely accepted definition, as scholars and laypeople alike use the term in many different ways. Ruch (1998) noted that a single definition of humor that scholars across—or even within—disciplines consensually accept and use does not exist. Accordingly, in their textbook, *The Psychology of Humor: An Integrative Approach*, Martin and Ford (2018) define humor very broadly to represent any phenomena related to the experience:

> Humor is a broad, multifaceted term that represents anything that people say or do that others perceive as funny and tends to make them laugh, as well as the mental processes that go into both creating and perceiving such an amusing stimulus, and also the emotional response of mirth involved in the enjoyment of it.
>
> *(Martin & Ford, 2018, p. 3)*

As a fundamental human experience, humor is inherently social, shared among people, and woven into the fabric of nearly every type of interpersonal relationship (Lefcourt, 2001; Martin & Ford, 2018). Indeed, a substantial body of research has shown that humor plays an integral and complex role in shaping the way we understand and interact with the social world. Thus, humor is a critical and relevant topic of social psychology.

Allport (1985) defined social psychology as the scientific attempt to explain how the *thoughts, feelings,* and *behaviours* of individuals are influenced by the *actual, imagined,* or *implied* presence of others (p. 5). Social psychologists, then, consider all the dynamic relationships between individuals and the people they interact with, both real and imagined, studying anything that contributes to an understanding of how people affect one another's thoughts, feelings, and behaviours (Baumeister & Finkel, 2010). Accordingly, social psychology offers a unique approach to the study of humor, addressing questions about *how* people use humor in daily life and *to what effect*.

Social psychologists and scholars in related disciplines have investigated the social uses and effects of humor at different "levels of analysis," relating to how broadly they conceptualise the social environment. From the narrowest perspective, scholars have studied the effects of humor on the psychological processes of the individual, investigating how humor shapes attitudes, feelings, and beliefs, as well as perceptions of others. Focusing more broadly on interpersonal relationships, scholars have studied how humor affects the quality of people's interactions and relationships with others. Still more broadly, researchers have investigated the patterns of humor used among people in larger group (organisational) contexts and the consequences of humor for group processes. Finally, scholars have addressed the role of humor in shaping the way people perceive and interact with others in intergroup settings.

Despite the universality of humor in the human experience and the integral role it plays in social relationships, social psychologists historically have given it little attention. We conducted a *PsycINFO* search using the classification codes, "Social Psychology," "Group & Interpersonal Processes," and "Social Perception & Cognition" to track the number of peer-reviewed journal articles published with the words "humor," "humour," "humor" or "laughter" in their titles by decade from 1900 to 2020. Our search revealed that social psychological research on humor was sporadic at best prior to 1970; only 20 articles were published between 1900 and 1969. However, with the emergence of positive psychology, there was a notable escalation of research on humor in social psychology (as well as personality and developmental psychology) in the 1970s (see Martin & Ford, 2018, for a more complete discussion). 39 social psychology articles were published in the 1970s, an increase of 875% over the four published in the previous decade, and a 95% increase over the 20 articles published in the previous 69 years. Another notable surge occurred in the 2000s that continues to the present day: 63 articles were published between 2000 and 2009 (an increase of 117% over the 29 published in the previous decade) and 106 between 2010 and June 2020.

Although the increasing number of peer-reviewed research conducted on humor over the last four decades is encouraging, there are some indications that humor is still regarded as a peripheral or "special" topic rather than one that has a central importance in mainstream social psychology. We searched the subject index of eight social psychology textbooks published between 2015 and 2020. Six of the eight textbooks briefly mentioned humor alluding to it as a positive personality trait, an emotion regulation strategy, persuasion technique, or a relationship maintenance strategy. None of the books, however, treated humor as an important topic in its own right. In fact, the term "humor" appeared in the index of only two of the eight textbooks. Similarly, authoritative, scholarly reference works allude to humor in a cursory manner, if at all. For instance, the 2016 *APA Handbook of Personality and Social Psychology*, spanning more than 2,700 pages, included only six sentences about a sense of humor and cited only six empirical studies (Martin & Ford, 2018). Similarly, the *Handbook of Social Psychology* (Fiske, Gilbert, & Lindzey, 2010) that contains 37 chapters—each written by an authoritative scholar in the field addressing different topics central to the study of social psychology—included references to only three empirical works on humor.

Martin and Ford (2018) argued that psychologists tend to relegate humor to secondary importance, in part, because of its non-serious nature; many views it as too frivolous for serious academic study. Consistent with this notion, McGhee (2010) concluded from a personal conversation that most psychologists are simply interested in more serious topics. Also, the complexity of humor and the difficulty of precisely defining it in a way that derives clear operational definitions could deter scientific investigation.

We propose, however, that the frivolity and complexity of humor contribute to the myriad of ways people experience it in interpersonal relationships and broader social contexts, underscoring rather than obviating the need for scholars to subject it to rigorous, scientific inquiry. Furthermore, as the current volume demonstrates, the cumulative efforts of social psychologists and scholars in related disciplines over the past four decades have made significant advances in theory and research on the social psychology of humor, illuminating the integral role that humor plays in the social-psychological experience.

This volume consists of 11 chapters that present state-of-the-art research on the social psychology of humor. We have organised the chapters into four parts according to the use and effects of humor among people in the social environment at different "levels of analysis." Each chapter reviews current research and new theoretical advancements, offering new, precise, and testable conceptions of humor in social processes and ends with a discussion of next steps for future research. The intended audience of this book are students and well-established scholars of social psychology and related disciplines (e.g., communication, sociology, anthropology, marketing, etc.) seeking to conduct their own research on humor in social life.

The first part of the book emphasises the role of humor in the psychological processes of the individual. In Chapter 1, Madelijn Strick presents research showing that humor has a strong persuasive potential. Persuasion researchers generally assume that humor is a positive emotion promoting peripheral-route persuasion in low-involvement contexts. In contrast, she proposes that humour often provokes mixed emotions (i.e. ambivalence) and, to an extent, encourages central-route persuasion in high-involvement contexts.

In Chapter 2 Jody Baumgartner examines research on the effects of political humor organised around four main political humor types: simple comedy, simple satire, complex satire, and self-deprecating humor. For each type, the chapter discusses the cognitive, attitudinal, and participatory effects that viewing has on individuals, as well as what we know about the reason viewership has these effects.

Then, in Chapter 3, Boaz Hameiri introduces a new approach to persuasion termed paradoxical thinking. Hameiri first introduces the paradoxical thinking conceptual framework. He then reviews supporting empirical evidence in the context of the Israeli-Palestinian conflict. He concludes the chapter by discussing the role humor might play in the paradoxical thinking process and the similarities and differences between paradoxical thinking messages and satire in promoting attitude change.

Part B addresses how humor affects the quality of people's interpersonal relationships. In Chapter 4 John Meyer proposes that the use of humor in interpersonal relationships falls along a continuum—from unifying, satisfying humor to dividing, uncomfortable humor. Meyer then elucidates four specific functions of humor along this continuum. He argues that all four functions of humor, however, serve to enhance creativity by presenting a perception of reality in new and unexpected ways, concluding that the major function served by all instances of humor may be to play.

Jeffrey Hall examines over 30 years of qualitative and quantitative research on the roles that humor plays in romantic relationships in Chapter 5 Hall explores whether people with different humor styles are more likely to experience romantic relationship satisfaction and the ways that one's partner's humor style relates to satisfaction. Accordingly, this chapter reviews the association between humor and other constructs relevant to romantic partners, such as partner embarrassment, stress relief and coping, teasing, and playfulness.

In Chapter 6, Herbert L. Colston examines the relationship between figurative language. In contrast to a traditional approach to understanding this relationship as a complex pragmatic effect produced by figurative language usage and comprehension, Colston adopts a newer and broader linguistic framework that views humor and figurative language as dance partners, as it were—one causing the other and the other causing the one, working together within a complex, highly interactive human social system in which we are compelled evolutionarily to inhabit.

More broadly, Part C addresses the use of humor among people in a larger group and organisational contexts. In Chapter 7, Barbara Plester explores the dynamics of humor in the workplace. Her ethnographic research shows that groups of people mostly navigate workplace humor successfully that it offers relief from pressurised work situations. However, while workgroups take care not to offend others through humor, this raises questions about whether humor is becoming overly 'politically correct' and is at risk of disappearing from work environments or only existing in its most insipid form. Plester reviews the complexity of workgroup humor dynamics, offers examples taken from actual workplaces, and speculates on the changing nature of humor at work.

Chapter 8, co-authored by Ann Bainbridge Frymier and Melissa Bekelja Wanzer, examines the functions of humor in an instructional setting, specifically the college classroom. The authors approach classroom humor from a competence perspective and argue that teachers should use humorous messages that are perceived by students as appropriate and effective (funny) to be competent users of humor. They provide a brief overview of communication competence, apply this framework to the teacher's use of humor in the classroom, and examine research on student perceptions of appropriate and inappropriate teacher humor. Then, they present original research testing the Instructional Humor Processing Theory as an explanation for why teacher humor is positively associated with student learning.

The last part, Part D, considers the role of humor in shaping the way people perceive and interact with others in intergroup settings. In Chapter 9, Thomas E. Ford and Andrew R. Olah review evidence that disparagement humor—humor that attempts to amuse through the denigration of a social group or individual (Ferguson & Ford, 2008)—can have a detrimental, exacerbating effect on intergroup prejudice in two ways. First, it *releases* or disinhibits prejudice by loosening the norms of a social setting to permit expressions of prejudice. Second, it *legitimises* prejudice by making targeted social groups seem more deserving of prejudice. Ford and Olah also propose that disparagement humor can have a beneficial consequence of *subverting* prejudice when people use it with constructive intentions.

In Chapter 10, Gordon Hodson and Elvira Prusaczyk review evidence showing that people higher in social dominance orientation or racism are drawn to the aggressive functions of humor. They present the Group-Based Dominance Model of Humor Appreciation, wherein Cavalier Humor Beliefs (CHB) (i.e. "jokes are just jokes" and are harmless) play a key role in promoting derision directed at low-status (but not high-status) outgroups and, in turn, exacerbate prejudice toward the targeted group. Further, they discuss the broader functions of humour as part of a delegitimising toolkit that rules targets "in" for negativity, alongside dehumanisation/objectification which rules targets "out" for compassion and concern.

Lastly, in Chapter 11, Julie A. Woodzicka and Robyn K. Mallett propose that one strategy to reduce the prevalence of disparagement humor (and future displays of prejudice) is the use of interpersonal confrontation. Woodzicka and Mallett review the literature on confronting disparagement humor and identifies how the ambiguity inherent in humor affects each stage of the Confronting Prejudiced Responses Model (Ashburn-Nardo, Morris, & Goodwin, 2008). They then review research that examines confrontation tactics that may reduce the social costs that typically accompany direct confrontation of non-humorous disparaging statements. Finally, they discuss their research on confronting sexist and racist humor with subtle strategies, including witty confrontation and judgement-free prodding.

We hope that by highlighting advances in theory and research, as well as intriguing questions that remain, established humor researchers will find this book with new insights and stimulate new ideas to tackle in future research. Further, we hope this volume will inspire a new generation of students to think about the myriad of ways that humor impacts social interaction and to pursue those ideas through empirical investigation.

—Maya Angelo

References

Allport, G. W. (1985). The historical background of social psychology. In G. Lindzey & E. Aronson (Eds.). *The handbook of social psychology* (pp. 1–46). New York: McGraw Hill.

Ashburn-Nardo, L., Morris, K. A., & Goodwin, S. A. (2008). The Confronting Prejudiced Responses (CPR) Model: Applying CPR in organizations. *Academy of Management Learning & Education*, 7(3), 332-342.

Baumeister, R. F., & Finkel, E. J. (Eds.). (2010). *Advance social psychology: The state of the science*. New York: Oxford University Press.

Fiske, S. T., Gilbert, D. T., & Lindzey, G. (Eds.). (2010). *Handbook of social psychology* (5th ed.). Hoboken, NJ: John Wiley and Sons.

Lefcourt, H. M. (2001). *Humor: The psychology of living buoyantly*. New York: Kluwer Academic.

Martin, R. A. & Ford, T. E. (2018). *The psychology of humor: An integrative approach* (2nd ed.). Academic Press: Boston.

McGhee, P. E. (2010). *Humor: The lighter path to resilience and health*. Bloomington, IN: Author House.

Ruch, W. (1998). Sense of humor: A new look at an old concept. In W. Ruch (Ed.), *The sense of humor: Explorations of a personality characteristic* (pp. 3–14). Berlin, Germany: Mouton de Gruyter.

PART I
Individual social psychological processes

1
HOW HUMOR CAN PROMOTE CENTRAL-ROUTE PERSUASION

The role of ambivalence

Madelijn Strick

One of my students recently asked a group of research participants to watch a video of British comedian Russell Howard. The video shows Howard on stage, telling the true story of a 14-year-old boy who has terminal cancer. The boy's parents send Howard an e-mail asking him to come and see the boy. During the visit, the boy turns out to have a great sense of humor. He shares with Howard a list of his favourite Russell Howard performances, including Mr Dildo, a TV show in which Howard dresses up in a six-foot-high phallus costume. The boy invites Howard to his funeral, and he asks Howard to come dressed as Mr Dildo. Russell hesitates but eventually agrees. By a miraculous turn of luck, however, the boy survives his cancer. At the end of the video, the boy joins Howard on stage, smiling broadly and dressed as Mr Dildo.

The research participants reported that they found the comedy piece very funny, but also 'touching' and 'moving.' It induced a reflective state in them. One participant reported the story had taught her 'to celebrate life.' Others wrote that the story convinced them that 'people should plan their funerals' and 'humor is the best way to fight fear.'

The example suggests that comedy can make people think and change their perspective on serious issues. But which aspect of the story made this happen? Was it the humor? To what extent was it important that the story also moved the viewers? Under what circumstances can humor persuade people to change their opinion about important matters?

Persuasion researchers generally assume that humor does not change people's perspective on significant topics. This assumption is based on the idea that humor reduces motivation and ability to elaborate on messages and thereby precludes high-involvement persuasion. In this chapter, I challenge the generalisability of that position. I discuss theory and evidence suggesting that humor can provoke mixed emotions (e.g., of sadness and joy). Research on ambivalence illustrates that the experience of mixed feelings mobilises effortful information processing. Based on these notions, I propose that to the extent humor elicits ambivalence, it encourages central-route processing and high-involvement persuasion.

I first review a research program illustrating the persuasive role of one-sided (i.e. purely positive) humor in advertising low-involvement products. I present studies showing that one-sided humor only persuades in low-involvement contexts, not in high-involvement contexts. Then, I provide preliminary evidence for the idea that two-sided humor (i.e. humor that elicits both positive and negative feelings) elicits effortful information processing and promotes high-involvement persuasion. The reviewed studies draw from a variety of communication settings, from advertising to political satire to stage comedy. I end with open questions and promising avenues for future research.

The Elusive Persuasive Effect of Humor

Persuasion can be defined as the process by which attitude change is brought about (Colman, 2015). Several strands of research suggest that humorous messages have more impact on people's thoughts, feelings, and behaviour than serious messages do. There is broad agreement among persuasion researchers that humor helps to draw attention to persuasive messages (e.g., Hansen, Strick, Van Baaren, Hooghuis, & Wigboldus, 2009; Madden & Weinberger, 1982). People generally have a better memory for humorous than non-humorous advertisements (Cline & Kellaris, 2007). Humor can increase the motivation of perceivers to process a message (Zhang & Zinkhan, 2006), and can positively bias thoughts about persuasive arguments (Eisend, 2011).

Yet, the persuasive effect of humor is not consistently found across different types of messages and contexts. A meta-analysis on humor in advertisements found that humor had a positive effect on persuasion in five studies, had mixed results in eight studies, and harmed persuasion in one study (Weinberger & Gulas, 1992). One problem is that humor may distract and thereby harm memory for persuasive arguments (e.g., Krishnan & Chakravarti, 2003). Humor is found to be persuasive when viewers have a pre-existing positive attitude toward a message, but not when their pre-existing attitude toward a message is negative (Chattopadhyay & Basu, 1990).

Another prominent moderator of the persuasive effect of humor, which is the focus of this chapter, is *involvement*: the extent to which the topic of a persuasive message has personal relevance and significant consequences for the viewer's own life (Petty & Cacioppo, 1986). For example, if a persuasive message is about a political candidate running for president in the viewers' own country, involvement will be high. If a persuasive message is about a political election in a faraway country, involvement will be lower. Research and theorising suggest that humor is effective for persuading people on low-involvement topics, not on high-involvement topics (e.g., Weinberger & Campbell, 1991; Weinberger, Spotts, Campbell, & Parsons, 1995; Zhang & Zinkhan, 2006). This is in line with predictions of a prominent theory about persuasion: The elaboration likelihood model.

Humor and Information Processing: Peripheral versus Central

Social-psychological research indicates that people process persuasive messages according to the *least effort principle* (Chaiken, Liberman, & Eagly, 1989). The principle holds that people are 'cognitive misers': they have a preference for efficiency and only spend cognitive effort when it is truly needed. In low-involvement contexts, the consequences of forming an inaccurate judgment are low, dissuading people from investing cognitive energy. In high-involvement contexts, however, the consequences of forming an inaccurate judgment are substantial, encouraging people to think harder about the message.

The dynamic between involvement and information processing is reflected in the elaboration likelihood model (ELM; Petty & Cacioppo, 1986). According to the ELM, persuasion may happen through two routes: a peripheral route and a central route. The routes differ in a) their focus of attention: peripheral cues vs. message arguments, and b) their depth of processing: superficial vs. deep. In peripheral route persuasion, the focus of attention is on peripheral cues associated with the message and the processing is rather superficial and effortless. Peripheral route persuasion depends on the presence of peripheral cues such as likeable communicators, source expertise, and message length. In central route persuasion, the focus of attention is on the quality of message arguments and the processing of that information is deep and effortful. Based on the level of argument strength, people will formulate cognitive responses that can be either positive or negative (e.g., 'I like this political candidate because of her focus on education'; 'I disagree with this candidate's ideas about foreign policy'). In central route persuasion, people are only persuaded when positive cognitive responses outweigh negative cognitive responses.

Humor reduces processing depth by eliciting a positive mood which comes with a sense of comfort and certainty (Schwarz, 1990; Tiedens & Linton, 2001). As feeling certain is an internal cue that one is already correct and accurate, it undermines people's motivation to process a message effortfully. On top of this, humor distracts and thereby reduces people's ability to fully process the underlying message arguments. One of the most important features of humor is incongruence, a violation of expectations or norms (Martin & Ford, 2018). Incongruencies draw on people's limited cognitive resources, which comes at the expense of processing other information presented in the context of humor, such as persuasive arguments. This reduces the level of message elaboration even more.

It should be noted that the problem of distraction is reduced by applying *related* humor, which is relevant to the message and directly tied to the persuasive arguments (Cline & Kellaris, 2007). Consider the health-slogan 'Drinking can cause memory loss, or worse, memory loss.' Elaborative processing of the humorous portion of this slogan automatically means elaborative processing of the central message that drinking is bad for memory because the joke and the message are strongly connected (Blanc & Brigaud, 2014). In more than 40% of humorous advertisements, however, humor is paired with a persuasive message without the two being meaningfully related (Weinberger & Campbell, 1991). In such cases, humor distracts perceivers from the underlying message arguments and reduces their ability to engage in effortful processing.

For these reasons, humor is generally thought to encourage peripheral route processing and discourage central route processing, thereby reducing persuasion of messages that require complex reasoning (central route processing). A study by Moyer-Gusé, Mahood, and Brookes (2011) illustrates this problem. They investigated a media campaign designed to warn people against the severe consequences of unsafe sex. The story of a young woman experiencing the negative consequences of unplanned pregnancy was integrated into a comedy series and presented in the context of pregnancy-related jokes. Viewers needed to go through a complex thought process to understand the intended message ('Ha-ha, this is funny! But wait … what if this would happen to me, wouldn't it be devastating? Yes, it would.'). However, as humor undermines critical thought, the message was bound to be misunderstood ('Ha-ha, this is funny! Unplanned pregnancy doesn't seem too bad'). Indeed, compared to a more serious control condition, watching the unplanned pregnancy storyline in a humorous context led viewers to be *more* inclined to engage in unprotected sex.

This effect of humor could be problematic since peripheral persuasion is superficial and not grounded in substantive reasoning. It is generally found to produce weak and fleeting attitudes that fail to guide behaviour when people think before they act. Indeed, there is general agreement among persuasion researchers that central route-processing generates more substantial and lasting attitude change than peripheral route-processing does (e.g., Wagner & Petty, 2011).

However, some studies show that humorous messages can – under some circumstances – be persuasive in high-involvement contexts. For example, humor had positive effects in persuasive messages about the importance of a healthy lifestyle (Blanc & Brigaud, 2014), the benefits of vaccination (Moyer-Gusé, Robinson, & McKnight, 2018), and, indeed, the risks of unprotected sex (Futerfas & Nan, 2017). Furthermore, humor is an essential ingredient of political satire, a genre that plays a significant role in informing people about issues in the political sphere (Hardy, Gottfried, Winneg, & Jamieson, 2014). Recent studies show that political satire influences learning, understanding and behaviour towards complex political issues, and can have a considerable effect on agenda-setting (Boukes, 2019). It thus seems that in some conditions, humor can elicit elaboration and persuasion on high-involvement topics.

What are these conditions? In this chapter, I highlight the possibility that the *two-sidedness* of humor (i.e., the extent to which humor elicits not only positive but also negative feelings), is an important moderator. I assume this is the case because, in contrast to one-sided (i.e., purely positive) humor, two-sided humor evokes uncertainty and consequently stimulates additional deliberation. Two-sided humor may therefore motivate people to reconsider and eventually abandon their pre-existing opinion. Before elaborating on this new idea, however, I will review an extensive research line in which my colleagues and I studied the persuasive effect of one-sided humor in low-involvement conditions.

Persuasion in Low-Involvement Contexts

One-sided humor is among the most employed strategies in advertising. Approximately 24% of television advertisements try to be funny, and advertisers apply humor to a similar extent in other media (e.g., Beard, 2005). In line with the notion that such humor elicits peripheral route processing, humor is more often used in advertisements for low-involvement products like soft drinks and candy than in advertisements for high-involvement products such as insurance and corporate identity (e.g., Weinberger & Campbell, 1991).

In a four-year research program comprising 17 experiments (summarised in Strick, Holland, Van Baaren, Van Knippenberg, & Dijksterhuis, 2013), my colleagues and I examined how humor affects attention, memory, attitudes, and behaviour towards low-involvement consumer products. We chose to study brand-unrelated humor because it is commonly applied in advertising for low-involvement products (Weinberger & Campbell, 1991). Furthermore, we studied only novel rather than familiar brands to get a clear view of the impact of humor on persuasion without having to take pre-existing brand attitudes into account.

We derived our experimental method from studies on evaluative conditioning, a research area that examines changes in the liking of stimuli due to pairing the stimuli with other positive or negative stimuli (De Houwer, Thomas, & Baeyens, 2001). A common experimental procedure in this field is to repeatedly pair neutral stimuli (e.g., an unknown brand) with positive stimuli (e.g., pictures of cute puppies) or negative stimuli (e.g., pictures of dangerous snakes), and afterward measure how the pairing affected the liking of the neutral stimuli. In our studies, we paired unknown brands with humorous or non-humorous stimuli and observed how this affected the attention, memory, attitudes, and behaviour towards the brands.

In a study that was representative of our experimental approach (Strick, Van Baaren, Holland, & Van Knippenberg, 2009, Experiment 3), we arranged a situation in which one unknown (but truly existing) energy drink brand was repeatedly paired with humor, while another unknown (but truly existing) energy drink brand was repeatedly paired with non-humor.

We asked our research participants to 'browse' through a digital magazine presented full screen on a computer monitor (Figure 1.1 gives an illustration of the stimulus presentation). Two pages were presented on screen for ten seconds, after which the computer program automatically jumped to the next two pages. From the perspective of the participants, it looked as if they were skimming through a magazine, with the pages turning automatically at a regular pace.

A picture of one of two energy drink brands (Enorm or Energy Slammers) was consistently shown on the same page as a humorous cartoon. A picture of the other energy drink brand (Energy Slammers or Enorm) was consistently shown on

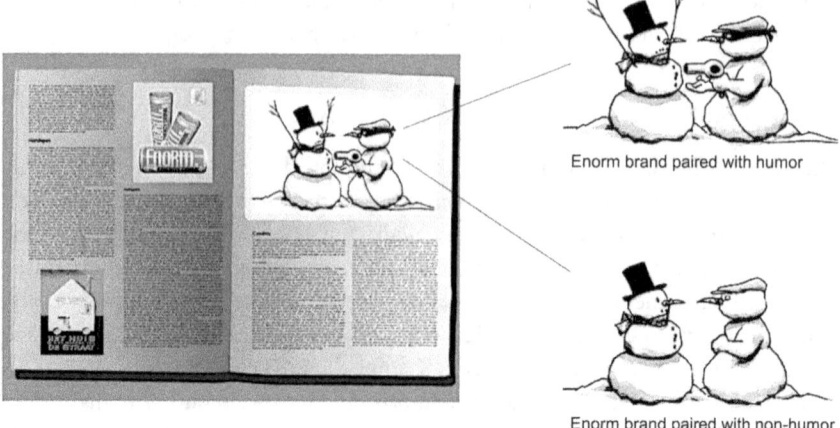

FIGURE 1.1 Illustration of the pairing of a brand with humor and non-humor in the 'magazine paradigm' used in Strick et al. (2009, Experiment 3).

the same page as a non-humorous cartoon (i.e., a cartoon with the humorous clue removed). This pairing of brands with humor (or non-humor) occurred on ten different pages per brand. Thus, throughout the magazine, one brand was paired with humor ten times, using ten different humorous cartoons. The other brand was paired with non-humor ten times, using ten different non-humorous cartoons. The pairing of brands with humor or non-humor was varied between participants to avoid the influence of differential liking of the two brand names.

After leafing through the magazine, brand attitudes were measured using an evaluative priming task (Fazio, Sanbonmatsu, Powell, & Kardes, 1986). In this task, participants are repeatedly asked to categorise target words (e.g., rainbow, headache) presented on a computer monitor into positive or negative categories by pressing a left 'negative' or right 'positive' key. Before each target word appears on the computer screen, a picture is presented that serves as *prime* (in this case, a picture of one of the two energy drink brands). The primed brands are thought to activate evaluations, and thereby facilitate responses to target words that are evaluatively similar and inhibit responses to target words that are evaluatively dissimilar. For example, if an energy drink brand activates a positive evaluation, responses on subsequently presented positive target words will be faster, and responses on subsequently presented negative target words will be slower. Brand attitude is calculated by subtracting the response time to positive target words from the response time to negative target words after priming with the brand. Higher numbers indicate a more positive brand attitude. As expected, the results showed that the participants had a positive attitude toward the brand paired with humor, but not towards the brand paired with non-humor.

In a later phase of the experiment, we measured overt brand choice. Participants were escorted to a room where a stack of cans of both energy drink brands (in equal numbers) was presented. Participants were asked to choose a can and take three sips. As justification for this task, we told the participants we wanted to measure the effect of energy drink consumption on reaction time task performance. After consuming the energy drink, participants completed a reaction time task to lend credibility to the cover story. However, our true interest was in the brand choice. In line with the assumption that humor is persuasive in low-involvement contexts, participants were twice as likely to choose the energy drink brand that was paired with humor compared to the brand paired with non-humor.

These findings show that one-sided humor in advertising positively influences attitudes and behaviour towards low-involvement consumer products (Strick et al., 2013). The positivity of such humor directly injects a positive attitude and behavioural preference towards brands.

When Attitudes Matter

Based on the ELM, one can predict that the strong persuasive power of one-sided humor in low-involvement conditions does not apply to high-involvement conditions. Indeed, experimental research on advertising generally confirmed this assumption.

In one study, research participants were given a booklet containing several articles and ads, including a target ad promoting a fictional brand of camera (Zhang & Zinkhan, 2006). In the low-involvement condition, participants were simply asked to skim through all ads and articles in the booklet. In the high-involvement condition, participants were informed that one of the ads featured a new camera that would be test-marketed in their own city, and for which they would receive a discount coupon. This experimental manipulation of involvement was crossed with an experimental manipulation of one-sided humor: for half of the participants, the camera ad was made humorous by including a funny cartoon. For the other half, the camera ad was made serious by including a non-humorous picture.

After reading the booklet, participants' attitudes towards the camera brand were measured. In line with the predictions of the ELM, the results indicated that the effects of humor varied across the different involvement levels. The humorous ad elicited a more positive attitude than the non-humorous ad under low-involvement conditions, not under high-involvement conditions.

The study by Zhang and Zinkhan (2006) confirms that humor is persuasive in low-involvement contexts, not high-involvement contexts. They provided evidence for this pattern in commercial advertising. However, humor is also often used in other types of persuasive communication like public service announcements, health promotion messages, and political satire. The opening example of the Russell Howard comedy illustrated that even stage comedy can have persuasive effects. To what extent do the predictions of the ELM apply to these domains?

In a recent study (Strick & Dijksterhuis, 2017), we explored the interplay between humor and involvement in political satire, a humorous genre that ridicules politicians and political institutions to stimulate societal change. As a humorous stimulus, we used a satirical video of Dutch comedian Arjen Lubach about U.S. President Donald Trump.[1] The video was an alleged tourism advertisement from the Dutch government introducing the 'tiny country' of the Netherlands to President Trump. As 'America First' was the slogan of Trump's presidential campaign, the Lubach video asked Trump whether the Netherlands could be second. The voice-over closely imitated Trump's speaking style, words, and mannerisms. Meanwhile, the video also ridiculed Trump's proposed policies such as his plans to build a wall against Mexican immigrants, as well as other controversies such his alleged tax evasion, his mocking a disabled reporter, and his *Grab-'em-by-the-pussy* remark.

At the time of our research, Donald Trump had just been inaugurated as the 45th president of the United States and was destined to lead the country in the upcoming years. We therefore reasoned that the election of Trump was a high-involvement topic to U.S. citizens. We also reasoned that The Netherlands, a faraway country with little direct consequences for the United States, would be a low-involvement topic for U.S. citizens.

We designed two experiments to examine whether the humorous video would change the attitude toward President Trump (Study 1) and toward The Netherlands (Study 2) among U.S. citizens of different political backgrounds (i.e., those who had voted for Hillary Clinton and those who had voted for Donald Trump). More specifically, we investigated the extent to which the perceived humorousness of the video predicted potential attitude change. Based on the predictions derived from the ELM that humor is not persuasive in high-involvement contexts, we hypothesised that the perceived humorousness of the video would not predict the level of attitude change towards President Trump but would predict the level of attitude change towards The Netherlands.

In the first study, we compared the humorous video with a non-humorous video criticising President Trump and to a no video control condition. First of all, the results showed that U.S. citizens found the Lubach video very funny. The perceived humorousness rating was $M = 5.54$ on a scale from 1 (*Not funny all*) to 7 (*Very funny*). Even Trump voters found it reasonably funny ($M = 4.32$). However, as expected, the humorousness of the video did not predict attitude change towards President Trump, among Clinton voters or Trump voters.

In the second study, we used the same satirical video by Arjen Lubach to explore its persuasive potential toward The Netherlands. In line with our expectations, the humorous video caused a positive attitude change towards the Netherlands, compared to a no video control condition. Further in line with our predictions, perceived humorousness was a significant predictor of this attitude change. These results confirmed that humor was a working ingredient in the attitude change towards The Netherlands.

In summary, the results of the research by Strick & Dijksterhuis (2017) imply that the findings from the ELM can be applied to the political satire of Arjen Lubach. Humor had persuasive power for low-involvement topics (e.g., The Netherlands), but not for high-involvement topics (e.g., President Trump).

The results so far suggest that humor has persuasive potential in commercial advertising and political satire, but only for persuasion on low-involvement issues, not on high-involvement issues. In what follows, I will propose that this limitation can be lifted by applying two-sided humor.

Ambivalence and Elaboration

Many studies in social psychology have investigated how the elicitation of an emotion by a first task (e.g., watching comedy or drama) affects the depth of processing in a second task (e.g., the processing of a persuasive message). A general finding is that negative emotions cause deep information processing, while positive emotions cause shallow information processing (e.g., Mackie & Worth, 1991; Schwarz, 1990). A prominent explanation is that positive emotions carry information that the situation is benign, and hence, that critical processing is not necessary (e.g., Schwarz, 1990).

A contrasting perspective that has gained support in recent years is that emotions affect information processing depending on the level of confidence or certainty they elicit. This idea is based on appraisal theory, which classifies emotions on the basis of their cognitive components or *appraisals*. According to this view, emotions differ on various cognitive dimensions such as the level of responsibility, pleasantness, control, and confidence they elicit (e.g., Smith & Ellsworth, 1985). The appraisal view crosscuts the categorisation into positive and negative emotions. For example, emotions like anger, disgust, contentment, and happiness are all accompanied by a sense of certainty, even though the first two are negative and the latter two are positive. Emotions like worry, shame, surprise, and hope are usually accompanied by a sense of uncertainty.

Studies show that the level of certainty or confidence elicited by an emotion affects the depth of processing a persuasive message. In one study (Tiedens & Linton, 2001, Experiment 2), students were induced to feel anger, contentment, worry or surprise. The first two emotions are high-certainty emotions, while the latter two are low-certainty emotions. Next, the students read an essay in which the author criticised 'grade inflation' and opted for harsher grading at universities. The essay was ostensibly written by a student from a nearby community college (low expert source) or by a distinguished professor of education (high expert source). The extent to which source expertise (a peripheral cue) influenced persuasion was taken as a measure of processing depth. In line with the expectations, participants who were induced to feel certainty emotions agreed more with the high expert source than the low expert source, indicating peripheral route processing. In contrast, source expertise had no influence on those who were induced to feel uncertainty emotions.

Within the emotional-appraisal framework, humor can be classified as a high-certainty emotion. Incongruity-resolution theories describe the understanding of a punchline as a moment of sudden insight providing a sense of control and being 'in the know' (e.g., Suls, 1972). Superiority theories contend that the essence of humor lies in the experience of sudden glory from which people derive a sense of pride and confidence (e.g., Gruner, 1978). Humor is a form of play that creates an atmosphere of levity in which actions are low-risk and inconsequential (Mulkay, 1988). Research has illustrated that humor creates a 'humor mindset' not to take information seriously, which undercuts effortful information processing (Martin & Ford, 2018).

However, a closer look suggests that humor is not necessarily purely positive, nor does it always elicit a sense of high confidence. Several scholars have noted that humor is an emotion that essentially derives from pain or sorrow. A classic theory on humor, ambivalence theory (Gregory, 1924) holds that humor stems from the simultaneous experience of incompatible emotions such as sadness and joy, envy and malice, or shame and pride. Laughter is the mechanism by which these conflicting emotions resolve themselves. Yet, the inner conflict caused by humor is not always completely removed and a feeling of uncertainty may linger. A more recent account of humor, benign violation theory (McGraw & Warren, 2010), proposed that humor arises when we experience something that physically or psychologically threatens our sense of how the world ought to be, while at the same time we appraise the situation as benign. Hence, this framework also assumes that humor is essentially two-sided and involves conflicting emotions.

Anecdotal evidence further suggests that the experience of humor can indeed be accompanied by feelings of inner contradictions and conflict. People find humor at funeral ceremonies of intimate loved ones, experiencing deep sadness and joy at the same time. People can thoroughly enjoy a sexist or racist joke, and simultaneously feel ashamed by their response. People can dread their own mistakes or setbacks and at the same time find humor in them.

A large body of research has mapped the nature and consequences of ambivalence, which can be defined as 'a psychological state in which a person holds mixed feelings (positive and negative) towards some psychological object' (Gardner, 1987, for a review see Van Harreveld, Nohlen, & Schneider, 2015). Research shows that ambivalence is associated with less confidence in one's evaluation. It is generally assumed that people mobilise cognitive resources to reduce ambivalence, which leads to the thorough processing of new information (Van Harreveld et al., 2015). Indeed, ambivalence is associated with systematic reasoning (Jonas, Diehl, & Broemer, 1997), higher activity of brain regions associated with elaboration (Cunningham, Johnson, Gatenby, Gore, & Banaji, 2003), and increased discrimination between strong and weak arguments (Maio, Bell, & Esses, 1996). Studies confirm that this heightened elaboration is functional, as increased receptiveness to a strong message reduces subsequent feelings of ambivalence (Maio et al., 1996). Furthermore, attitudes formed through ambivalence-induced processing tend to be strong and firmly grounded in reasoning. Consequently, although ambivalence itself is associated with doubt and uncertainty, it eventually leads to strong attitudes that are predictive of future behaviour (Jonas et al., 1997; Maio et al., 1996).

These findings suggest that the general assumption that humor elicits peripheral route processing may need further qualification. Humor is not always clearly positive and may elicit conflict and uncertainty. Here, I propose that to the extent humor induces ambivalence, it promotes effortful information processing (see Figure 1.2 for the proposed model). If evidence confirming this idea were found, it would mean that the range of persuasion contexts where humor can be fruitfully applied extends beyond messages on low-involvement topics. Humor could be used to evoke critical thought and contemplation, guiding people into awareness and attitude change towards important issues.

Preliminary Evidence for the Hypothesis

First evidence comes from a study using the Russell Howard comedy about the boy suffering from cancer, which I discussed at the start of this chapter (Verhoeven & Strick, 2018). In our study, we measured the extent to which the comedy 'moved' viewers, a feeling that is colloquially defined as 'crying for joy.' Being moved has recently been identified as a distinct emotion involving both positive and negative components (Cova & Deonna, 2014; Zickfeld, Schubert, Seibt, & Fiske, 2019). Based on the assumption that ambivalence predicts effortful processing, we reasoned that to the extent the comedy piece moved viewers, it would stimulate elaboration.

After watching the video, participants (100 university students) indicated their level of elaboration by indicating their agreement with three statements: 'This video sets me to thinking'; 'This video has made me reflect'; and 'This video made me stop and think,' on 7-point Likert scales ranging from 1 (*Totally Disagree*) to 7 (*Totally agree*). Because the reliability of the three items was excellent, they were averaged into one elaboration variable. Participants also rated the level of perceived humorousness ('I thought this video was funny'; 'This video made me laugh'; and 'I thought this video was humorous') and the level of being moved ('This video touched me'; 'I thought this video was moving'; and 'This video evoked emotions in me'), again by indicating their agreement on 7-point scales. The three humor items and the three being moved items were merged into single perceived humorousness and being moved variables, respectively.

The participants rated the video as highly humorous ($M = 5.06$) and highly moving ($M = 4.69$). The video also elicited high elaboration ($M = 5.20$). We

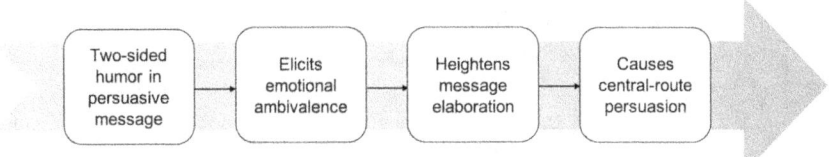

FIGURE 1.2 Illustration of the proposed theoretical model.

regressed elaboration on perceived humorousness and being moved. The data revealed no association between perceived humorousness and elaboration. However, as expected, higher levels of being moved related to higher levels of elaboration, providing preliminary evidence that ambivalence predicts heightened elaboration.

It should be noted that the Russell Howard study suffered from a number of limitations. While being moved has positive and negative components, it is not the same as ambivalence. Moreover, the study did not measure persuasion. A full examination of the proposed model would entail a more extensive analysis of the mediating role of elaboration between ambivalence and persuasion (see Figure 1.2).

We tested the complete model in a different study, which benefited from the help of Dutch comedian Guido Weijers (Strick & Weijers, 2017). The study revolved around Weijers' *Oudejaarsconference,* a Dutch tradition in which a prominent comedian creates a show especially for New Year's Eve as a way to round off the year. The comedian typically conveys his or her viewpoint on topical issues in Dutch politics and society in a humorous way, and hence, the Oudejaarsconference can be considered a humorous persuasive message on high-involvement topics.

From September to December 2017, Weijers performed try-outs in theatres with live audiences to fine-tune his show. During this period, audience members could voluntarily participate in our study by clicking on a link on Weijers' website, which led to our online questionnaire.

Weijers' routine consisted of 14 thematic 'pieces,' each lasting about five to ten minutes and addressing a different societal topic in a different emotional tone. Examples of topics were gender neutrality, animal rights, Dutch political elections, Turkish President Erdogan, and the Fipronil scandal (a worldwide incident in 2017 involving the spread of a toxic pesticide contaminating chicken eggs destined for human consumption). We chose to collect data at the level of a single piece. This was operationalised in the questionnaire by asking participants to first select one of the 14 pieces from a dropdown list and to focus all their answers on this bit of the show.

A total of 98 participants filled out the questionnaire. Participants indicated the level of perceived humorousness of the piece they had selected by answering the question 'How funny did you find this piece?' Then they indicated the extent to which the bit evoked ambivalence by answering the question 'To what extent did the piece release mixed feelings in you (i.e., both positive and negative)?' Elaboration was measured with two items: 'To what extent did the piece make you aware of a societal issue?' and 'To what extent did the piece induce you to societal reflection?' of which the scores were merged. Persuasion was measured with one item: 'To what extent did the piece change your attitude on a societal issue?'

The participants rated the selected piece as highly humorous ($M = 3.95$, on a scale from 1 to 5, with 5 indicating high humorousness). The level of ambivalence ($M = 3.04$), elaboration ($M = 3.10$), and persuasion ($M = 2.61$) fluctuated around the mid-point of the scale.

We used a bootstrapping procedure (Preacher & Hayes, 2008) to estimate the indirect effect of ambivalence on persuasion via heightened elaboration. The results corresponded with the hypothesised mediation model (see Figure 1.3 for a graphic representation). The level of ambivalence predicted more elaboration, and more elaboration predicted more persuasion. When heightened elaboration was included in the model, ambivalence no longer predicted persuasion, which is in line with a full mediation model.

The mediation was not found when ambivalence was replaced with perceived humorousness in the analysis. This confirms that humorousness itself does not promote high-involvement persuasion via elaboration. Overall, this study provided preliminary evidence for the full model: two-sided humor in persuasive messages elicits ambivalence, which increases elaboration, which in turn promotes persuasion on high involvement topics.

Next Steps

The Guido Weijers study provided evidence for the full model, but replication using solid research methods is needed to draw firm conclusions. The evidence presented here is correlational, and control conditions with one-sided humor and no humor are needed to establish causality. Future studies may measure persuasion behaviourally instead of using self-report. A useful procedure would be to elicit ambivalence in a first task (e.g., having participants watch the Russell Howard comedy show), and measuring persuasion in a second task using the ELM framework (e.g., assessing differentiation between strong and weak arguments or the influence of peripheral cues).

Another challenge for future studies is to pinpoint the kind of ambivalence that elicits elaboration. Ambivalence can refer to cognitive conflict, emotional conflict, or conflict between cognitions and emotions (Van Harreveld et al., 2015).

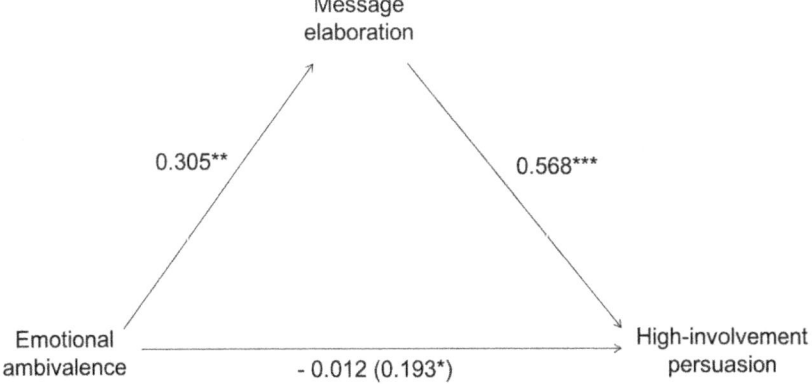

FIGURE 1.3 Graphic illustration of the mediating effect of heightened elaboration between emotional ambivalence and persuasion on high-involvement topics in Strick and Weijers (2017). *p < .05, **p < .01, ***p < .001.

Ambivalence may be held with respect to events, attitude objects, goals, or behaviours. Some measures tap the existence of positive and negative evaluative responses (objective ambivalence, e.g., 'How positive (negative) are your feelings with respect to X?'), others tap the experience of conflict (subjective ambivalence, e.g., 'I feel torn between the two sides of X').

It would also be valuable to explore the impact of different emotion combinations. Based on appraisal theory, we may predict that humor elicits most ambivalence when combined with uncertainty-emotions, such as sadness, shame, or concern. Sadness may be elicited by the tragicomedy in the style of Charlie Chaplin or Woody Allen. Concern may be elicited by socially critical comedy. Shame may be elicited by harsh humor, especially when it succeeds in making people laugh and feeling ashamed about their amused response at the same time. In contrast, aggressive and disgusting humor will probably not heighten elaboration, as anger and disgust are certainty-emotions (Tiedens & Linton, 2001).

Another avenue for future research is to compare effects of different types of humor. Current theorising identifies two humor varieties (e.g., Ruch, 1992). Incongruity-resolution humor is the variety where the conflict elicited by the joke can be completely resolved leaving the perceiver with the subjective certainty of 'getting the point.' Nonsense humor, in contrast, is the variety where the incongruity cannot be completely resolved, leaving the listener with a sense of bizarreness or absurdity. Based on the framework presented here, nonsense humor may elicit heightened elaboration and cause central route processing, while incongruity-resolution humor may not. As explained before, however, improved elaboration only benefits persuasion if the humor is meaningfully related to the persuasive message.

It would also be interesting to examine whether citizens of Western and Eastern cultures respond differently to two-sided humor in persuasive messages, as Eastern cultures are found to have a greater tolerance for ambivalence (Peng & Nisbett, 1999). This difference appears to be based on the Eastern tradition of dialectical thinking, a thought process that recognises the importance of opposites.

A question that lingers is whether the model advanced here is specific to humor or could be accommodated within the broader literature of non-humorous ambivalence. I am inclined to think there is something special about the ambivalence elicited by humor. Feelings of sadness, shame, or concern create an unusual context for humor. A cheerful joke expressed in the midst of tragedy can be highly surprising and therefore have strong emotional impact. Indeed, the emotional response to positive events is elevated when they occur in a negative context (Strick & Van Soolingen, 2018). Thus, comedy may be a particularly fruitful vehicle for eliciting strong ambivalent feelings, and consequently, for eliciting contemplation.

The best stories make us laugh while also touching us on a deeper, more serious level. In this chapter, I have argued that the same can be said about the most impactful persuasive messages. Persuading people on high-involvement topics is not easy and cannot be done based on humor alone. A more complex emotional experience combining joy and sorrow may be required to make people feel, think, and eventually change their mind.

Note

1 For the Lubach video with English subtitles see https://www.youtube.com/watch?v=pD7xIxLWjNc&t=13s.

References

Beard, F. K. (2005). One hundred years of humor in American advertising. *Journal of Macromarketing*, 25, 54–65.

Blanc, N., & Brigaud, E. (2014). Humor in print health advertisements: Enhanced attention, privileged recognition, and persuasiveness of preventive messages. *Health Communication*, 29, 669–677.

Boukes, M. (2019). Agenda-setting with satire: How political satire increased TTIP's saliency on the public, media, and political agenda. *Political Communication*, 36, 426–451.

Chaiken, S., Liberman, A., & Eagly, A. H. (1989). Heuristic and systematic information processing within and beyond the persuasion context. In J. S. Uleman & J. A. Bargh (Eds.), *Unintended thought* (pp. 212–252). New York, NY: Guilford.

Chattopadhyay, A., & Basu, K. (1990). Humour in advertising: The moderating role of prior brand evaluation. *Journal of Marketing Research*, 27, 466–476.

Cline, T. W., & Kellaris, J. J. (2007). The influence of humor strength and humor–message relatedness on ad memorability: A dual process model. *Journal of Advertising*, 36, 55–67.

Cline, T. W., & Kellaris, J. J. (2014). The joint impact of humor and argument strength in a print advertising context: A case for weaker arguments. *Psychology & Marketing*, 16, 69–86.

Colman, A. M. (2015). *A dictionary of psychology* (4th ed.). Oxford: Oxford University Press.

Cova, F., & Deonna, J. A. (2014). Being moved. *Philosophical Studies*, 169, 447–466.

Cunningham, W. A., Johnson, M. K., Gatenby, J. C. G., Gore, J. C., & Banaji, M. R. (2003). Neural components of social evaluation. *Journal of Personality and Social Psychology*, 85, 639–649.

De Houwer, J., Thomas, S., & Baeyens, F. (2001). Associative learning of likes and dislikes: A review of 25 years of research on human evaluative conditioning. *Psychological Bulletin*, 127, 853–869.

Eisend, M. (2011). How humour in advertising works: A meta-analytic test of alternative models. *Marketing Letters*, 22, 115–132.

Fazio, R. H., Sanbonmatsu, D. M., Powell, M. C., & Kardes, F. R. (1986). On the automatic activation of attitudes. *Journal of Personality and Social Psychology*, 50, 229–238.

Futerfas, M. L., & Nan, X. (2017). Role of humor in the persuasiveness of entertainment narratives on unprotected sexual behavior. *Journal of Health Communication*, 22, 312–318.

Gardner, P. L. (1987). Measuring ambivalence to science. *Journal of Research in Science Teaching*, 24, 241–247.

Gregory, J. C. (1924). *The nature of laughter*. London: Kegan Paul.

Gruner, C. R. (1978). *Understanding laughter: The workings of wit and humor*. Chicago: Nelson-Hall.

Hansen, J., Strick, M., Van Baaren, R. B., Hooghuis, M., & Wigboldus, D. H. J. (2009). Exploring memory for product names advertised with humour. *Journal of Consumer Behaviour*, 8, 135–148.

Hardy, B. W., Gottfried, J. A. Winneg, K. M., & Jamieson, K. H. (2014) Stephen Colbert's civics lesson: How Colbert super PAC taught viewers about campaign finance. *Mass Communication and Society*, 17, 329–353.

Jonas, K., Diehl, M., & Broemer, P. (1997). Effects of attitudinal ambivalence on information processing and attitude-intention consistency. *Journal of Experimental Social Psychology, 33,* 190–210.

Krishnan, H. S., & Chakravarti, D. (2003). A process analysis of the effects of humorous advertising executions on brand claims memory. *Journal of Consumer Psychology, 13,* 230–245.

Mackie, D. M., & Worth, L. T. (1991). Feeling good, but not thinking straight: The impact of positive mood on persuasion. In J. P. Forgas (Ed.), *Emotion and social judgments* (pp. 201–220). New York, NY: Wiley.

Madden, T. J., & Weinberger, M. C. (1982). The effects of humour on attention in magazine advertising. *Journal of Advertising, 11,* 8–14.

Madden, T. J., & Weinberger, M. C. (1984). Humour in advertising: A practitioner view. *Journal of Advertising Research, 24,* 23–29.

Maio, G. R., Bell, D. W., & Esses, V. M. (1996). Ambivalence and persuasion: The processing of messages about immigrant groups. *Journal of Experimental Social Psychology, 32,* 513–536.

Martin, R. A., & Ford, T. (2018). *The psychology of humor: An integrative approach.* Burlington, MA: Academic Press.

McGraw, A. P., & Warren, C. (2010). Benign violations: Making immoral behavior funny. *Psychological Science, 21,* 1141–1149.

Menninghaus, W., Wagner, V., Hanich, J., Wassiliwizky, E., Kuehnast, M., & Jacobsen, T. (2015). Towards a psychological construct of being moved. *PLoS One, 10,* 1–33.

Morreall, J. (1983). Humor and emotion. *American Philosophical Quarterly, 20,* 297–304.

Moyer-Gusé, E., Mahood, C., & Brookes, S. (2011). Entertainment-education in the context of humor: Effects on safer sex intentions and risk perceptions. *Health Communication, 26,* 765–774.

Moyer-Gusé, E., Robinson, M., & McKnight, J. (2018). The role of humor in messaging about the MMR vaccine. *Journal of Health Communication, 23,* 514–522.

Mulkay, M. J. (1988). *On humor: Its nature and place in modern society.* Oxford: Blackwell.

Peng, K., & Nisbett, R. E. (1999). Culture, dialectics and reasoning about contradiction. *American Psychologist, 54,* 741–754.

Petty, R. E., & Cacioppo, J. T. (1986). The Elaboration Likelihood Model of persuasion. *Advances in Experimental Social Psychology, 19,* 124–205.

Preacher, K. J., & Hayes, A. F. (2008). Asymptotic and resampling strategies for assessing and comparing indirect effects in multiple mediator models. *Behavior Research Methods, 40,* 879–891.

Ruch, W. (1992). Assessment of appreciation of humor: Studies with the 3WD humor test. In J. N. Butcher & C. D. Spielberger (Eds.), *Advances in personality assessment* (pp. 27–75). Hillsdale, NJ: Erlbaum.

Schwarz, N. (1990). Feelings as information: Information and motivational function of affective states. In E. T. Higgins & R. M. Sorrentino (Eds.), *Handbook of motivation and cognition* (Vol. 2, pp. 527–561). New York, NY: Guilford.

Smith, C. A., & Ellsworth, P. C. (1985). Patterns of cognitive appraisal in emotion. *Journal of Personality and Social Psychology, 48,* 813–838.

Strick, M., & Dijksterhuis, A. (2017). *The persuasive impact of humor in politics: What did the Lubach video do in the US?* Unpublished manuscript. Available via https://osf.io/6rtva/?view_only=56efeb3b8735444a80b688fa289a0404.

Strick, M., Holland, R. W., Van Baaren, R. B., Van Knippenberg, A., & Dijksterhuis, A. (2013). Humour in advertising: An associative processing model. *European Review of Social Psychology, 24,* 32–69.

Strick, M., Van Baaren, R. B., Holland, R. W., & Van Knippenberg, A. (2009). Humour in advertisements enhances product liking by mere association. *Journal of Experimental Psychology: Applied, 15,* 35–45.

Strick, M., & Van Soolingen, J. (2018). Against the odds: Human values arising in unfavourable circumstances elicit the feeling of being moved. *Cognition and Emotion, 32,* 1231–1246.

Strick, M., & Weijers, G. (2017). Ambivalent humor and persuasion at the *Oudejaarsconference* 2017. Unpublished raw data. Available via https://osf.io/c6jt4/?view_only=35210ebc5cdd4f9f95fadb94ce740f51.

Suls, J. M. (1972). A two-stage model for the appreciation of jokes and cartoons: An information processing analysis. In J. H. Goldstein & P. E. McGee (Eds.), *The psychology of humour: Theoretical perspectives and empirical issues* (pp. 81–100). New York, NY: Academic Press.

Tiedens, L. Z., & Linton, S. (2001). Judgment under emotional certainty and uncertainty: The effects of specific emotions on information processing. *Journal of Personality and Social Psychology, 81,* 973–988.

Van Harreveld, F., Nohlen, H. U., & Schneider, I. K. (2015). The ABC of ambivalence: Affective, behavioral, and cognitive consequences of attitudinal conflict. In J. M. Olson & M. P. Zanna (Eds.), *Advances in experimental social psychology* (pp. 285–324). New York, NY: Academic Press.

Verhoeven, R., & Strick, M. (2018). The effect of being moved on the relationship between humor and reflective state. Unpublished master's thesis, available via https://dspace.library.uu.nl/handle/1874/367482.

Wagner, B. C., & Petty, R. E. (2011). The elaboration likelihood model of persuasion: Thoughtful and non-thougful social influence. In D. Chadee (Ed.), *Theories in social psychology* (pp. 96–116). Oxford: Blackwell.

Wegener, D. T., & Petty, R. E. (1994). Mood management across affective states: The hedonic contingency hypothesis. *Journal of Personality and Social Psychology, 66,* 1034–1048.

Weinberger, M. G., & Campbell, L. (1991). The use and impact of humour in radio advertising. *Journal of Advertising Research, 31,* 44–52.

Weinberger, M. G., & Gulas, C. S. (1992). The impact of humour in advertising: A review. *Journal of Advertising, 21,* 36–59.

Weinberger, M. G., Spotts, H. E., Campbell, L., & Parsons, A. L. (1995). The use of humour in different advertising media. *Journal of Advertising Research, 35,* 44–56.

Zhang, Y., & Zinkhan, G. M. (2006). Responses to humorous ads: Does audience involvement matter? *Journal of Advertising, 35,* 113–127.

Zickfeld, J. H., Schubert, T. W., Seibt, B., & Fiske, A. P. (2019). Moving through the literature: What is the emotion often denoted being moved? *Emotion Review, 11,* 123–139.

2
POLITICAL HUMOR

Jody C. Baumgartner

This chapter reviews research focused on the cognitive, attitudinal, and participatory effects of individuals' exposure to political humor (PH). Summarised, findings demonstrate that PH is 'more than a joke.' Before proceeding, a few notes are in order. First, many studies examine various aspects of the content (targets, tone, etc.) of PH (e.g., Brewer & Marquardt, 2007; Feldman, 2013a; Niven, Lichter, & Amundson, 2003) and how politicians use PH (e.g., Alisky, 1990; Gardner, 1994; Yarwood, 2001). These subjects are outside of the scope of this essay.

Second, although this essay will not focus on the content of PH, it is important to differentiate between basic types of PH when examining its effects. These types include political comedy, simple satire, complex satire, and self-deprecating humor. Political comedy is humor whose primary function is to make people laugh and which happens to be centred around politics. Examples are jokes told by the hosts of late-night talk shows (e.g., Jimmy Fallon) during the monologue segment of their shows. The humor is about politics, but it is non-political in that the political content is only used to make people laugh.

Political satire (hereafter, satire), on the other hand, is designed to make a political point but is delivered in a humorous fashion. Simple satire contains a singular, straightforward message, easy to understand and interpret. Jon Stewart's presentations on *The Daily Show* (*TDS*) are a good example. Few people misunderstood what Stewart was saying about a particular subject. Complex satire contains dual messages, both explicit and implicit. Here, what the satirist is explicitly saying is *not* what they really mean. Examples include Jonathan Swift's *A Modest Proposal*, or Stephen Colbert's *The Colbert Report* (*TCR*). Finally, self-deprecating PH humor is when a politician makes fun of him or herself. It is important to distinguish between these types because the effects of each may differ from other types.

The Pre-History of Humor Effects Research

Systematic study of PH effects has been largely non-existent until fairly recently. Various studies prior to the year 2000 or so examined *humor* effects, but there were few lasting streams of research and relatively few studies devoted to the effects of exposure to *political* humor. Existing research spans several disciplines, primarily education, psychology, marketing, and communication.

Much of the early research on the effects of viewing humor was conducted by marketing and advertising scholars. Most examined whether humorous advertisements affected attention to and comprehension of the ads, aided in the retention of brand name recall or recognition, affected subjects' intention to purchase the advertised product, purchasing decisions, and the credibility of the source of the ad (Gelb & Zinkhan, 1986; Weinberger & Gulas, 1992).

Attitudes

Most scholarship devoted to humor effects deals with whether and how humor exposure might influence attitudes. Early reviews suggested that while there were various methodological challenges to this research (e.g., the use of student populations as subjects, problems with experimental realism), humor did have the potential to change attitudes, at least in some cases (Gruner, 1996; Markiewicz, 1974).

The earliest empirical examinations of humor effects on attitudes focused on editorials and editorial cartoons, and results were inconclusive (Annis, 1939; Asher & Stansfield, 1941). Early research on humorous versus non-humorous speeches found that the former was not significantly more persuasive than the latter (Lull, 1940). Another pioneering study found evidence of a 'boomerang effect,' where subjects' opinion moved in a direction opposite from what was expected after listening to complex satire in the form of a radio drama (Berlo & Kumata, 1956).

A significant amount of scholarship has been devoted to the influence of humorous advertisements on consumers. While many of these studies use terms like 'brand recognition' and 'purchase intention,' the underlying dependent variable is attitude change. In other words, this scholarship is germane to a discussion of PH effects. The consensus view of this scholarship is that at least for some individuals, humorous ads can affect attitudes (see, e.g., Cline & Kellaris, 1999; Nelson, Duncan, & Frontczak, 1985; Zhang, 1996a, 1996b; Zhang & Zinkhan, 1991; see Eisend, 2009, for a review).

More immediately relevant to a discussion of PH effects is a review of research in psychology and communication. This research, mainly experimental, often relied on explicitly *political* humor. Much of the early psychology research on humor effects focused less on the presence or absence of direct effects, but rather the cognitive mechanisms responsible for such effects, particularly persuasion. Two such mechanisms are prominent in this regard, both of which are employed in later research.

The first is known as the counterargument disruption (a.k.a., distraction) thesis, which suggests that when individuals are exposed to a humorous message, appreciation of the humor distracts them such that they are less likely to argue with the message. According to this logic, they are more likely to experience a message-consistent attitude shift. Some research supports this thesis (Festinger & Maccoby, 1964; Grote & Cvetkovich, 1972).

The second theory, known as the elaboration likelihood model (ELM), outlines a process similar to counterargument disruption. This model suggests that individuals process messages in one of two ways, or routes. Message processing in the central route involves cognition or actually thinking about the message or argument being presented. Processing messages in the peripheral route is more affective, relying less on cognition (Petty & Cacioppo, 1986). According to this logic, humorous messages, which admittedly often require cognition in order to 'get the joke,' are more likely to be processed in the peripheral route. Because of this relative lack of cognitive processing (counterargument), the humorous message may be more likely to persuade. This was the proposition used by Lyttle (2001), who found attitude change as the result of humor exposure. This said it is also possible that the humorous message will be discounted, or not taken seriously, making the message *less* likely to persuade (more on this in the concluding section).

Most early research on the effect of PH on attitudes was produced by scholars whose interest in the subject was somewhat fleeting. One exception was Charles Gruner, a communication scholar. In his early work, Gruner found little evidence of persuasive effects from PH exposure (1965, 1966, 1967, 1971). However, he often used hard-to-understand satirical messages in his experiments, so any potential persuasive effect was likely mitigated. In a later review, he acknowledged this, also noting that much subsequent research had found evidence of humor's persuasive power (1996).

A few other communication scholars examined the persuasive effects of PH as well. Some of this research complemented Gruner's, finding the interpretation of satire was often challenging for subjects (Brinkman, 1968; Carl, 1968). Others focused on factors that might moderate PH's impact on attitude change. For example, research showed that individuals with pre-existing attitudes toward the subject of a message were less likely to be persuaded (Pokorny & Gruner, 1969), while those to whom the the subject mattered less were more likely to be persuaded (Powell, 1977, 1978).

A distinct subgroup of early research addressed humor effects on attitudes related to how group membership might moderate its influence. Various scholars examined differences in how humor disparaging one's own group (the 'in-group') and others (the 'out-group') was perceived. Early studies suggested that people found out-group disparaging humor to be funnier and that it had some ability to change attitudes about the targeted group (Husband, 1977; LaFave, 1972; Wolff, Smith, & Murray, 1934). This stream of research is inherently political, particularly with respect to issues of race, ethnicity, and partisanship. For example, studies show that partisans find jokes targeting the opposition party to be funnier than those targeting their own (Priest, 1966; Priest & Abrahams, 1970; Weise, 1996). In the same vein, exposure to the hit television sitcom *All in the Family* tended to reinforce pre-existing negative views about minorities and women, based on Archie's (the protagonist) bigoted views (Brigham & Giesbrecht, 1976; Vidmar & Rockeach, 1974).

Cognition

A second stream of early research focused on the effect humorous messages had on cognition, including learning, memory and understanding of the content. Regarding the latter, several studies echoed Gruner's early findings that individuals often misunderstand the message of political satire (McMahon, 1999; Pfaff & Gibbs, 1997), especially complex satire.

Much of what we know in this area comes from marketing and education research. One early review of marketing research on the efficacy of humor in advertising suggested that while humor may have a detrimental effect on comprehension it increases attention to the message (Sternthal & Craig, 1973). Some early education research found similar results, noting that increased attention did not necessarily translate to greater recall or retention of information (Bryant, Alan, Silberberg, & Elliott, 1981; Cantor & Venus, 1980; Taylor, 1964) or comprehension of the materials being presented (Kaplan & Pascoe, 1977). However other research found positive cognitive effects of humorous messages. For example, while humorous ads did not increase brand *recall*, there was a positive effect on brand *recognition* (Berg & Lippmanm, 2001). Still others suggested that humor had a positive effect on both comprehension and recall (Duncan, Nelson, & Frontczak, 1984; Schmidt, 1994, 2002; Schmidt & Williams, 2001).

Early research on the effects that humor, and PH, had on individuals pointed in a few directions. First, not all PH is well understood by the audience, which has implications for any attitudinal and cognitive effects it may have. Second, the research suggested that humor might have the power to affect attitudes. Finally, earlier scholarship showed that humor might have a positive effect on some aspects of learning.

Political Humor and Its Effects

Since the year 2000, a small handful of communication, psychology and political science scholars have been systematically examining the question of how specifically *political* humor affects individuals' understanding of, and engagement in, politics. Most of these contemporary studies, whether based on survey or experimental research designs, have focused on PH on late-night talk shows on television. Some have been grounded in research reviewed in the previous section, and for the most part, findings are in line with that research.

Attitudes

A plurality of contemporary scholarship on PH effects focuses on how it might influence attitudes and opinion. Given the volume of work on this subject, this section will be divided according to the humor types introduced at the beginning of this essay: self-deprecating humor, simple political comedy and satire, and complex political satire. Following this will be a short discussion of recent studies that examine PH's effect on attitudes toward various outgroups, including racial and ethnic outgroups.

Self-Deprecating Humor

Early research on how self-deprecating humor affected various attitudes toward the speaker (e.g., Chang & Gruner, 1981; Eisend, 2009; Hackman, 1988; Powell, 1978; Smith & Powell, 1988; Stocking & Zillmann, 1976) proved inconclusive. However recent research paints a simpler picture. Politicians speaking ill of themselves, even in a joking manner, is so unusual that the resulting incongruity is pleasantly surprising to most (Nerhardt, 1976; Rothbart, 1976; but see Becker, 2011). One study used a representation of President George W. Bush in an animated clip, in effect a *faux* first-person clip of the president mocking himself, to show that self-deprecating humor had a positive effect on evaluations of him (Baumgartner, 2007). In later research Baumgartner and colleagues found a similar positive effect, this time employing a short clip of NJ Governor Chris Christie making light of his weight and eating habits (Baumgartner, Morris, & Coleman, 2018). Others have found similar results (Becker & Haller, 2014; Stewart, 2011).

Simple Political Comedy and Political Satire

Numerous studies in the past two decades show that simple PH has a message-consistent effect on evaluations of its target. The message in PH is typically negative (Niven *et al.* 2003), and this translates into a negative effect of the opinion of the target. Young's (2004) study found that less knowledgeable viewers of late-night talk shows rated both presidential candidates in 2000 (George W. Bush and Al Gore) lower after seeing them lambasted by hosts of the programs. Baumgartner and Morris' seminal research showed that viewing clips from *TDS* mocking Bush and John Kerry during the 2004 campaign lowered evaluations of both, irrespective of partisan identification (2006).

Morris (2009) also examined the effect of *TDS* coverage of the 2004 Republican and Democratic conventions had on viewers. He showed first that coverage of Republicans was harsher than that for Democrats, then, that evaluations of President Bush and Vice President Dick Cheney were lowered. Numerous studies have confirmed the idea that simple PH (comedy and satire) lowers opinions of its target (Baumgartner, 2008; Baumgartner & Morris, 2012; Baumgartner, Morris, & Walth, 2012; Becker, 2014a; Brewer & McKnight, 2015;

Matthes, Rauchfleisch, & Kohler, 2011; Nabi, Moyer-Gusé, & Byrne, 2007; Neuberger & Krcmar, 2008; Xenos, Moy, & Becker, 2011; Young, 2012).

Some research findings have been more nuanced. For example, one study found that those with lower levels of political interest and political knowledge were more likely to base their judgment of political candidates on traits caricatured by late-night talk show hosts (Young, 2006; see also Baum, 2005). As noted earlier, partisans think jokes about the opposing party's candidates are funnier than those targeting co-partisans (Priest, 1966; Priest & Abrahams, 1970). Furthermore, individual attitudes are less likely to be affected when the topic or issue in the message is important to the individual (Chung & Zhao, 2003; Cline & Kellaris, 1999; Powell, 1977, 1978). Finally, those who have a high need for cognition (who enjoy critical thinking) are also less likely to be affected by humorous messages (Zhang, 1996a, 1996b).

Another aspect of attitude change that has been examined is external and internal political efficacy. External political efficacy is an individual's perception of how responsive government is to the public (Niemi, Craig, & Mattei, 1991). Related to external political efficacy is trust in government and the media as well as cynicism regarding the political system (Cappella & Jamieson, 1997). Employing both survey and experimental data, Baumgartner and Morris (2006) showed that viewership of *TDS* was associated with lowered faith in the electoral system and the media among young adults (Morris & Baumgartner, 2008). Baumgartner's (2013) experimental research showed that exposure to animated clips lampooning presidential candidates lowered trust in political institutions in a 'spillover effect.'

Other studies showed lowered evaluations of television news programming among at least some who viewed *TDS* or *TCR* (Holbert, Lambe, Dudo, & Carlton, 2007; Littau & Stewart, 2015). Another analysis found that those exposed to 'comedy talk' (e.g., David Letterman, Jay Leno) were more distrustful of politicians, while those exposed to political satire (e.g., *TDS*) displayed greater levels of 'systemic cynicism' (Guggenheim, Kwak, & Campbell, 2011).

Internal political efficacy is a measure of one's belief in their ability to understand the political world and affect change (Niemi et al., 1991). Interestingly, experimental research by Baumgartner and Morris (2006) showed that while viewership of *TDS* *lowered* external efficacy among young adults, it *raised* internal efficacy. The authors reasoned that this increase may have resulted from increased confidence in viewers' 'getting the joke,' or from simple PH's simplification of the political world. Two other studies focused on young adults, suggested there may be a positive relationship between viewing simple political comedy and political participation, where the mediating variable was increased internal political efficacy (Hoffman & Thomson, 2009; Hoffman & Young, 2011; see also Becker, 2011, 2014b; Holbert et al., 2007).

Complex Political Satire

Unlike simple PH, complex satire contains two messages, both explicit and implicit. For example, on *TCR*, Colbert would explicitly state that George W. Bush was the best president ever. His implicit message, or what he actually meant, was that Bush was one of the *worst* presidents ever. The dual-message nature of complex satire has important implications for predicting attitude change. Research suggests that because additional cognitive resources are required to process the implicit message, viewers often process only the explicit message. In short, in complex satire, the explicit message is the one most likely to be processed.

Thus, complex PH also has a message-consistent effect on attitudes toward its target, but viewers are moved to agree with its *explicit* message. For example, research has shown that although Colbert was implicitly mocking Bush, Republicans and conservatives, viewers of his show were moved to see those targets more favourably (Baumgartner & Morris, 2008a, 2012). This finding is reminiscent of that of Berlo and Kumata (1956), who found that listeners of complex satire in the form of a radio play explicitly supporting (implicitly condemning) the McCarthy hearings of the 1950s were moved to evaluate McCarthy more positively. This 'boomerang effect' was also found among viewers of the 1970s sitcom *All in the Family*, another complex satire. Here, viewers were moved to agree with the sexist, bigoted views of the protagonist Archie (Brigham, 1975; Vidmar and Rockeach, 1974).

Other Research on Attitudinal Effects

There are a few other areas of research into the effects of PH on attitudes that should be mentioned. Humor targeting historically disadvantaged groups, although not, strictly speaking, political, has political ramifications. Psychologist Thomas Ford has examined how racist, ethnic, and sexist humor might affect attitudes toward the targeted groups. His findings are consistent with other research on the effects of viewing simple PH on attitudes toward the target: other-disparaging humor moves attitudes in a message-consistent direction – in other words, in a negative direction (Ford, 1997; Ford, Boxer, Armstrong, & Edel, 2008; Ford & Ferguson, 2004).

One area of research that has received scant attention is how PH about a particular subject might affect subjects' perceptions regarding the importance of the subject. Here, two studies have examined humor about various foreign policy and security issues, and perceptions about how serious these issues were declined as the result of exposure to such humor in both (Baumgartner & Morris, 2015; Tsfati, Tukachinsky, & Peri, 2009).

Researchers have also begun to examine various aspects of PH appreciation. One stream of this research focuses on the idea that most people interpret PH to fit their own views. LaMarre and her colleagues' landmark study showed that liberal viewers of *TCR* perceived Colbert as a liberal, while viewers who were conservative thought he was conservative (LaMarre, Landreville, & Beam, 2009). This same bias coloured viewers' opinions of content from *TDS* (Coe et al., 2008). Other research has gone further, suggesting that viewing satirical news programming may reduce subsequent exposure to news that disagrees with their own views (Stroud & Muddiman, 2013). Biased perception or interpretation of humor also extends to how funny people think the humor may be. As noted earlier, partisans are less appreciative of humor targeting their own political party as opposed to their rivals' (Priest, 1966; Priest & Abrahams, 1970; Weise, 1996; see also Knobloch-Westerwick & Lavis, 2017).

Cognition

Research on the relationship between PH and political cognition has focused on how PH associates with political knowledge and whether people learn from exposure to PH. With respect to the former, one early study found that viewing 'television comedy (e.g., *Saturday Night Live* [*SNL*])' had a negative relationship with an index of 'political expertise, which included political knowledge' (Pfau, Houston, & Semmler, 2005, 53). But overall research shows a positive relationship between PH exposure and political knowledge. Several analyses using cross-sectional data found associations between knowledge of the presidential candidates and viewership of late-night talk shows and comedy during the 2000 and 2004 election cycles (Brewer & Cao, 2006; Cao, 2008; Moy, 2008). Another, which combined viewership of broadcast network talk shows on late-night television (e.g., Leno, Letterman) and *TDS* into a single measure, found evidence of greater political knowledge during the 2004 campaign among viewers, especially those who were previously less informed (Baek & Wojcieszak, 2009; see also Baumgartner & Morris, 2011).

Overall, the evidence suggests that there is a relationship between PH exposure and political knowledge. However, the aforementioned studies did not test for a *causal* relationship between PH exposure and political knowledge. It is possible that those who are already politically knowledgeable are those who are viewing PH. Some research suggests that people believe they learn about politics from viewing political comedy (e.g., Brewer & Cao, 2008; Young & Tisinger, 2006), although this may not be the case.

Do people actually *learn* about politics and public affairs from viewing PH? Findings from experimental research, ideal for answering this question, have varied somewhat over the past few years. Some early research suggested that such learning was possible, but sceptics argued that learning was minimal (Baum, 2003; Hollander, 2005). One study found that the use of Jon Stewart's *America: The Book* in introductory American government classes did not raise test scores of students (Baumgartner & Morris, 2008b). Another found increased attentiveness to and interest in the material among subjects resulting from exposure to humor, but results were mixed with respect to learning (Xenos & Becker, 2009).

The weight of the evidence, however, suggests that viewing PH can raise political knowledge, at least in some cases or with some groups. One study found a learning effect among viewers when presidential candidates appear on late-night television and engage in humorous banter with the host (Parkin, 2010). Another found that although viewers might not be able to remember discrete facts (e.g., those used in multiple-choice questions) after viewing PH, they can learn enough to be able to come to reasoned political decisions, such as voting (Kim & Vishak, 2008). Still, another found that learning occurs as the result of viewing PH if individuals see the program in question as a valid news source (Feldman, 2013b).

Much of the existing research on learning from PH has focused on the effects of viewing *TDS* and *TCR* and other satire. Two studies, for example, showed that those who watched *TCR* while the host focused the subject of Super PACs (political action committees that have no caps on the amount of money they can accept from individuals or organisations) became more knowledgeable about these groups (Hardy, Gottfried, Winneg, & Jamieson, 2014; Warner, Hawthorne, & Hawthorne, 2015). Others have found increases in political knowledge resulting from viewing other satirical programming (Becker, 2013, 2018; LaMarre, 2013; Matthes, 2013; Young & Hoffman, 2012).

In short, there is an association between exposure to PH and political knowledge. Moreover, evidence suggests that at least some people, especially those who may not be particularly attentive to or knowledgeable about politics, learn from exposure to PH.

Participation

The final area of inquiry into how viewing PH might affect political behaviour focuses on the subject of political engagement. Here, scholarship lags behind, at least relative to studies which look at attitudinal and cognitive effects. The existing research can be divided into two main areas. The first examines engagement with or attentiveness to politics. Two studies, drawing on survey data, demonstrate that late-night talk show viewership, in particular satire viewership, is associated with greater attentiveness to political news (Cao, 2010; Feldman & Young, 2008; see also Feldman, Leiserowitz, & Maibach, 2011).

The second, larger area, examines how PH viewership affects political participation. One early study of young adults found a null effect of viewership of entertainment talk shows, including late-night talk shows on the broadcast networks, on the likelihood of voting (Kwak, Wang, & Guggenheim, 2004). Another, examining a sample of all adults, found a null effect of viewing late-night talk shows on broadcast network television and a small but significant negative effect among viewers of *TDS*, *SNL*, and *Politically Incorrect* on voter turnout in 2004 (Moy, 2008). Yet another found a negative effect of viewership of *SNL* and *MadTV* on participation (Pfau, Houston, & Semmler, 2007).

This said, most of the evidence points to a positive relationship between exposure to PH and various forms of political participation. Two early studies found such a positive effect, mediated by increased levels of internal political efficacy (Hoffman & Young, 2011), among high school students (Hoffman & Thomson, 2009). Other cross-sectional research, also focused on young adults, found similar associations, for those viewing online PH (Baumgartner, 2008), and low-to-medium frequency *TDS* viewing (Baumgartner & Morris, 2011). Others, using national samples of all adults, found evidence of a positive relationship between viewing PH on various late-night television shows and different measures of political participation (e.g., attending a political event or joining a political organisation; Cao and Brewer, 2008), overall participation, or the inclination to talk politics with others (Young & Esralew, 2011; see also Moy, Xenos, & Hess, 2005). One recent study, using national panel data, distinguished between viewership of televised political comedy and satire, finding null effects of the former and a positive relationship of the latter on various measures of political participation in 2012 (Baumgartner & Lockerbie, 2018).

Next Steps

Humorists routinely claim that their material, including politically oriented material, should be taken as a joke. However, research in the past two decades has clearly demonstrated that PH is more than 'just a joke.' Political comedy and political satire contribute to how people understand, how they think about, and engage in politics.

Exposure to self-deprecating PH seems to raise evaluations of the person (politician) poking fun at themselves. However, PH directed at other targets lowers evaluations not only of the target of the humor, but the larger political system as well. This is also true of complex satire, which serves to lower opinion of the explicit target of the humor. Exposure to simple PH also seems to raise individuals' confidence in their ability to understand and effectively navigate the political world. Humor about various groups increases negative attitudes about those groups, and finally, humor crafted around various issues may decrease their perceived importance.

Cognitively, many people believe that they learn about politics from exposure to PH. Such exposure does have a positive association with political knowledge and has also been shown to aid in some learning. Finally, there seems to be little question that exposure to PH has a positive effect on political engagement, including political participation.

One major area of research that is underdeveloped centres around the psychological mechanisms of how and why PH affects attitudes, learning and engagement. A fair amount of research has been done in this regard with respect to attitudes (e.g., Becker & Waisanen, 2016; Boukes, Boomgaarden, Moorman, & De Vreese, 2015), but there is no consensus regarding the underlying psychological mechanism of humor's ability to change attitudes as of yet. Earlier work, as well as some recent research, employed the elaboration likelihood model of persuasion (Petty & Cacioppo, 1986). But it is still unclear why peripheral route processing might result in attitude change. It may be the result of the positive mood created by viewing humor, an increase in likeability of the source of the humor, or a reduction in cognitive resources available to scrutinise the argument contained in the message (LaMarre & Walther, 2013). Another theory that has been used to explain attitude change resulting from PH viewing is the theory of priming (see, e.g., Esralew & Young, 2012), in which certain objects are ideas are 'primed' for subsequent activation by various messages (Iyengar, Peters, & Kinder, 1982). In other words, if a particular frame or idea is activated, or primed by the message, individuals will be more likely to agree with that frame or idea.

Alternatively, some theorists suggest a discounting cue theory. Contrary to the bulk of the research that exists, this theory posits that attitude change *cannot* occur as the result of exposure to PH. This is because humor cannot be very persuasive given that most individuals know they are hearing a joke (Nabi et al., 2007; Xenos & Becker, 2009; Young, 2008; see also Jennings, Bramlett, & Warner, 2018; LaMarre, Landreville, Young, & Gilkerson, 2014). According to this logic, they simply 'discount' the message. Clearly more research is needed to clarify our understanding of the mechanisms promoting attitude change.

Other aspects of attitude change that require further investigation include how lasting the effects of viewing PH are. Because of typical research design limitations, most of what we know confirms short-term attitude change as the result of PH exposure, but how long does this change last, and under what circumstances? It is also unclear how the issue of salience or previously held beliefs factors into attitude change resulting from PH exposure. Strongly held beliefs might mitigate attitude change about these beliefs (Baumgartner, 2018) and the converse may be true, but this question has not been sufficiently explored.

Another avenue of research that is less well developed involves how various humor appreciation factors affect attitudes. Some work, for example, has been done examining how attitude change is mediated by a need for cognition or affinity for PH (Hmielowski, Holbert, & Lee, 2011), although the latter may have issues of face validity. Further testing or development of an alternative scale would be a positive contribution. It might also be useful to specify what type of PH (if any) the individual prefers in analytical models. Is it simple political comedy, simple political satire, or more nuanced complex satire? Some researchers have begun distinguishing between Horatian and Juvenalian satire (Holbert, Hmielowski, Jain, Lather, & Morey, 2011) in analyses, but this distinction is less useful than the one employed in this essay for empirical analyses of the effects of PH exposure.

With respect to cognition, why is it that people think they learn from exposure to PH – even if they do not? Greater attention could also be paid to the question of how useful the information gained as an incidental by-product of PH viewership is. One school of thought is that although such learning comes at a minimal cognitive cost, its utility is marginal (Prior, 2003). More, what drives learning that occurs subsequent to and as a consequence of viewing PH (the 'gateway' theory; Feldman & Young, 2008)? Is it pre-existing interest in the subject, or does the humor spark new interest?

Several questions remain with respect to humor's effect on political participation as well. Here too, much of what remains to be uncovered revolves around the mechanics, or how and why, humor might drive participation. This question is especially interesting because, on the one hand, we know that PH has a negative effect on external political efficacy. As the result, we might expect lower rates of participation due to the cynicism produced. Does this cynicism have a demobilising effect? Or, because most PH increases internal political efficacy, should we expect higher rates of participation? Which of these mechanisms is stronger, or more proximate? More research is needed to uncover the nuances of these effects. Another question that bears investigation: because disparaging humor helps foster negative attitudes toward out-groups, does it also lead to discriminatory behaviour?

In all, much has been learned over the past two decades about the impact of exposure to this sub-genre of political speech. We know that PH is more than simply a laughing matter regarding how people understand and feel about the political world. What remains is to continue to explore the various reasons how and why this might be the case.

References

Alisky, M. (1990). White House wit: Presidential humor to sustain policies, from Lincoln to Reagan. *Presidential Studies Quarterly, 20*(2), 373–381.

Annis, A. D. (1939). The relative effectiveness of cartoons and editorials as propaganda media. *Psychological Bulletin, 36,* 628.

Asher, R., & Stansfield, S. S. (1941). Shifts in attitude caused by cartoon caricatures. *The Journal of General Psychology, 24*(2), 451–455.

Baek, Y. M., & Wojcieszak, M. E. (2009). Don't expect too much! Learning from late-night comedy and knowledge item difficulty. *Communication Research,* 36(6), 783–809.

Baum, M. A. (2003). Soft news and political knowledge. Evidence of absence or absence of evidence? *Political Communication, 20*(2), 173–190.

Baum, M. A. (2005). Talking the vote: Why presidential candidates hit the talk show circuit. *American journal of Political Science, 49*(2), 213–234.

Baumgartner, J. C (2007). Humor on the next frontier: Youth, online political humor, and the JibJab effect. *Social Science Computer Review, 29,* 319–338.

Baumgartner, J. C (2008). Polls and elections: Editorial cartoons 2.0: The effects of digital political satire on presidential candidate evaluations. *Presidential Studies Quarterly, 38*(4), 735–758.

Baumgartner, J. C (2013). No laughing matter? Young adults and the 'spillover effect' of candidate-centered political humor. *Humor, 26*(1), 23–43.

Baumgartner, J. C (2018). The limits of attitude change: Political humor during the 2016 campaign. In J. C Baumgartner & A. B. Becker (Eds.), *Political humor in a changing media landscape: A new generation of research* (pp. 61–78). Lanham, MD: Lexington.

Baumgartner, J. C, & Lockerbie, B. (2018). Maybe it is more than a joke: Satire, mobilization, and political participation. *Social Science Quarterly, 99*(3), 1060–1074.

Baumgartner, J. C, & Morris, J. S. (2006). The Daily Show effect: Candidate evaluations, efficacy, and American youth. *American Politics Research, 34*(3), 341–367.

Baumgartner, J. C, & Morris, J. S. (2008a). One 'nation' under Stephen? The effects of *The Colbert Report* on American youth. *Journal of Broadcasting and Electronic Media, 52*(4), 622–643.

Baumgartner, J. C, & Morris, J. S. (2008b). Jon Stewart comes to class: The learning effects of *America (The Book)* in introduction to American government courses. *Journal of Political Science Education, 4*(2), 169–186.

Baumgartner, J. C, & Morris, J. S. (2011). Stoned slackers or super-citizens? 'Daily Show' viewing and political engagement of young adults. In A. Amarasingam (Ed.), *The Stewart/Colbert effect: Essays on the real impacts of fake news* (pp. 63–78). Jefferson NC: McFarland & Co.

Baumgartner, J. C, & Morris, J. S. (2012). Research note: The 2008 presidential primaries and differential effects of 'The Daily Show' and 'The Colbert Report' on young adults. *Midsouth Political Science Review, 12*, 87–102.

Baumgartner, J. C, & Morris, J. S. (2015). The serious business of late-night political humor: Foreign policy issue salience in the 2014 mid-term elections. In J. A. Hendricks & D. Schill (Eds.), *Communication and mid-term elections: Media, message, and mobilization* (pp. 131–142). New York, NY: Palgrave.

Baumgartner, J. C, Morris, J. S., & Walth, N. L. (2012). The Fey effect: Young adults, political humor, and perceptions of Sarah Palin in the 2008 presidential election campaign. *Public Opinion Quarterly, 76*(1), 95–104.

Baumgartner, J. C, Morris, J. S., & Coleman, J. M. (2018). Did the 'road to the White House run through' Letterman? Chris Christie, Letterman, and other-disparaging versus self-deprecating humor. *Journal of Political Marketing, 17*(3), 282–300.

Becker, A. B. (2011). Political humor as democratic relief? The effects of exposure to comedy and straight news on trust and efficacy. *Atlantic Journal of Communication, 19*(5), 235–250.

Becker, A. B. (2013). What about those interviews? The impact of exposure to political comedy and cable news on factual recall and anticipated political expression. *International Journal of Public Research, 25*(3), 344–356.

Becker, A. B. (2014a). Humiliate my enemies or mock my friends? Applying disposition theory of humor to the study of political parody appreciation and attitudes toward candidates. *Human Communication Research, 40*(2), 137–160.

Becker, A. B. (2014b). Playing with politics: Online political parody, affinity for political humor, anxiety reduction, and implications for political efficacy. *Mass Communication and Society, 17*(3), 424–445.

Becker, A. B. (2018). Interviews and viewing motivations: Exploring connections between political satire, perceived learning, and elaborative processing. In J. C Baumgartner & A. B. Becker (Eds.), *Political humor in a changing media landscape: A new generation of research* (pp. 79–94). Lanham MD: Lexington.

Becker, A. B., & Haller, B. A. (2014). When political comedy turns personal: Humor types, audience evaluations, and attitudes. *Howard Journal of Communication, 25*(1), 34–55.

Becker, A. B., & Waisanen, D. J. (2016). Laughing or learning with the chief executive? the impact of exposure to president' jokes on message elaboration. *Humor, 30*(1), 23–41.

Berg, E. M., & Lippmanm, L. G. (2001). Does humor in radio advertising affect recognition of novel product brand names? *The Journal of General Psychology, 128*(2), 194–205.

Berlo, D. K., & Kumata, H. (1956). The investigator: The impact of a satirical radio drama. *Journalism Quarterly, 33*(3), 187–198.

Boukes, M., Boomgaarden, H. G., Moorman, M., & De Vreese, C. H. (2015). At odds: Laughing and thinking? The appreciation, processing, and persuasiveness of political satire. *Journal of Communication, 65*(5), 721–744.

Brewer, P., & Cao, X. (2008). Late night comedy as news sources: What the polls say. In J. C Baumgartner & J. S. Morris (Eds.), *Laughing matters: Humor and American politics in the media age* (pp. 263–278). New York, NY: Routledge.

Brewer, P. R., & Marquardt, E. (2007). Mock news and democracy: Analyzing *The Daily Show*. *Atlantic Journal of Communication, 15*(4), 249–267.
Brewer, P. R., & Cao, X. (2006). Candidate appearances on soft news shows and public knowledge about primary campaigns. *The Journal of Broadcasting and Electronic Media, 50*(1), 18–35.
Brewer, P. R., & McKnight, J. (2015, August 3). Climate as comedy: The effects of satirical television news on climate change perceptions. *Science communication, 37*(5), 635–657.
Brigham, J. C. (1975). Ethnic humor on television: Does it reduce/reinforce racial prejudice? Presented at the *Annual convention of the American Psychological Association*. Chicago, IL.
Brigham, J. C., & Giesbrecht, L. B. (1976). 'All in the Family': Racial attitudes. *Journal of Communication, 26*(4), 69–74.
Brinkman, D. (1968). Do editorial cartoons and editorials change opinions? *Journalism Quarterly, 45*(4), 724–726.
Bryant, J., Alan, D. B., Silberberg, R., & Elliott, S. M. (1981). Effects of humorous illustrations in college textbooks. *Human Communication Research, 8*(1), 43–57.
Campbell, A., Converse, P. E., Miller, W. E., & Stokes, D. E. (1960). *The American voter*. Chicago, IL. University of Chicago Press.
Cantor, J., & Venus, P. (1980). The effect of humor on recall of a radio advertisement. *Journal of Broadcasting. 24*(1), 13–22.
Cao, X. (2008). Political comedy shows and knowledge about primary campaigns: The moderating effects of age and education. *Mass Communication & Society, 11*(1), 43–61.
Cao, X. (2010). Hearing it from Jon Stewart: The impact of *The Daily Show* on public attentiveness to politics. *International Journal of Public Opinion Research, 22*(1), 26–46.
Cao, X., & Brewer, P. R. (2008). Political comedy shows and public participation in politics. *International Journal of Public Opinion Research, 20*(1), 90–99.
Cappella, J. N., & Jamieson, K. H., (1997). *Spiral of cynicism: The press and the public good*. Oxford University Press.
Carl, L. M. (1968). Editorial cartoons fail to reach many readers. *Journalism Quarterly, 45*(3), 533–535.
Chang, M., & Gruner, C. R. (1981). Audience reaction to self-disparaging humor. *Southern Speech Communication Journal, 46*, 419–426.
Chung, H., & Zhao, X. (2003). Humour effect on memory and attitude: Moderating role of product involvement. *International Journal of Advertising, 22*(1), 117–144.
Cline, T. W., & Kellaris, J. J. (1999). The joint impact of humor and argument strength in a print advertising context: A case for weaker arguments. *Psychology & Marketing, 16*(1), 69–86.
Coe, K., Tewksbury, D., Bond, B. J., Drogos, K. L., Porter, R. W., Yahn, A., & Yuanyuan Z. (2008). Hostile news: Partisan use and perceptions of cable news programming. *Journal of Communication, 58*(2), 201–219.
Duncan, C. P., Nelson, J. E., & Frontczak, N. T. (1984). The effect of humor on advertising comprehension. *Advances in Consumer Research Volume, 11*(1), 432–437.
Eisend, M. (2009). A meta-analysis of humor in advertising. *Journal of the Academy of Marketing Science, 37*(2), 191–203.
Esralew, S., & Young, D. G. (2012). The influence of parodies on mental models: Exploring the Tina Fey-Sarah Palin phenomenon. *Communication Quarterly, 60*(3), 338–352.
Feldman, L. (2013a). Cloudy with a chance of heat balls: The portrayal of global warming on *The Daily Show* and *The Colbert Report*. *International Journal of Communication, 7*(1), 430–451.

Feldman, L. (2013b). Learning about politics from *The Daily Show*: The role of viewer orientation and processing motivations. *Mass Communication and Society*, *16*(4), 586–607.

Feldman, L., & Young, D. G. (2008). Late-night comedy as a gateway to traditional news: An analysis of time trends in news attention among late-night comedy viewers during the 2004 presidential primaries. *Political Communication*, *25*(4), 401–422.

Feldman, L., Leiserowitz, A., & Maibach, E. (2011). The science of satire: *The Daily Show* and *The Colbert Report* as sources of public attention to science and the environment. In A. Amarasingam (Ed.), *The Stewart/Colbert effect: Essays on the real impacts of fake news* (pp. 25–46). Jefferson, NC: McFarland & Company.

Festinger, L., & Maccoby, N. (1964). On resistance to persuasive communications. *The Journal of Abnormal and Social Psychology*, *68*(4), 359–366.

Ford, T. E. (1997). Effects of stereotypical television portrayals of African-Americans on person perception. *Social Psychology Quarterly*, *60*(3), 266–275.

Ford, T. E., Boxer, C. M., Armstrong, J. A., & Edel, J. R. (2008). More than just a joke: The prejudice-releasing function of sexist humor. *Personality and Social Psychology Bulletin*, *34*(2), 159–170.

Ford, T. E., & Ferguson, M. A. (2004). Social consequences of disparagement humor: A prejudiced norm theory. *Personality and Social Psychology Review*, *8*(1), 79–94.

Gardner, G. (1994). *Campaign comedy: Political humor from Clinton to Kennedy*. Detroit, MI: Wayne State University.

Gelb, B. D., & Zinkhan, G. M. (1986). Humor and advertising effectiveness after repeated exposures to a radio commercial. *Journal of Advertising*, *15*(2), 15–20, 34.

Grote, B., & Cvetkovich, G. (1972). Humor appreciation and issue involvement. *Psychonomic Science*, *27*(4), 199–200.

Gruner, C. R. (1965). An experimental study of satire as persuasion. *Speech Monographs*, *32*(2), 149–154.

Gruner, C. R. (1966). A further experimental study of satire as persuasion. *Speech Monographs*, *33*(2), 184–185.

Gruner, C. R. (1967). Editorial satire as persuasion: An experiment. *Journalism Quarterly*, *44*(4), 727–730.

Gruner, C. R. (1971. Ad hominem satire as a persuader: An experiment. *Journalism Quarterly*, *48*(1), 128–131.

Gruner, C. R. (1996). Wit and humour in mass communication. In J. Chapman & H. C. Foot (Eds.), *Humor and laughter: Theory, research, and applications* (pp. 287–311). New Brunswick, NJ: Transaction Publishers.

Guggenheim, L., Kwak, N., & Campbell, S. W. (2011). Nontraditional news negativity: The relationship of entertaining political news use to political cynicism and mistrust. *International Journal of Public Opinion Research*, *23*(3), 287–314.

Hackman, M. Z. (1988). Audience reactions to the use of direct and personal disparaging humor in informative public addresses. *Communication Research Reports*, *5*(2), 126–130.

Hardy, B. W., Gottfried, J. A., Winneg, K. M., & Jamieson K. H. (2014). Stephen Colbert's civics lesson: How Colbert's super PAC taught viewers about campaign finance. *Mass Communication and Society*, *17*(3), 329–353.

Hmielowski, J. D., Holbert, R. L., & Lee, J. (2011). Predicting the consumption of political TV satire: Affinity for political humor, *The Daily Show*, and *The Colbert Report*. *Communication Monographs*, *78*(1), 96–114.

Hoffman, L. H., & Thomson, T. L. (2009). The effect of television viewing on adolescents' civic participation: Political efficacy as a mediating mechanism. *Journal of Broadcasting & Electronic Media*, *53*(1), 3–21.

Hoffman, L. H., & Young, D. G. (2011). Satire, punch lines, and the nightly news: Untangling media effects on political participation. *Communication Research Reports*, 28(2), 159–168.

Holbert, R. L., Lambe, J. L., Dudo, A. D., & Carlton, K. A. (2007). Primacy effects of *The Daily Show* and national TV news viewing: Young viewers, political gratifications, and internal political self-efficacy. *Journal of Broadcasting & Electronic Media*, 51(1), 20–38.

Holbert, R. L., Hmielowski, J., Jain, P., Lather, J., & Morey, A. (2011). Adding nuance to the study of political humor effects: Experimental research on Juvenalian satire versus Horatian satire. *American Behavioral Scientist*, 55(3), 187–211.

Hollander, B. A. (2005). Late-night learning: Do entertainment programs increase political campaign knowledge for young viewers. *Journal of Broadcasting & Electronic Media*, 49(4), 402–415.

Husband, C. (1977). The mass media and the functions of ethnic humour in a racist society. In A. J. Chapman & H. C. Foot (Eds.), *It's a funny thing, humour* (pp. 267–272). Oxford, UK: Pergamon Press.

Iyengar, S., Peters, M. D., & Kinder, D. R. (1982). Experimental demonstrations of the 'not-so-minimal' consequences of television news programs. *The American Political Science Review*, 76(4), 848–858.

Jennings, F. J., Bramlett, J. C., & Warner, B. R. (2018). Comedic cognition: The impact of elaboration on political comedy effects. *Western Journal of Communication*, 83(3), 365–382.

Kaplan, R. M., & Pascoe, G. C. (1977). Humorous lectures and humorous examples: Some effects upon comprehension and retention. *Journal of Educational Psychology*. 69(1), 61–65.

Kim, Y. M., & Vishak, J. (2008). Just laugh! You don't need to remember: The effects of entertainment media on political information acquisition and information processing in political judgment. *Journal of Communication*, 58(2), 338–360.

Knobloch-Westerwick, S., & Lavis, S. M. (2017). Selecting serious or satirical, supporting or stirring news? selecting exposure to partisan versus mockery news online videos. *Journal of Communication*, 67(1), 54–81.

Kwak, N., Wang, X., & Guggenheim, L. (2004). Laughing all the way: The relationship between television entertainment talk show viewing and political engagement among young adults. Paper presented at the Annual meeting of the Association for Education in Journalism and Mass Communication, Toronto, Canada.

LaFave, L. (1972). Humor judgments as a function of reference groups and identification classes. In J. H. Goldstein & P. E. McGhee (Eds.), *The psychology of humor: Theoretical perspectives and empirical issues* (pp. 195–210). New York, NY: Academic Press.

LaMarre, H. (2013). When parody and reality collide: Examining the effects of Colbert's super PAC satire on issue knowledge and policy engagement across media formats. *International Journal of Communication*, 7(1), 394–413.

LaMarre, H. L., Landreville, K. D., & Beam, M. A. (2009). The irony of satire: Political ideology and the motivation to see what you want to see in *The Colbert Report*. *The International Journal of Press/Politics*, 14(2), 212–231.

LaMarre, H. L., Landreville, K. D., Young, D., & Gilkerson, N. (2014). Humor works in funny ways: Examining satirical tone as a key determinant in political humor message processing. *Mass Communication and Society*, 17(3), 400–423.

LaMarre, H. L., & Walther, W. (2013). Ability matters: Testing the differential effects of political news and late-night political comedy on cognitive responses and the role of ability in micro-level opinion formation. *International Journal of Public Opinion Research*, 25(3), 303–322.

Lewis-Beck, M. S., Norpoth, H., Jacoby, W. G., & Weisberg, H. F. (2008). *The American voter revisited*. University of Michigan Press.

Littau, J., & Stewart, D. R. (2015). 'Truthiness' and second-level agenda setting satire news and its influence on perceptions of television news credibility. *Electronic News, 9*(2), 122–136.

Lull, P. E. (1940). The effectiveness of humor in persuasive speech. *Speech Monographs, 7*(1), 26–40.

Lyttle, J. (2001). The effectiveness of humor in persuasion: The case of business ethics training. *The Journal of General Psychology, 128*(2), 206–216.

Markiewicz, D. (1974). Effects of humor on persuasion. *Sociometry,* 37(3), 407–422.

Matthes, J. (2013). Elaboration or distraction? Knowledge acquisition from thematically related and unrelated humor in political speeches. *International Journal of Public Opinion Research, 25*(3), 291–302.

Matthes, J., Rauchfleisch, A., & Kohler, F. (2011, September). Getting the joke: The negative effects of late-night political parody on the evaluation of politicians. In *WAPOR 64th Annual Conference: Public Opinion and the Internet*, University of Zurich, 21–23.

McMahon, M. 1999. Are we having fun yet? Humor in the English class. *The English Journal, 88*(4), 70–72.

Morris, J. S. (2009). *The Daily Show with Jon Stewart* and audience attitude change during the 2004 party conventions. *Political Behavior, 31*(1), 79–102.

Morris, J. S., & Baumgartner, J. C (2008). *The Daily Show* and attitudes toward the news media. In J. C. Baumgartner & J. S. Morris (Eds.), *Laughing matters: Humor and American politics in the media age* (pp. 315–332). New York, NY: Routledge.

Moy, P. (2008). The political effects of late night comedy and talk shows. In J. C. Baumgartner & J. S. Morris (Eds.), *Laughing matters: Humor and American politics in the media age* (pp. 295–314). New York, NY: Routledge.

Moy, P., Xenos, M. A., & Hess, V. K. (2005). Communication and citizenship: Mapping the political effects of infotainment. *Mass Communication & Society, 8*(2), 111–131.

Nabi, R. L., Moyer-Gusé, E., & Byrne, S. (2007). All joking aside: A serious investigation into the persuasive effect of funny social issue messages. *Communication Monographs, 74*(1), 29–54.

Nelson, J. E., Duncan, C. P., & Frontczak, N. T. (1985). The distraction hypothesis and radio advertising. *Journal of Marketing, 49*(1), 60–71.

Nerhardt, G. (1976). Incongruity and funniness: Towards a new descriptive model. In A. J. Chapman & H. C. Foot (Eds.), *Humour and laughter: Theory, research, and applications* (pp. 37–54). New York, NY: Wiley.

Neuberger, L., & Krcmar, M. (2008). Exploring the effects of editorial cartoons on attitude change: An experimental analysis. In: *Annual Meeting of the International Communication Association*, Montreal, Quebec, Canada.

Niemi, R. G., Craig, S. C., & Mattei, F. (1991). Measuring internal political efficacy in the 1988 national election study. *American Political Science Review, 85*(4), 1407–1413.

Niven, D., Lichter, S. R., & Amundson, D. (2003). The political content of late night comedy. *Harvard International Journal of Press/Politics, 8*(3), 118–133.

Parkin, M. (2010). Taking late night comedy seriously: How candidate appearances on late night television can engage viewers. *Political Research Quarterly, 63*(1), 3–15.

Petty, R. E., & Cacioppo, J. T. (1986). *Communication and persuasion: Central and peripheral routes to attitude change*. Berlin, Germany: Springer-Verlag.

Pfaff, K. L., & Gibbs, R. W., Jr. (1997). Authorial intentions in understanding satirical texts. *Poetics. 25*(1), 45–70.

Pfau, M., Houston, J. B., & Semmler, S. M. (2005). Presidential election campaigns and American democracy: The relationship between communication use and normative outcomes. *American Behavioral Scientist, 49*(1), 48–62.

Pfau, M., Houston, J. B., & Semmler, S. M. (2007). *Mediating the vote: The changing media landscape in U.S. presidential campaigns.* Langham, MD: Rowman & Littlefield.

Pokorny, G. F., & Gruner, C. R. (1969). An experimental study of the effect of satire used as upport in persuasive speech. *Western Speech, 33*(3), 204–211.

Powell, L. 1977. Satirical persuasion and topic salience. *Southern Speech Communication Journal, 42*(2), 151–162.

Powell, L. (1978). Topic salience and responses to the source of satirical messages. *Southern Speech Communication Journal, 44*(1), 60–72.

Priest, R. F. (1966). Election jokes: The effects of reference group membership. *Psychological Reports. 18*(2), 600–602.

Priest, R. F., & Abrahams, J. (1970). Candidate preference and hostile humor in the 1968 elections. *Psychological Reports, 26*(3), 779–783.

Prior, M. (2003). Any good news in soft news? The impact of soft news preferences on political knowledge. *Political Communication, 20*(2), 149–171.

Rothbart, M. K. (1976). Incongruity, problem-solving and laughter. In A. J. Chapman & H. C. Foot (Eds.), *Humour and laughter: Theory, research, and applications* (pp. 54–62). New York, NY: Wiley.

Schmidt, S. R. (1994). Effects of humor on sentence memory. *Journal of Experimental Psychology: Learning, Memory, and Cognition. 20*(4), 953–967.

Schmidt, S. R. (2002). The humour effect: Differential processing and privileged retrieval. *Memory, 10*(2), 127–138.

Schmidt, S. R., & Williams, A. R. (2001). Memory for humorous cartoons. *Memory & Cognition. 29*(2), 305–311.

Smith, C. M., & Powell, L. (1988). The use of disparaging humor by group leaders. *The Southern Speech Communication Journal, 53*, 279–292.

Sternthal, B., & Craig, C. S. (1973). Humor in advertising. *Journal of Marketing, 37*(4), 12–18.

Stewart, P. A. (2011). The influence of self-and other-deprecatory humor on presidential candidate evaluation during the 2008 US election. *Social Science Information, 50*, 201–222.

Stocking, H. S., & Zillmann, D. (1976). Effects of humorous disparagement of self, friend and enemy. *Psychological Reports, 39*(2), 455–461.

Stroud, N. J., & Muddiman, A. (2013). Selective exposure, tolerance, and satirical news. *International Journal of Public Opinion Research, 25*(3), 271–290.

Taylor, P. M. (1964). The effectiveness of humor in informative speaking. *Central States Speech Journal 15*(1), 295–296.

Tsfati, Y., Tukachinsky, R., & Peri, Y. (2009). Exposure to news, political comedy, and entertainment talk shows: Concern about security and political mistrust. *International Journal of Public Opinion Research, 21*(4), 399–423.

Vidmar, N., & Rockeach, M. (1974). Archie bunker's bigotry: A study in selective perception and exposure. *Journal of Communication, 24*(1), 36–47.

Warner, B. R., Hawthorne, H. J., & Hawthorne, J. (2015). A dual-processing approach to the effects of viewing political comedy. *Humor, 28*(4), 541–558.

Weinberger, M. G., & Gulas, C. S. (1992). The impact of humor in advertising: A review. *Journal of Advertising, 21*(4), 35–59.

Weise, R. E. (1996). Partisan perceptions of political humor. *Humor, 9*(2), 199–207.

Wolff, H. A., Smith, C. E., & Murray, H. A. (1934). The psychology of humor: A study of responses to race-disparagement jokes. *Journal of Abnormal and Social Psychology, 28*(4), 341–365.

Xenos, M. A., Moy, P., & Becker, A. B. (2011). Making sense of *The Daily Show*: Understanding the role of partisan heuristics in political comedy effects. In A. Amarasingam (Ed.), *The Stewart/Colbert effect: Essays on the real impacts of fake news* (pp. 47–62). Jefferson, NC: McFarland.

Xenos, M. A., & Becker, A. B. (2009). Moments of Zen: Effects of *The Daily Show* on information seeking and political learning. *Political Communication, 26*(3), 317–332.

Yarwood, D. L. (2001). When Congress makes a joke: Congressional humor as serious and purposeful communication. *Humor: International Journal of Humor Research, 14*(4), 359–394.

Young, D. (2016). Humor and satire, political. In G. Mazzoleni, K. G. Barnhurst, K. Ikeda, R. C. M. Maia, & H. Wessler (Eds.), *The international encyclopedia of political communication* (pp. 487–494). Hoboken, NJ: Wiley-Blackwell.

Young, D. G. (2004). Late-night comedy in election 2000: Its influence on candidate trait ratings and the moderating effects of political knowledge and partisanship. *Journal of Broadcasting & Electronic Media, 48*(1), 1–22.

Young, D. G. (2006). Late-night comedy and the salience of the candidates' caricatured traits in the 2000 election. *Mass Communication & Society, 9*(3), 339–366.

Young, D. G. (2008). The privileged role of the late-night joke: Exploring humor's role in disrupting argument scrutiny. *Media Psychology, 11*(1), 119–142.

Young, D. G. (2012). A flip-flopper and a dumb guy walk into a bar: Political humor and priming in the 2004 campaign. *Humor, 25*(3), 215–231.

Young, D. G., & Esralew, S. E. (2011). Jon Stewart a heretic? Surely you jest: Political participation and discussion among viewers of late-night comedy programming. In A. Amarasingam (Ed.), *The Stewart/Colbert effect: Essays on the real impacts of fake news* (pp. 99–115). Jefferson, NC: McFarland & Company.

Young, D. G., & Hoffman, L. (2012). Acquisition of current-events knowledge from political satire programming: An experimental approach. *Atlantic Journal of Communication, 20*(5), 290–304.

Young, D. G., & Tisinger, R. M. (2006). Dispelling late-night myths: News consumption among late-night comedy viewers and the predictors of exposure to various late-night shows. *Press/Politics, 11*(3), 113–134.

Zhang, Y. (1996a). Responses to humorous advertising: The moderating effect of need for cognition. *Journal of Advertising, 25*(1), 15–32.

Zhang, Y. (1996b). The effect of humor in advertising: An individual-difference perspective. *Psychology & Marketing, 13*(6), 531–546.

Zhang, Y., & Zinkhan, G. M. (1991). Humor in television advertising: The effects of repetition and social setting. In R. H. Holman & M. R. Solomon (Eds.), *Advances in consumer research* (pp. 813–818). Provo, UT: Association for Consumer Research.

3
PARADOXICAL THINKING AS A PARADIGM OF ATTITUDE CHANGE

Comparison to satire and the role of humor (or lack thereof)

Boaz Hameiri

Intergroup conflicts, inequality, global warming, racism and prejudice toward minorities are just a handful of prominent examples of societal issues that plague the world. Solutions to these problems in many cases require tangible resources, such as redistribution of wealth, or funding to support research; however, they also require that large segments of societies and policymakers change their beliefs and attitudes regarding the issue at stake. As an example, in order to mitigate global warming, it is pivotal to persuade people that it is indeed taking place, it is harmful, and that humans cause it. And although there is a consensus among scientists that this the case (Stocker et al., 2013), various organisations, groups and individuals dispute this conclusion and do not attribute global warming to human actions (see Bliuc et al., 2015). Similarly, curbing the spread of the coronavirus outbreak is dependent upon the general public adherence to guidelines issued by the authorities, such as isolation, quarantine, and social distancing. However, this was found to be dependent on people's knowledge and attitudes toward the pandemic (Zhong et al., 2020), as well as their political affiliation (Kushner Gadarian, Goodman, & Pepinsky, 2020), and personality traits (Maaravi, Hameiri, & Gur, 2020), which could also potentially be associated with resistance to scientific information (Hornsey & Fielding, 2017).

A similar, and perhaps even more arduous challenge is the case of intractable conflicts,[1] that still rage in, e.g., Kashmir, Turkey and the Middle East, with their devastating consequences on the involved societies. Given the psychological underpinnings of intractable conflicts, peacefully solving them necessitates a dramatic change in the conflict-supporting beliefs and attitudes that are held by the vast majority of members of the involved societies (Bar-Tal, 2013). This challenge is particularly difficult among the society members who hold these conflict-supporting beliefs and attitudes strongly and confidently due to the intense socialisation they undergo when living in this intense conflict context (Bar-Tal,

Diamond, & Nasie, 2017; Persianis, 2017). Different psychological interventions that were based on different psychological principles have proven to be only partially successful in changing people's beliefs and attitudes when applied in the context of intractable conflicts (e.g., Bar-Tal & Hameiri, 2020; Tropp, 2015).

By and large, most of the interventions aimed at changing beliefs and attitudes to promote intergroup conflict resolution try to provide information or messages that are inconsistent with the conflict-supporting held beliefs and attitudes shared by the majority of individuals living in these contexts. However, if at all willing to be exposed to alternative information (Hameiri, Bar-Tal, & Halperin, 2017), individuals who adhere to conflict-supporting beliefs and attitudes tend to reject attitude-inconsistent information, or initiate different defence mechanisms automatically, and thus reject the new attitude-inconsistent information (Baumeister, Dale, & Sommer, 1998; Kruglanski, 2004; Kunda, 1990). This is especially true when the information starkly negates the held beliefs and attitudes (Sherif & Hovland, 1961). These psychological processes render these interventions to be only partially effective in this challenging context.

In the present chapter, I will introduce an alternative paradigm to attitude change, termed paradoxical thinking, that we recently developed to address the limitations of many of the existing interventions (for a review, see Bar-Tal, Hameiri, & Halperin, in press). I will begin by introducing the paradoxical thinking conceptual framework. I will then review empirical evidence—mostly obtained in the difficult context of intractable conflicts—which establishes the effectiveness of the paradoxical thinking approach and provides some indications for the underlying psychological mechanisms. This context, in which we conducted most of our research, is considered to be particularly challenging as it leads to deeply-entrenched and frozen conflict-supporting beliefs and attitudes (for a review, see Bar-Tal, 2013).

The remainder of the chapter will be devoted to potential new avenues for future research on paradoxical thinking, focusing specifically on how the literature on satire can inform the literature on paradoxical thinking and vice versa. Through the years, we observed that when we presented some of our paradoxical thinking intervention materials to other academics, and in general to audiences that were not the intended target of our interventions, many found them to be funny and satirical. This was unexpected, since, and as I will elaborate below, we did not initially consider humor to be a part of the psychological process when we developed the paradoxical thinking conceptual framework. However, this observation clearly indicates that there are similarities and differences between paradoxical thinking and satire that should be explored theoretically and empirically. Thus, as the first step in an endeavour to bridge this gap, following the review on paradoxical thinking, I will briefly review the literature on humor and satire as tools for attitude change and integrate it with the literature on paradoxical thinking, focusing on the similarities and differences between these two constructs. I will conclude the chapter by suggesting potential next steps on the role (or lack thereof) humor plays in paradoxical thinking, and the similarities and differences between paradoxical thinking and satire as means to promote societal change through attitude change.

Paradoxical Thinking

In the paradoxical thinking conceptual framework, we (Bar-Tal et al., in press) argued that '… when individuals with well anchored extreme views are exposed to consistent messages that are *formulated in an amplified, exaggerated, or even absurd manner,* their level of disagreement, resistance and/or psychological defences are not fully triggered, and they embark on a deliberative thinking process… Furthermore, such paradoxical messages… raise *threats to the identity* of the message recipient, *instigating a re-evaluation process of the held beliefs and attitudes that in turn may stimulate their unfreezing* [namely, an increased willingness to reevaluate held beliefs and attitudes]. Eventually, unfreezing may lead to openness to alternative viewpoints that may be adopted. Specifically, the paradoxical thinking message is intended to lead individuals to perceive their currently held societal beliefs or the current situation as implausible and farfetched and then eventually move them towards more moderate positions.' (Bar-Tal et al., in press, p. 5). Paradoxical thinking is largely based on the classic debating technique *reductio ad absurdum* (Rescher, n.d.), as well as on paradoxical clinical psychological treatments (e.g., Frankl, 1960, 1975; Miller & Rollnick, 2002; for a review, see Riebel, 1984). These treatments argue that patients who are provided with amplified or exaggerated information that is in line with their beliefs, attitudes, or behaviour, might change them, even in cases when they are extremely entrenched and negative. Using the coronavirus as an example, a paradoxical thinking message targeting the young individuals who played down the risk of contracting the virus and infecting others (Miller, 2020) might be that 'indeed, you are invincible and nothing you do can hurt you or the people that surround you. You should start licking random surfaces and strangers, young and old' (see Bar-Tal et al., in press; see also Miller & Rollnick, 2002; Swann, Pelham, & Chidester, 1988).

Although a thorough review of the paradoxical thinking conceptual framework is beyond the scope of this chapter, there are several elements of the paradoxical thinking definition that I would like to highlight at this point. These elements will also serve us in the discussion on paradoxical thinking, satire, and humor. First, paradoxical thinking messages are consistent with held beliefs and attitudes but are provided in an amplified, exaggerated or even absurd manner. This means that, when compared to attitude-inconsistent messages, these messages should seem to message recipients as more in line with their views, and therefore lead to less disagreement, resistance, and rejection of these messages. Second, the paradoxical thinking messages are nonjudgmental, leaving out the message source intentions or stance on the issue at stake. This increases message processing (e.g., Perloff, 2010), and reduces the likelihood that the message will be perceived as ridiculing the message recipients, or as being manipulative, with a hidden goal of changing their beliefs and attitudes. Bar-Tal et al. (in press) argued that attribution of any of these goals to the message source by the recipients—particularly the sense that they are the 'butt of a joke'—may hinder the whole process by triggering resistance and automatic rejection of the message (see Frankl, 1975; Miller & Rollnick, 2002).

Third, and as I elaborate below, the exaggeration and amplification of the recipient's own beliefs and attitudes are meant to elicit surprise, as well as a sense of absurdity regarding the held attitudes or the current situation. This should promote more thorough message processing (e.g., Petty, Fleming, Priester, & Feinstein, 2001). Fourth, the paradoxical thinking messages create a sense of ambiguity, as they are absurd, but not entirely attitude-inconsistent (or consistent). Therefore, it is hypothesised that they demand greater processing of the message, but hinder the creation of sound counterarguments, which can lead to the weakening of the held beliefs and attitudes (Petty, Tormala, & Rucker, 2004). Finally, the research on paradoxical thinking suggests that it is likely that these interventions do not have an immediate effect on unfreezing. Arguably, this is because a single exposure is not sufficient for individuals to perceive the absurdity of the message (Hameiri, Bar-Tal, & Halperin, 2019; Hameiri, Nabet, Bar-Tal, & Halperin, 2018).

To establish the paradoxical thinking conceptual framework, we conducted a study in the context of the Israeli–Palestinian intractable conflict (Hameiri, Porat, Bar-Tal, Bieler, & Halperin, 2014). Jewish-Israeli participants were randomly assigned to one of two conditions. In the paradoxical thinking condition, participants watched a video campaign with messages related to the Israeli–Palestinian conflict. These five-minute-long videos included three television commercials, unrelated to the conflict, and three short paradoxical thinking video clips. In the control condition, participants watched a video of a similar length comprised of television commercials, unrelated to the Israeli–Palestinian conflict. Participants were asked to watch these materials across six waves with three to four days between each wave. The paradoxical thinking campaign included video clips expressing ideas that were consistent with conflict-supporting societal beliefs shared by the majority of Jewish-Israelis but in an amplified, exaggerated manner. These 30-second video clips emphasised how Jewish-Israelis construe their identity based on their conflict-related experiences. Each video-clip presented one core Jewish-Israeli identity theme—a conflict-supporting belief of ethos of conflict (e.g., belief in self-glorification, unity, or victimhood; see Bar-Tal, 2013)—and ended by suggesting that Israelis cannot afford to peacefully end the Israeli–Palestinian conflict, as its continuation helps maintain these societal beliefs of the ethos of conflict. Importantly, the clips did not refute the core conflict-supporting beliefs but rather amplified them to extrapolate an absurd conclusion, such as that in order for them to be moral, Jewish-Israelis probably need the conflict.

As we expected, the results showed that the paradoxical thinking intervention, compared to the control condition, led participants to show more cognitive unfreezing. It also led centrist and (marginally significantly) rightist[2] participants to express increased support for conciliatory statements toward the Palestinians, indicating that Palestinians were perceived as less responsible for the continuation of the conflict. The paradoxical thinking intervention effects were long-lasting as, when reassessed a year later, participants in the intervention condition (vs. the control condition) expressed more willingness to compromise in order to promote a peaceful conflict resolution. Finally, the intervention even influenced participants' actual voting patterns in the 2013 Israeli general elections: Participants who were exposed to the paradoxical thinking intervention, which took place in proximity to the general elections, reported that they tended to vote more for dovish parties which advocated a peaceful resolution to the conflict (Hameiri et al., 2014).

Following these results, we next sought to examine the paradoxical thinking intervention in a more naturalistic environment among individuals who are not necessarily aware of their participation in an experiment. In order to do so, Hameiri, Porat, Bar-Tal, and Halperin (2016) designed a multi-channelled campaign based on the intervention materials used in Hameiri et al. (2014). This campaign included three channels of dissemination: online video-clips and banners, billboard posters, and fieldwork in which t-shirts, balloons and brochures were handed out. The campaign was administered in a small city in the centre of Israel during a period of six weeks. In order to assess the campaign's effectiveness, the study used a pre-post field quasi-experiment design. The paradoxical thinking condition was compared to a control condition in which participants were sampled from the area surrounding the targeted city and were matched to those sampled in the city in terms of their socio-political parameters. Results showed that the rightist participants in the paradoxical thinking condition decreased their adherence to conflict-supporting beliefs across time, while the levels remained constant for the participants in the control condition. These effects were obtained despite the fact that shortly after the campaign began, the Israeli–Palestinian conflict re-escalated and violence erupted throughout Israel and the West Bank. Furthermore, compared to participants in the control condition, rightist participants in the paradoxical thinking condition expressed less support for aggressive policies and more support for conciliatory policies by the Israeli government in the face of the eruption of violence.

Thus, in two large-scale studies, we established the paradoxical thinking paradigm as an effective means to moderate attitudes in the context of the Israeli–Palestinian conflict, which is a prototypical intractable conflict. This held true in both an online field experiment with long-lasting behavioural manifestations and a real-world campaign. Importantly, these effects were more pronounced among the more rightist, or hawkish, participants who tend to adhere to more conflict-supporting beliefs and attitudes in this context. It should be noted that both of these studies examined the effectiveness of 'The Conflict' campaign. Later in this chapter, I will return to this campaign and how it was perceived by our participants, as well as other people who were exposed to it. Finally, while the majority of research on paradoxical thinking was conducted in the context of the Israeli–Palestinian conflict, interventions that were based on the paradoxical thinking principles were found to be effective in additional contexts involving intergroup relations, including gender relations in the US (Swann et al., 1988) and attitudes toward refugees and asylum seekers in Germany (Knab & Steffens, 2020). These additional studies were based on a leading questions paradigm, rather than 'The Conflict' campaign, on which I will elaborate next.

Paradoxical Thinking Mechanisms

After establishing that paradoxical thinking interventions are effective in changing beliefs and attitudes in various contexts, and in particular, the Israeli–Palestinian conflict, we turned our attention to conceptualising and empirically examining the underlying psychological mechanism of paradoxical thinking (for a thorough discussion, see Bar-Tal et al., in press). We focused on four variables: surprise, disagreement with the message, identity threat, and unfreezing. To the extent that the paradoxical thinking messages do not lead to strong disagreement and complete rejection, surprise is probably the first reaction to the perceived absurdity of the message. Indeed, when a stimulus or a message is surprising, it prompts individuals to focus their attention on it, which heightens processing and in-depth exploration. Eventually, it may also make the message more persuasive (e.g., Petty et al., 2001). This can cause individuals to process the message thoroughly, which in turn should motivate individuals to examine and reevaluate their held beliefs and attitudes, leading to their unfreezing.

However, for this to take place, one crucial aspect of the paradoxical thinking approach must occur – it must challenge the most central aspects of the message recipient's identity. Identity is a central component of the self, and individuals strive to achieve and maintain a positive identity (Tajfel, 1978). Individuals do not want to be considered as holding the senseless, implausible and absurd beliefs and attitudes expressed in the paradoxical thinking message, and therefore feel the need to liberate themselves from the threatening feeling by moderating their beliefs and attitudes away from the views expressed in the message. Individuals also do not want to be associated with a group or with a source of information which holds senseless, farfetched and absurd beliefs and attitudes (this is similar to what Sherif and Hovland's, 1961, termed a contrast effect). These comparisons can lead to a dissonance-like state (Festinger, 1957), which is invoked when the conveyed paradoxical thinking message is primarily dissonant with the individual's and/or her ingroup positive self-image, rather than with the individual's held beliefs and attitudes in general. The threat to the individuals' identity should be seen as the key instigator to unfreezing of the beliefs and attitudes through a thoughtful process of meaning-making. This sense of threat may result, eventually, in attitude change to avoid an unpleasant self-perception as extremists (Bar-Tal et al., in press; see also Brown, Ryan, Creswell, & Niemiec, 2008).

To examine these hypothesised psychological mechanisms, Hameiri et al. (2018) conducted two studies in the context of the Israeli–Palestinian conflict. The first was a conceptual replication of the study conducted by Swann et al. (1988) and utilised a leading questions paradigm. Participants who held conflict-supporting beliefs observed in a pretest conducted a few weeks prior to the manipulation were invited to the lab for an interview. The interviews were introduced as if the researchers wanted to better understand the views expressed in the pretest questionnaire. Participants were then asked ten leading questions that were either paradoxical, encouraging them to respond with statements that were consistent, but blatantly more extreme than their own conflict-supporting beliefs (e.g., 'Why do you think that the real and only goal the Palestinians have in mind is to annihilate us, in a manner that transcends their basic needs such as food and health?'); or inconsistent, encouraging participants to respond with statements that negated their held beliefs (e.g., 'Why do you think the real goal of the Palestinians is ultimately to live with us in peace?').

These interviews were coded by two trained judges, who rated the participants' levels of surprise and general disagreement. Hameiri et al. (2018) found, as expected, an interaction between the condition and participants' political orientation on general disagreement, such that while rightist participants showed lower levels of disagreement with the questions they were asked in the paradoxical thinking condition (that were consistent with their conflict-supporting beliefs), they showed higher levels of disagreement in the inconsistent condition. Additionally, levels of surprise among participants in the paradoxical thinking condition were higher than those of participants in the inconsistent condition, regardless of participants' political orientation. Furthermore, rightist participants showed more unfreezing and openness to alternative information in the paradoxical thinking condition, compared to the inconsistent condition. There were no significant differences between the conditions for the more centrist participants.

In the second study, Hameiri et al. (2018) aimed to add another layer to the hypothesised mechanism and examined participants' sense of identity threat following exposure to the paradoxical thinking messages. We also wanted to provide a comprehensive account of the examined psychological mechanism. This study conceptually replicated the study conducted by Hameiri et al. (2014), but this time we added a third, attitude-inconsistent, condition. In this condition, participants were presented with an attitude-inconsistent campaign arguing that, contrary to what most Jewish-Israelis believe, Palestinians are credible partners for peace. The results replicated and extended those found in the previous study, indicating that the paradoxical thinking intervention was more effective in promoting unfreezing and openness to alternative information with the rightist participants, compared to both the attitude-inconsistent and the neutral control conditions. Furthermore, replicating the results from the previous study, the paradoxical thinking intervention (vs. the attitude-inconsistent intervention) led the rightist participants to show more surprise and less disagreement with the message, as it was consistent with the message recipients' held conflict-supporting beliefs. Importantly, the results also indicated that participants in the paradoxical thinking condition sensed more threat to their identities compared to those in the attitude-inconsistent and neutral control conditions. These psychological mechanisms mediated the effect of the paradoxical thinking intervention (compared to both attitude-inconsistent and neutral control conditions) on unfreezing and openness to alternative information.

Additionally, Hameiri et al. (2018) examined the delicate interplay and possible inter-relations *among* identity threat, surprise, and general disagreement across time among the rightist participants. We were also able to examine how these processes affect and are affected by participants' levels of unfreezing across time. We found that, at first, identity threat led to more unfreezing, but then, the more participants unfroze, the *less* they sensed a threat to their identity. General disagreement predicted lower levels of unfreezing across time, and surprise did not predict unfreezing across time but was positively correlated with unfreezing measured at the same wave. These results correspond with the overall pattern of supplementary longitudinal analysis Hameiri et al. (2018) conducted in which, most notably, rightist participants in the paradoxical thinking condition showed a decrease in identity threat across time, while at the same time, they showed an increase in unfreezing.

Finally, in a recent experiment, Hameiri, Idan, Nabet, Bar-Tal, and Halperin (2020) examined whether the paradoxical thinking messages need to hit a 'sweet spot' in that they should be sufficiently extreme, but not *too* extreme, to be effective, and that this is also dependent on the message recipients' characteristics. Jewish-Israeli participants were asked to read an opinion editorial piece arguing that the National Health Insurance Law in Israel should be applied to cover the refugees' health needs, not only for humane, just, and moral reasons but also because it was prescribed by law (Haaretz Editorial, 2016). Those who tended to disagree with the editorial were invited to participate in the study. They were asked to read a second opinion editorial that was ostensibly written by a rightist Knesset (Israel's parliament) member as a response to the original editorial. Participants were randomly assigned to one of four conditions that differed in the extremity and absurdity of the message. All texts had the same underlying message, consistent with their own views that Israel should not grant free health care to the refugees, but rather make an effort to expel them from Israel. The difference between the conditions was in the way the text was written, such that the first condition, i.e., Text 1, was moderate, Texts 2 and 3 were increasingly more extreme, and Text 4 was *very* extreme. The materials were pilot tested and found to vary in the degree to which they were perceived as extreme and absurd.

Results generally replicated previous studies, in that the more the texts were extreme and absurd, the more they surprised participants. Hameiri et al. (2020) also found some indications that the more the texts were extreme and absurd, the more participants sensed a threat to their identities, particularly among participants who were high in moral conviction (i.e., 'a strong and absolute belief that… [something] … is right or wrong, moral or immoral'; Skitka, Bauman, & Sargis, 2005, p. 896), which served as an indicator for the extent to which participants would be willing to process different messages thoroughly. Importantly, Text 4, with its outrageous linguistic extremity, rendered the text to be so outlandish (at least for some of the participants) that, even though it was consistent with the participants' views, they immediately dismissed it and processed it superficially, yielding an automatic rejection. This was manifested in high levels of disagreement with the opinion editorial, compared to all other conditions, assessed in questionnaires and in content analysis of comments written by the participants to respond to the editorial writer. In contrast, Text 3, which was less extreme and absurd, was considered consistent with the participants' attitude, and evoked an in-depth deliberative cognitive processing of the message, as was found in other studies.

Furthermore, Hameiri et al. (2020) found a significant interaction between the manipulation and (immigration-related) moral convictions on unfreezing. Interestingly, this analysis generally indicated that, for the low morally convicted participants, it was Text 1, the most moderate condition, that, to some extent, led to more unfreezing. At the same time, as hypothesised, for the high morally convicted participants it was Text 3, the extreme and absurd, but not *very* extreme and absurd, condition that led to the highest levels of unfreezing. To summarise, it seems that for the low morally convicted participants, the text had to be only slightly exaggerated or amplified to lead to more unfreezing. For the high morally convicted participants, the text had to be substantially more extreme and absurd to obtain these effects. When the text was *very* extreme and absurd, it led to a knee-jerk disagreement and defensive reactions regardless of participants' levels of moral conviction.

Paradoxical Thinking, Satire, and Humor

The research on paradoxical thinking so far has yielded a comprehensive conceptual framework, established the existence of this phenomenon in the lab and the field, and provided initial evidence for its underlying psychological mechanisms. While important progress has been made, the conducted research sparks additional important questions, which call for further research to fully understand the external validity and applicability (Hameiri et al., 2019), as well as the theoretical, practical, and ethical aspects of the conceptual framework (Bar-Tal et al., in press). In the current chapter, I would like to focus for the first time on potential research questions that are based on (1) the possible association between paradoxical thinking and satire, and (2) whether humor plays a significant role as part of the psychological process underlying paradoxical thinking.

These ideas were sparked by the following observation our research group made: Whenever we showed 'The Conflict' campaign video-clips to academics (who tend to be liberal/leftist; see Inbar & Lammers, 2012) in, for example, conferences, their response was laughter while making the assertion that these videos are satirical. This observation is interesting when contrasted with findings from when we pilot tested 'The Conflict' video-clips among the general public in Israel that tends to be skewed to the right. We found that at least some participants perceived the videos literally. This was manifested in stronger feelings of pride for being Israeli, compared to a control condition (Hameiri et al., 2014). Unfortunately, we never directly assessed whether participants perceived the video-clips to be humorous or satirical. This observation sparked the initial interest in examining the connections between paradoxical thinking and satire. The following review and integration between the literature clearly indicate that paradoxical thinking and satire have several similarities and differences that can inform the research and theoretical thinking on both of these constructs.

Satire is generally defined as a 'literary form [that] often seeks to both educate and entertain as it tries to persuade' (Holbert, Hmielowski, Jain, Lather, & Morey, 2011, p. 191; see also Ruch, Heintz, Platt, Wagner, & Proyer, 2018). Satire scholars argue that absurdity and *reductio ad absurdum* are key characteristics in satire (for a recent review, see Park-Ozee, 2019). One prime example of *reductio ad absurdum* in satire was the persona Stephen Colbert portrayed on *The Colbert Report*, and in particular, his roasting of President George W. Bush, at the White House Correspondents' Association dinner in 2006 (Schiller, 2009). As part of Colbert's *reductio ad absurdum* satire, he parodied conservative pundits, such as Bill O'reilly and *The O'reilly Factor*, which generally followed this rhetoric structure: First, Colbert started with a plausible premise that could be perceived literally, and as such is consistent with conservative recipients (e.g., 'The greatest thing about this man [President Bush] is he's steady...'). The premise was then followed by an exaggerated hyperbole, which reflected on the original premise, showing that it was nonsensical, or absurd ('He believes the same thing Wednesday that he believed on Monday, no matter what happens Tuesday. Events can change; this man's beliefs never will'). Thus, both paradoxical thinking and satire are rooted in absurdity and *reductio ad absurdum*. It is the driving force that leads message recipients to question their held beliefs and attitudes and the current situation (Bar-Tal et al., in press; Frankl, 1960, 1975; Park-Ozee, 2019).

In a more nuanced examination, Colbert's approach to satire is sometimes labelled as Juvenalian, which is normally contrasted with Horatian satire. Both approaches to satire are based on humorous content, and both attack a particular target. However, whereas Horatian satire seeks to make the truth more palatable with laughter, as a means to circumvent message recipients' resistance (Highet, 1962); Juvenalian satire humor is supposed to wound, and be fierce and merciless (Sander, 1971). Research on exposure to satirical messages found that provided the satirical message was relevant to the participants (i.e., they had the motivation), and they had the ability to process it, Juvenalian satire (vs. Horatian satire and control) was generally more effective. It received more attention, but at the same time led to fewer counterarguments and message scrutiny, and was also perceived to be somewhat more humorous (Holbert et al., 2011; LaMarre, Landreville, Young, & Gilkerson, 2014). Thus, both paradoxical thinking and satire reduce counterarguing and resistance to the messages. However, while in the case of paradoxical thinking we argue that this is due to the fact that the messages are consistent with the message recipients held beliefs and attitudes (Bar-Tal et al., in press; Hameiri et al., 2018); with satire, it is humor that is argued to reduce counterarguing and help recipients swallow the bitter pill (Highet, 1962; Nabi, Moyer-Gusé, & Byrne, 2007).

However, the efficacy of satire to change attitudes and promote societal change has been questioned by researchers (e.g., Day, 2011; Gournelos & Greene, 2011; LaMarre, Landerville, & Beam, 2009; Nabi et al., 2007) and comedians, such as Hannah Gadsby (Krefting, 2019), Jon Stewart, and Stephen Colbert, alike (Schiller, 2009). It seems that one potential explanation for the lack of consistent effects of (Juvenalian) satirical messages on attitude change is that it triggers two opposing processes (Boukes, Boomgaarden, Moorman, & de Vreese, 2015). On the one hand, it leads to more focused attention and less counterarguing, which is supposed to increase attitude change (see elaboration likelihood model; Petty & Cacioppo, 1986; see also Chapter 1, this volume). But, on the other hand, it is also funny, which was found to be associated with less attitude change, as it leads to more message discounting, more positive thoughts toward the message target, and relieved tension or a catharsis effect, which goes against the satirist's goals (Boukes et al., 2015; Coe, 2013; Krefting, 2019). Nevertheless, it should also be noted that these mixed results might also be the product of a sleeper effect, in that the satirical political humor potentially serves as a discounting cue (being 'just a joke') only in the immediate term, while it leads to more significant attitude change after some time has passed (Nabi et al., 2007).

Furthermore, having prior knowledge of the premise of the satire or the goals and stance of the message source was argued to be a necessary condition for satire to be perceived as such (Caufield, 2008; Knight, 2004; Park-Ozee, 2019), and to lead to perceiving the satirical message as more humorous. Interestingly, Boukes et al. (2015) found that the more the satirical message was in line with the message recipients' prior beliefs and attitudes, the more they found it to be funny, which, as mentioned above, was found to lead to more discounting and less attitude change. To paint a more nuanced picture, in some cases, satirical messages that are consistent with the held beliefs and attitudes of the message recipients can even backfire among some message recipients who have prior knowledge of the premise of the satire, but feel that they themselves are being attacked (Boukes et al., 2015; Simpson, 2003). One example for that is when Hannah Gadsby addressed serious illnesses of society, such as misogyny, homophobia, and violence in *Nanette*. Her use of angry messages that do not provide tension relief seemed to have more impact on some of her audiences, while at the same time elicited a strong backlash from those who sensed that they were under attack. While Gadsby's *Nanette* pushed the boundaries of satire, it also raised questions as to whether it is, in fact, satire (Krefting, 2019).

Thus, satire is intended to use (more or less) humor to attack a target in order to persuade and does not necessarily rely on exaggeration or amplification of recipients' held beliefs and attitudes (e.g., Highet, 1962; Knight, 2004; Park-Ozee, 2019), which might also undermine the satirists' goal to persuade (Boukes et al., 2015; Coe, 2013). Paradoxical thinking messages, however, aim to change beliefs and attitudes and do not intend to be perceived as humorous. Therefore, if a message recipient perceives the paradoxical thinking message to be funny, it means that the message was either not effective at all (i.e., poorly crafted), or that it was intended to target other message recipients. As an example, returning to the reaction we encountered when presenting 'The Conflict' video-clips to other researchers, I argue that they reacted with laughter because they either were not Israelis, did not hold the targeted conflict-supporting beliefs, or were 'in on the joke' as we, the identified source, provided them with the premise of the video-clips and our goals, prior to playing the video clip. Had these audiences perceived that they were not 'in the joke,' but in fact the 'butt of the joke,' then regardless of whether they were exposed to paradoxical thinking messages or to satirical messages, the messages would have backfired, as people would have rejected these messages (Bar-Tal et al., in press; Simpson, 2003). Finally, there is some evidence to suggest that in both paradoxical thinking and satire, time and exposure play a significant role in the persuasiveness of the messages. However, the reasoning for these effects is different in each literature. While in paradoxical thinking we argued that perceiving the absurdity of the messages takes time and multiple exposures (Hameiri et al., 2019); the argument in the literature on satire is that after people stop discounting the message as being 'just a joke' they start to process the strong arguments that were embedded in it (Nabi et al., 2007).

Not having any prior knowledge of the premise of the satire or of the goals and stance of the message source, which leaves the satirical messages' goals ambiguous, generally does not harm the degree to which the message is perceived to be funny. However, if left ambiguous, research has shown that audiences tend to interpret satirical messages either literally, or in a manner that is in line with their views (Park-Ozee, 2019). For example, there were many instances in the past in which legitimate news outlets, including *The New York Times*, reported satirical 'news' published by *The Onion* as real (Sinkovich & Brindisi, 2016). Moreover, liberals were more likely to think that *The Colbert Report* is satirising conservative pundits; whereas, conservatives were more likely to think that Colbert is in fact conservative, and is mocking liberalism (LaMarre et al., 2009). Similarly, in a classic study conducted by Vidmar and Rokeach (1974), nonprejudiced viewers perceived the character of Archie Banker from the 1970s sitcom, *All in the Family*, to be a satirical character, whereas prejudiced viewers perceived this character literally, as someone who expresses their own views on primetime television. Thus, it is likely that for both paradoxical thinking and satire the ambiguity of the message can sometimes lead to unintended effects when the messages are perceived in the literal meaning, rather than in the paradoxical or implied meaning (Hameiri et al., 2014; Hameiri et al. 2016; Park-Ozee, 2019).

In sum, I argue that while indeed paradoxical thinking and satire share several similarities, they are fundamentally different. Sometimes paradoxical thinking messages can be perceived as satirical by some people, and in some cases, satirical messages can follow the paradoxical thinking principles. Furthermore, the literature on satire did not examine the potential role of surprise and identity threat, which were found to play key psychological mechanisms in the research on paradoxical thinking (Bar-Tal et al., in press; Hameiri et al., 2018). However, given these similarities and differences, we are left with the following question: In what way can the literature on satire inform what we know on paradoxical thinking and vice versa?

Next Steps

Based on the current review, I argue that the similarities between paradoxical thinking and satire raise interesting and important questions that should be examined in future research. These include: (1) Under what circumstances are paradoxical thinking messages be perceived as funny? (2) Is perceiving these messages as funny associated with reduced effectiveness in their aim to promote better intergroup relations? (3) How would knowing the premise of the paradoxical thinking intervention, or the goals of the message source, affect its effectiveness? (4) Do paradoxical thinking messages, similar to satirical messages, elicit fewer counterarguments compared to other, attitude-inconsistent, interventions? Bar-Tal et al. (in press) hypothesised that paradoxical thinking messages do indeed elicit fewer counterarguments, and paradoxical thinking interventions were found to lead to less self-reported disagreement with the messages (Hameiri et al., 2018); however, the actual number of produced counterarguments was never assessed. (5) Do levels of extremity and absurdity of the paradoxical thinking messages affect the degree to which they are perceived as humorous or satirical? For example, in Hameiri et al. (2020), were the more moderate, or the *very* extreme and absurd texts perceived by participants as satirical? If not, what is the key ingredient that is missing? Finally, (6) does age play a role in the effectiveness of paradoxical thinking interventions, as it does when examining satirical messages (Boukes et al., 2015)?

Similarly, I believe that the paradoxical thinking literature can yield interesting research questions in the study of satire, particularly with regard to the underlying psychological mechanism. Most notably, do surprise and identity threat play a role in the extent to which satirical messages are persuasive? Does perceiving the satirical message as funny relieve message recipients from the sense of identity threat, or is it the case that experiencing identity threat renders the satirical message to be less funny? These and related important questions that can promote our knowledge on paradoxical thinking and on satire as tools to promote positive societal change await future research.

Notes

1 Intractable conflicts have the following characteristics: They are fought over goals viewed as existential, they are violent, perceived as being of zero-sum nature and unsolvable, occupy a central position in the lives of the involved societies, require immense investments of material and psychological resources, and last for at least 25 years (Bar-Tal, 2013; Kriesberg, 1998).
2 Rightists, also referred to as hawks in Israel, tend to hold uncompromising positions toward the Israeli–Palestinian conflict and to view Palestinians negatively (Arian & Shamir, 2011).

References

Arian, A., & Shamir, M. (2011). Introduction. In A. Arian & M. Shamir (Eds.), *The elections in Israel 2009* (pp. 1–18). New Brunswick, NJ: Transaction Publishers.

Bar-Tal, D. (2013). *Intractable conflicts: Socio-psychological foundations and dynamics.* Cambridge, UK: Cambridge University Press.

Bar-Tal, D., Diamond, A., & Nasie, M. (2017). Political socialization of young children in intractable conflicts. *International Journal of Behavioral Development, 41*, 415–425.

Bar-Tal, D., & Hameiri, B. (2020). Interventions for changing well-anchored attitudes in the context of intergroup conflict. *Social and Personality Psychology Compass, 14,* e12534.

Bar-Tal, D., Hameiri, B., & Halperin, E. (in press). Paradoxical thinking as a paradigm of attitude change in the context of intractable conflict. *Advances in Experimental Social Psychology*.

Baumeister, R. F., Dale, K., & Sommer, K. L. (1998). Freudian defense mechanisms and empirical findings in modern social psychology: Reaction formation, projection, displacement, undoing, isolation, sublimation, and denial. *Journal of Personality, 66*, 1081–1124.

Bliuc, A. M., McGarty, C., Thomas, E. F., Lala, G., Berndsen, M., & Misajon, R. (2015). Public division about climate change rooted in conflicting socio-political identities. *Nature Climate Change, 5*, 226–229.

Boukes, M., Boomgaarden, H. J., Moorman, M., & de Vreese, C. H. (2015). At odds: Laughing and thinking? The appreciation, processing, and persuasiveness of political satire. *Journal of Communication, 65*, 721–744.

Brown, W. K., Ryan, M. R., Creswell, D. J., & Niemiec, P. C. (2008). Beyond me: Mindful responses to social threat. In H. A. Wayment & J. J. Bauer (Eds.), *Transcending self-interest: Psychological explorations of the quiet ego* (pp. 75–84). Washington, DC: American Psychological Association.

Caufield, R. (2008). The influence of 'infoenterpropagainment:' Exploring the power of political satire as a distinct form of political humor. In J. Baumgartner, & J. Morris (Eds.), *Laughing matters: Humor and American politics in the media age* (pp. 3–20). New York, NY: Routledge.

Coe, J. (2013, July 18). Sinking giggling into the sea. *London Review of Books, 35*. Retrieved from https://www.lrb.co.uk/the-paper/v35/n14/jonathan-coe/sinking-giggling-into-the-sea

Day, A. (2011). *Satire and dissent: Interventions in contemporary political debate*. Bloomington, IN: Indiana University Press.

Festinger, L. A. (1957). *A theory of cognitive dissonance*. Evanston, IL: Row Peterson.

Frankl, V. E. (1960). Paradoxical intention: A logotherapeutic technique. *American Journal of Psychotherapy, 14*, 520–535.

Frankl, V. E. (1975). Paradoxical intention and dereflection. *Psychotherapy, 12*, 226–237.

Gournelos, T., & Greene, V. (Eds.) (2011). *A decade of dark humor: How comedy, irony, and satire shaped post 9-11 America*. Jackson, MS: The University Press of Mississippi.

Haaretz Editorial. (2016, August 7). Israel must provide health care for asylum seekers. *Haaretz*. Retrieved from http://www.haaretz.co.il [in Hebrew]

Hameiri, B., Bar-Tal, D., & Halperin, E. (2017). Self-censorship as a socio-psychological barrier to peacemaking. In D. Bar-Tal, R. Nets-Zehngut, & K. Sharvit (Eds.), *Self-censorship in contexts of conflict: Theory and research* (pp. 61–78). New York, NY: Springer.

Hameiri, B., Bar-Tal, D., & Halperin, E. (2019). Paradoxical thinking interventions: A paradigm for societal change. *Social Issues and Policy Review, 13*, 36–62.

Hameiri, B., Idan, O., Nabet, E., Bar-Tal, D., & Halperin, E. (2020). The paradoxical thinking 'sweet spot': The role of recipients' latitude of rejection in the effectiveness of paradoxical thinking messages targeting anti-refugee attitudes in Israel. *Journal of Social and Political Psychology, 8*, 266–283.

Hameiri, B., Nabet, E., Bar-Tal, D., & Halperin, E. (2018). Paradoxical thinking as a conflict resolution intervention: Comparison to alternative interventions and examination of psychological mechanisms. *Personality and Social Psychology Bulletin, 44*, 122–139.

Hameiri, B., Porat, R., Bar-Tal, D., Bieler, A., & Halperin, E. (2014). Paradoxical thinking as a new avenue of intervention to promote peace. *Proceedings of the National Academy of Sciences, 111*, 10996–11001.

Hameiri, B., Porat, R., Bar-Tal, D., & Halperin, E. (2016). Moderating attitudes in times of violence through paradoxical thinking intervention. *Proceedings of the National Academy of Sciences, 113*, 12105–12110.

Highet, G. (1962). *The anatomy of satire*. Princeton, NJ: Princeton University Press.

Holbert, R. L., Hmielowski, J., Jain, P., Lather, J., & Morey, A. (2011). Adding nuance to the study of political humor effects: Experimental research on Juvenalian satire versus Horatian satire. *American Behavioral Scientist, 55*, 187–211.

Hornsey, M. J., & Fielding, K. S. (2017). Attitude roots and Jiu Jitsu persuasion: Understanding and overcoming the motivated rejection of science. *American Psychologist, 72*, 459–473.

Inbar, Y., & Lammers, J. (2012). Political diversity in social and personality psychology. *Perspectives on Psychological Science, 7*, 496–503.

Knab, N., & Steffens, M. C. (2020). *'Why do you think Christmas will never ever be celebrated again?' A paradoxical intervention's potential to reduce destructive intergroup conflict in the asylum context*. Manuscript submitted for publication.

Knight, C. A. (2004). *The literature of satire*. Cambridge, UK: Cambridge University Press.

Krefting, R. (2019). Hannah Gadsby: On the limits of satire. *Studies in American Humor, 5*, 93–102.

Kriesberg, L. (1998). Intractable conflicts. In E. Weiner (Ed.), *The handbook of interethnic coexistence* (pp. 332–342). New York, NY: Continuum.

Kruglanski, A. W. (2004). *The psychology of closed mindedness*. New York, NY: Psychology Press.

Kunda, Z. (1990). The case for motivated reasoning. *Psychological Bulletin, 108*, 480–498.

Kushner Gadarian, S., Goodman, S. W., & Pepinsky, T. B. (2020). *Partisanship, health behavior, and policy attitudes in the early stages of the COVID-19 pandemic*. Preprint available at SSRN: https://ssrn.com/abstract=3562796.

LaMarre, H. L., Landerville, K. D., & Beam, M. A. (2009). The irony of satire: Political ideology and the motivation to see what you want to see in The Colbert Report. *International Journal of Press/Politics, 14*, 212–231.

LaMarre, H. L., Landreville, K. D., Young, D., & Gilkerson, N. (2014). Humor works in funny ways: Examining satirical tone as a key determinant in political humor message processing. *Mass Communication and Society, 17*, 400–423.

Maaravi, Y., Hameiri, B., & Gur, T. (2020). Fighting coronavirus one personality at a time: Need for structure, trait victimhood and adherence to COVID-19 health guidelines. *Frontiers in Psychology, 11*, 576450. doi:10.3389/fpsyg.2020.576450

Miller, R. W. (2020, March 19). 'If I get corona, I get corona': Coronavirus pandemic doesn't slow spring breakers' party. *USA Today*. Retrieved from https://www.usatoday.com/story/travel/destinations/2020/03/19/spring-break-beaches-florida-look-packed-despite-coronavirus-spread/2873248001/

Miller, W. R., & Rollnick, S. (2002). *Motivational interviewing: Preparing people for change*. New York, NY: Guilford Press.

Nabi, R. L., Moyer-Gusé, E., & Byrne, S. (2007). All joking aside: A serious investigation into the persuasive effect of funny social issue messages. *Communication Monographs, 74*, 29–54.

Park-Ozee, D. (2019). Satire: An explication. *Humor, 32*, 585–604.

Perloff, R. M. (2010). *The dynamics of persuasion: Communication and attitudes in the twenty-first century*. New York, NY: Routledge.

Persianis, P. (2017). How have the two separate educational systems in Cyprus shaped the perspectives of the local communities? In I. Psaltis, N. Anastasiou, H. Faustmann, M. Hadjipavlou, H. Karahasan, & M. Zackheos (Eds.). *Education in a multicultural Cyprus* (pp. 80–92). Newcastle upon Tyne, UK: Cambridge Scholars Publishing.

Petty, R. E., & Cacioppo, J. T. (1986). The elaboration-likelihood model of persuasion. *Advances in Experimental Social Psychology, 19*, 123–205.

Petty, R. E., Fleming, M. A., Priester, J. R., & Feinstein, A. H. (2001). Individual versus group interest violation: Surprise as a determinant of argument scrutiny and persuasion. *Social Cognition, 19*, 418–442.

Petty, R. E., Tormala, Z. L., & Rucker, D. D. (2004). Resisting persuasion by counterarguing: An attitude strength perspective. In J. T. Jost, M. R. Banaji, & D. A. Prentice (Eds.), *Perspectivism in social psychology: The Yin and Yang of scientific progress* (pp. 37–51). Washington, DC: American Psychological Association Press.

Rescher, N. (n.d.). Reductio ad absurdum. *Internet Encyclopedia of Philosophy*. Retrieved from http://www.iep.utm.edu/reductio/.

Riebel, L. (1984). Paradoxical intention strategies: A review of rationales. *Psychotherapy: Theory, Research, Practice, Ttraining, 21*, 260–272.

Ruch, W., Heintz, S., Platt, T., Wagner, L., & Proyer, R. T. (2018). Broadening humor: Comic styles differentially tap into temperament, character, and ability. *Frontiers in Psychology, 9*, 6.

Sander, C. (1971). *The scope of satire*. Glenview, IL: Scott, Foresman.

Schiller, A. A. (Ed.) (2009). *Stephen Colbert and philosophy: I am philosophy (and so can you!)*. Chicago, IL: Open Court.

Sherif, M., & Hovland, C. I. (1961). *Social judgment: Assimilation and contrast effects in communication and attitude change*. New Haven, CT: Yale University Press.

Simpson, P. (2003). *On the discourse of satire: Toward a stylistic model of satirical humor*. Amsterdam: John Benjamins.

Sinkovich, J. & Brindisi, J. (2016). The art, influence and business of satire: Peeling back the layers of The Onion. *International Journal of Arts Management, 18*, 75–85.

Skitka, L. J., Bauman, C. W., & Sargis, E. G. (2005). Moral conviction: Another contributor to attitude strength or something more? *Journal of Personality and Social Psychology, 88*, 895–917.

Stocker, T. F., Qin, D., Plattner, G.-K., Tignor, M., Allen, S. K., Boschung, J. ... Wuebbles, D. (Eds.) (2013). *Climate change 2013: The physical science basis. Contribution of working group I to the fifth assessment report of the intergovernmental panel on climate change*. New York, NY: Cambridge University Press.

Swann, W. B., Pelham, B. W., & Chidester, T. R. (1988). Change through paradox: Using self-verification to alter beliefs. *Journal of Personality and Social Psychology, 54*, 268–273.

Tajfel, H. (1978). Social categorization, social identity and social comparison. In H. Tajfel (Ed.), *Differentiation between social groups* (pp. 61–76). London, UK: Academic Press.

Tropp, L. R. (2015). Dismantling the ethos of conflict: Strategies for improving intergroup relations. In E. Halperin & K. Sharvit (Eds.), *The social psychology of intractable conflict: Celebrating the legacy of Daniel Bar-Tal* (Vol. 1, pp. 159–171). New York, NY: Springer.

Vidmar, N., & Rokeach, M. (1974). Archie Bunker's bigotry: A study in selective perception and exposure. *Journal of Communication, 24*, 36–47.

Zhong, B. L., Luo, W., Li, H. M., Zhang, Q. Q., Liu, X. G., Li, W. T., & Li, Y. (2020). Knowledge, attitudes, and practices towards COVID-19 among Chinese residents during the rapid rise period of the COVID-19 outbreak: A quick online cross-sectional survey. *International Journal of Biological Sciences, 16*, 1745–1752.

PART II
Interpersonal relationships

4

UNITING AND DIVIDING IN PERSONAL INTERACTIONS

Four key functions of humor in communication

John Meyer

Humor pervades communication. It can be found in all settings and all types of messages. In so many conversations, one sees a common temptation to try for humor or to respond with humor. Often, parties seem to seek a balance between serious and humorous communication—as one becomes dominant, people will seek or slip in a dose of the other. Humor can be found in all situations—even those considered serious or threatening. Humor has the potential for enjoyment, even as emotions like pleasure, fear, or anger could overwhelm that sense. Yet people can still joke or find humor in fearful or tragic circumstances. Since humor can be found anywhere in communication, it is worth exploring further as to what it does for us in communication, or what functions it serves.

As communication develops, a motivation for variety or entertainment often manifests in the form of humor. People generally want routine patterns they can recognise, but also seek stimulation by novel patterns or ideas. These new patterns can be confusing or threatening, but they can also serve as an exhilarating puzzle or problem to solve. Humor serves as a source of variety that, in the end, poses no threat or harm. Humor involves a 'mirth experience' (Martin & Ford, 2018) that engages forms of ambiguity in the mind. One's mind needs a sense of expectations, or a planned pattern, along with some sort of violation of that expected pattern for humor to exist (Veatch, 1998). Some perception of change is also necessary for perceiving humor. This could be referred to as a 'pleasant psychological shift' (Morreall, 1983). Enough change must be perceived to be noteworthy as opposed to being trivial, but not too much so as to be perceived as alarming or dangerous. Thus, according to the benign violation theory of humor, a violation must be perceived as not harmful, and thus benign, and must be in mind simultaneously with the sense of a normal pattern (McGraw & Warren, 2010). Perceiving such benign changes to expected life patterns leads to experiencing humor (McGraw & Warner, 2014), and can allow humans to be more creative and adaptable. Humor use and appreciation have multiple benefits for us, and in general, have been found to improve communication, enhance learning, and promote a sense of social presence (Dormann & Biddle, 2009).

In essence, humor can be defined as a benign pattern violation, whether communicated through a series of events or through symbols that create messages (McGraw & Warner, 2014). 'A welcome disruption to the life pattern may indeed serve, then, as an apt descriptor of humor' (Meyer, 2015, p. 29). Such pattern violations, when not threatening and recognised as strikingly different from expectations, provide for an amusing reaction. This reaction, often pleasant, becomes a desired stimulant for more such entertainment through similar events or communication. Humor, thus, becomes sought out and welcome as an entertaining diversion during ongoing communication or tasks. Like any variation, though, it may not always be pleasant. Being the subject of humor may not be an enjoyable situation; similarly, not understanding humor that others see can be similarly alienating. One may understand the humor attempt but view it as an attack or a put-down—a serious event. Alternatively, one may not understand a particular social or symbolic pattern and how it was violated, thereby not 'getting' the joke. In spite of that variation, however, humans enjoy understanding and sharing humor with others. We seek and value humor across cultures. Clearly, 'having a sense of humor' is viewed as one of the most valued personal qualities in those people we live, work, and otherwise communicate with.

The power of humor inherent in its being desired or sought in so many settings makes humor more compelling. We seek it, we enjoy it, we communicate it, but how does it really work? What can humor do for us? Why is it so pervasive in our messages? It can be found in all sorts of communication, in all sorts of situations ranging from comic to serious and varies widely by topic. Yet it seems to be a human 'universal,' occurring in all cultures and settings. There must be some commonalities or constants one can expect from humor. Indeed, it turns out that humor does, among other purposes, reveal social boundaries, communication norms, and relationship status.

Social Functions of Humor

Social boundaries can be shown by who 'gets' or experiences humor during a conversation, and who does not. Those familiar with a pattern can see a funny violation of that pattern. At the same time, those who do not understand a relevant cultural or communication pattern do not perceive any humor. Social groupings, then, are key to understanding and sharing instances of humor. Cultural differences seem to shrink the number of available shared patterns to spark humor. People who cannot speak the same language, for instance, have a much smaller set of shared symbols or experiences through which to appreciate humor mutually. Such shared situations are further complicated when others see humor in a situation or message, but not for the same reasons (or for different relevant pattern violations). Communicators can then 'share' humor, but still are not perceiving it or the message in the same way. Yet, the social sharing of humor is so valuable, we take pleasure in the shared humor often without exploring to see if we all see the humor in the same way or for the same reasons.

One most common source of humor is to violate an expected norm. People will 'break a rule' and see what happens. If this is done in a benign, non-threatening or playful way, it often sparks humor-filled situations and communication. Paradoxically, this can also reinforce those very social norms that are being violated and subject to humor (Lynch, 2010). It is the power of those norms, and the moral suasion implied by them, that give the patterns power and make their violation compelling in a humorous way (Veatch, 1998). What sparks humor, then, often shows what people do care about and social and communication norms that are valued, in some way, or their violation would be hardly worthy of note rather than being found funny and the source of much humor.

A very common marker of a growing or strong relationship is the ability to share humor with the other person (Meyer, 2012). A seemingly bare minimum criterion for an acceptable relationship is colloquially referred to in this way, as 'at least they have a good sense of humor,' as if that is one basic requirement for a good relationship. Healthy relationships seem to have some shared sense of humor, and unhealthy relationships are often marked by one or the other party refusing to accept attempts at humor by the other (Bippus, 2003). Even in serious situations or conflicts, a healthy relationship can involve one party 'defusing' the situation or helping both cope with it by using humor. This adds variety to the number of potential message strategies that can influence or grow the relationship. The loss of humor, or the ability to joke with someone, seems to indicate restrictive communication and less shared meaning in a relationship, causing it to decline or become distant.

Humor can be perceived as present or absent in a relationship, depending on several factors. Some pattern or expectation is set up by personal experience, education, or social routines. Understanding of such a pattern, along with some contradiction or displacement of it, and a positive mood toward it, add up to an appreciation of humor (Meyer, 2015; Veatch, 1998). A sense of play, or creative possibilities, also opens relationship interactions to humor use. One tries out statements or phrases with the other person to test out perspectives and reactions to them. This capacity to explore patterns and break expectations seems ingrained in thinking and reasoning humanity. Even very small children can recognise the 'play with expectations' that inheres in humor appreciation (Airenti, 2016). With my own infant son, we shared laughter at times even when neither of us could explain the specific pattern we were violating, but the sense of play, difference, and uniqueness was palpable.

Communication Functions of Humor: Uniting and Dividing

Humor has a capacity both to unite and divide. Groups share in the understanding of humor and are drawn to its expression. People form connections through mutual laugher at something. Others, however, might not understand the humor perceived by some or take such humor as a put-down or threat. 'Laughter forms a bond and simultaneously draws a line' (Lorenz, 1963, p. 253). 'In-groups' get the humor, and understand and appreciate it. 'Out-groups,' though, fail to perceive or understand the humor that others may see. Alternatively, they may understand the humor but view it as a serious verbal attack that threatens, rather than deserving to be viewed humorously. A sense of key importance to the issue, as essential to their identity, can lead people to take discussions of or references to the issue as serious, having a high level of ego-involvement in the issue (Meyer, 2015). Consider the potential varying responses to the following post spread around the internet depending on one's religious affiliation:

> The Reverend Billy Powell tells of a time early in his career when he arrived in a small town to preach a sermon. Wanting to mail a letter, he asked a young boy where the post office was. When the boy told him, Reverend Powell thanked him and said, "If you'll come to the Baptist church this evening, you can hear me telling everyone how to get to Heaven." The boy said, "I don't think I'll be there. You don't even know your way to the post office."

Some who are Baptists or strong Christians may find the story outrageous and not funny, knowing that the post office and heaven are completely different places and concepts and that learning about getting to heaven is a crucial task. Yet, others may find it a funny twist on their religious belief. Non-religious people may enjoy the implied put-down of religious belief, while others may just laugh at the enhanced perception of the young boy. Paradoxically, humor can simultaneously unite a group even while setting it apart from a teased other. One can see humor even when someone gets angry about an issue. The angered person takes the issue quite seriously, and thus feels threatened and responds with anger or other strong emotions, while another, who takes the issue less seriously, may find still more humor in the dramatic or angry reactions. Thus, some may find unity through humor even as its use divides others who do not 'get it' or are outraged and angered by it and do not find it benign due to the topic or event in question being perceived as more serious.

Divisive humor can be distinguished from unifying humor by which aspect is emphasised. Given that humor requires a perception of an expected pattern along with its simultaneous violation, stress on either the desired pattern or its violation as dominant sets the stage for humor's function in communication (Meyer, 2000). Stressing what is normal, or the expected pattern leads to a unifying function. 'Unifying humor involves the ingratiating, rewarding functions that people enjoy the most, as the comfortable, secure, expected norms are highlighted as dominant' (Meyer, 2015, p. 42). Stress the violation more, however, and division through humor is likely to occur. If the violation of an expected moral order serves as the key focus of the humor, a social division is likely to follow. As humans communicate, we can pursue humor use for these socially unifying and dividing functions. Humor can pull a group together by engaging similarities and enhancing unity, or it can highlight differences in perceptions or expectations as noteworthy, humorous, but a source of division.

Four key functions of humor can be delineated, moving from high levels of unity to high levels of division: identification, clarification, enforcement, and differentiation (Meyer, 2000). Research in organisations and classrooms suggests that unifying humor, or the more positive functions enacted by identification and clarification, associates with higher morale and learning outcomes, while the divisive or more negative humor styles involving enforcement or differentiation associate with the opposite outcomes (Banas, Dunbar, Rodriguez, & Liu, 2011; Wanzer, Frymier, & Irwin, 2010). Varied measures of personal humor styles have found similar differences between prosocial styles, that enhance morale and unity, and antisocial ones that obtain humor from the putdown of self or others (Martin, Puhlik-Doris, Larsen, Gray, & Weir, 2003).

According to Martin et al.'s (2003) humor style model, persons use humor in certain ways that affect personal relationships. Self-enhancing humor involves benign uses of humor to enhance the self, and affiliative humor enhances relationships with others. These prosocial styles fall into the identification and clarification functions detailed below. Conversely, self-defeating humor serves to improve relationships with others at the expense of oneself, often through self-deprecating humor. Such humor demotes oneself yet may be benign and prosocial toward others. Enforcement or differentiation functions are likely involved to put oneself down in relation to others. Aggressive humor, though, is the most antisocial style as it enhances the self at the expense of others and is most akin to the differentiation function explored here. Damage to interpersonal relationships is quite likely for those invoking high levels of aggressive humor. The latter antisocial style leads to lower morale and lost productivity, while prosocial humor use leads to its benefits that people seek throughout many settings and forms of communication.

Identification

One key function of humor is identification, involving humor where the perceiver understands the topic, agrees with perspectives expressed about it, and finds a mutually agreeable variation of the expected pattern to appreciate. Identification humor pulls people together. There is a sense of shared meaning, as parties all understand some aspect of humor. A joke or one-liner that sparks mutual enjoyment due to shared understanding of expected patterns is a classic enactment of identification humor. Although a violation of the pattern must spark humor, the dominant sense is that the norm is solid and such violation is no threat—it may be laughed at together. Some examples shared on the internet capitalise on the shared norm that is perceived by all who can understand the humor. Thus, one person noted, 'I totally take back all those times I didn't want to nap when I was younger.' Now, most of us as adults can notice times that we would love a nap—and recognise the humor. A similar statement that capitalises on a wide knowledge of a pattern for the humor goes, 'you will never find anybody who can give you a clear and compelling reason why we observe daylight saving time.' Many of us do not really know—and those who do when they try to explain must launch into a long explanation. Most of us can recognise that pattern and the contrasting truths behind such statements and potentially share in finding them funny. The pattern—and those experiencing the humor—are in no danger and free to appreciate some unexpected or creative violation of the pattern.

Humor through identification builds group cohesiveness and sharedness by invoking a sense of unity. Shared scripts are invoked, along with shared values which lead to the disruptive instance of humor being mutually recognised and shared, often through joint laughter. Leaders can use humor to unify workers as part of a team and motivate them to perform (Daugherty, 2019; Romero & Cruthirds, 2006). Some intriguing evidence shows that humor use by a leader or manager does enhance creativity within a work team (Hu & Luo, 2020). Humor use also encourages trust and willingness to seek feedback among followers (Karakowsky, Podolsky, & Elangovan, 2020). Teams with strong job security climates showed definite production benefits from shared group humor which fit the identification function (Lehmann-Willenbrock & Allen, 2014). Positive humor used in the workplace has a variety of positive effects on morale and productivity (Mesmer-Magnus, Glew, & Viswesvaran, 2012; Robert & Wilbanks, 2012). Workers use humor to unite around shared expectations and norms and rebel against or resist threats to those norms or group unity (Lynch, 2010). The identification function of humor provides a sense of safety and unity that humans in groups strive for.

Identification humor also allows formation and reification of social or group norms in a benign way. Encountering what groups find funny, unifying them in laughter, teaches outsiders or new members what is valued in a group and which norms are expected (Meyer, 1997). We learn through noticing what friends and colleagues laugh at. Researchers have found humor used by both organisational newcomers and long-term members reinforces norms and establishes specific expectations for all members and clarifies social practices for those just joining an organisation (Heiss & Carmack, 2012). Inside jokes or truths that group members can quickly recognise lead to clear instances of identification humor. Those who are husbands, for instance, may recognise the dominant pattern of expectations behind the story, 'a little boy asked his father, "Daddy, how much does it cost to get married?" The father replies, "I don't know, son, I am still paying."' Similarly, 'a young son asked, "Is it true, Dad, that in some parts of the world a man doesn't know his wife until he marries her?" This time the father replies, "That happens in every country, son."' Most husbands can relate to such jokes in some way. Many instances of groups growing more cohesive through humor can be found (Graham, Papa, & Brooks, 1992; Romero & Pescosolido, 2008). Often, we can tell how cohesive a group is by how often members share in laughter.

Those who have shared an experience can laugh together at odd or unusual aspects of it that both parties perceive. This engagement of identification leads to good feelings toward the persons engaged in creating such humor, which can enhance believability and lead to persuasion. When we identify with someone, we are more likely to be persuaded by them, as shared identity leads to more comfortable mutual influence. For instance, a joke aimed at elderly people proved highly relatable to many:

> I feel like my body has gotten totally out of shape, so I got my doctor's permission to join a fitness club and start exercising. I decided to take an exercise class for seniors. I bent, twisted, gyrated, jumped up and down, and perspired for an hour. But, by the time I got my leotards on, the class was over.

The tendency of such humor use that shows similarity to ourselves is to boost positive feelings toward its source (Bolkan & Goodboy, 2015), increasing credibility and enhancing one's attention and possible persuasion in the situation. There is a sense that laughing together, or experiencing humor together, opens the mind to considering other alternatives through having experienced and enjoyed the contradictions perceived in humor.

The social sharing that occurs through identification humor may transcend many social differences. Shared social patterns enhance the mutual appreciation of humor. One of the joys of sharing humor is the sense that participants are 'in it together' as both 'get' the joke or understand why something can be found funny. Laughing together suggests that differences can be managed, or overcome, as apparently people will get along fine. Humor use that is mutually appreciated can overcome differences since the unifying characteristics shared increase perceptions of sociability (Chen, Joyce, Harwood, & Xiang, 2017). The human search for belonging, and love, seems partially answered by encountering and participating in the identification function of humor. The social unity and sharing of meaning are strong for this humor function, and many find promotion of such social closeness the most welcome and desirable attribute of humor use.

Clarification

The second key humor function is clarification. This kind of humor involves a flash of insight, or a new perspective, on an issue already well-understood by the perceiver, but now viewed suddenly in a different way. Memorable humorous one-liners or anecdotes with a key point fulfil this function well. A point is made memorably using humor. Emphasis is still on the operative norm or pattern, but now the clashing violation of it has an unusual, novel twist or generates surprise excitement. 'Aha! I have never thought of it that way before!' This phrase is operative and is part of the spark or source for the appreciation of the humor. There is still a mutual appreciation of the humor, but along with it more of a shocking 'sharp edge' brought by the defiance of a norm, or an unexpected happening or statement. A point is made, a contradiction noted, two clashing perspectives come together, and humor is experienced in a memorable yet benign and prosocial manner.

Often, through a memorable short phrase or anecdote, people who share a basic understanding of an issue may have one perspective clarified or reinforced in an unusual way. The pattern violation that causes the humor also causes a re-thinking or re-evaluation of the topic. Even as an expected norm or pattern is broken, upended, or contradicted, that very norm is re-emphasised. Most people, for instance, have encountered vacation or away notifications when attempting to email or contact a friend or co-worker. One person came up with a twist on the standard form those messages usually take:

> I am currently out of the office on vacation. I know I'm supposed to say that I'll have limited access to email and won't be able to respond until I return—but that's not true. My iPhone will be with me, but I promised myself that I am going to try to disconnect, get away and enjoy my vacation as much as possible. However, if your email is urgent and you need a response while I am away, please resend it to interruptmyvacation@urkiddingme.com.

Often, violations of a norm in the form of mistakes can be laughed at as uniquely reinforcing the very same social norm (Meyer, 2015). Stories told in a workplace about unusual events or family members portraying themselves in unique ways can spark laughter and new ways of thinking about them. Sudden juxtapositions of concepts through humor may be memorable and thought-provoking. One can find that 'the incongruity of a message's violation of expectations makes it stand out all the more due to its error, yet its intended message is still implied…. the clarification function is memorably expressing a position on an issue through a humorous remark' (Meyer, 2015, p. 37).

Much study has been made of how people can teach and learn through humor use. Apparently, this cannot be done directly, in that simply making messages funnier to people does not help them learn more or faster. They merely become more and more entertained and take retaining information or knowledge less seriously and put out less effort. Yet humor does enhance attention to and enjoyment of the experience. Humor use (in moderate amounts) has been found to enhance learning in many ways, in multiple formats and settings (Goodboy, Booth-Butterfield, Bolkan, & Griffin, 2015). The clarification and identification functions likely both contribute to such learning, one by memorably presenting concepts, and the other by enhancing a mutual sense of goodwill and unity.

Humor use can also be emancipatory as it reframes and clarifies one's position on issues or social norms. President Barack Obama used such humor to clarify his own positions rhetorically while upending social contradictions involving black males (Isaksen, 2017). Also, in politics, one widespread email clarified a position this way:

> The United States Department of Agriculture is proud to be distributing this year the greatest amount of free meals and food stamps ever, to 46 million people.

Meanwhile, the National Park Service, administered by the United States Department of Interior, asks us: 'Please do not feed the animals.' Their stated reason for the policy is because 'the animals will grow dependent on handouts and will not learn to take care of themselves.' Thus ends today's lesson in irony.

In a less political situation, loving cats and men were dramatically juxtaposed in a widespread humorous email:

> I've never understood why women love cats. Cats are independent, they don't listen, they don't come in when you call, they like to stay out all night, come home and expect to be fed and stroked, then want to be left alone and sleep. In other words, every quality that women hate in a man, they love in a cat.

A group can explore a topic using humor, and so evaluate group procedures or recent events that took place (Keyton & Beck, 2010). Social changes can then follow, as people feel comfortable enough with some evolution or alteration in the face of solid social norms mutually understood. Yet, by laughing at expectations while clarifying how one's own position may contradict others' expectations, humor can free those who appreciate it from constraint by serious social norms—since they are treated humorously. People are granted leeway, for instance, to joke about qualities they themselves have, or groups of which they themselves are a part. Persuasive appeals by members of an opposed group were more influential when they used humor at the group's own expense (Nir & Halperin, 2019). Even those who disagreed with a speaker were more likely to listen to and be swayed by messages that included humorous jokes or asides making light of the speaker or group making the appeal. A sense that one can laugh at oneself or one's own group seems to open others to new ideas to clarify positions on issues.

Clarification humor has a strong element of creativity within it. To be able to make a point memorably or unusually or tell a story is socially valued, as many able to perform in that way do find. People find new unity based on the mutually appreciated twist or contradiction to an old and well-understood pattern. People of many religious backgrounds, for instance, along with nonbelievers, may laugh at the quick witticism expressing that 'many folks want to serve God, but only as advisors.' Humans universally can recognise the tendency to laziness, and the social norm that resists or contradicts it. In such humor, both the identification and clarification functions serve as social unifiers, pulling people together through a social experience of humor. The next two functions serve to enact social divisions, in a pleasant way for many participants, but in a divisive and unwelcome way for others.

Enforcement

The enforcement function has a disciplinary element—a different pattern or unusual event sparking the humor is assumed to need correction or is considered some kind of social violation. It is viewed as funny, humor is experienced, but the pattern or norm being violated is being more forcefully asserted, and the violation is emphasised more strongly. Teases serve as the most common fulfilment of this function. At this point, the stress is on the violation of the pattern rather than solid expectations for it. The violation is viewed as potentially subversive, and the instance of humor may evoke 'discipline by laughter' (Duncan, 1962). This kind of humor can have a unifying aspect to it, but there is always the possibility that the person sparking the humor, the butt of the joke, or the target of the tease, will take it seriously as criticism or as an attack. Social divisions may quickly become evident between those who choose to appreciate the humor, and those who do not (Meyer, 2015). The enforcement function of humor seems focused on pointing out and making light of some kind of social pattern or norm violation. Behind the humor, however, may lurk some serious criticism, depending on how much (or how little) one chooses to appreciate the humor involved.

With the enforcement function, some social norms are being violated, and they seem to be worth mention and focus through invoking humor. Even as this aberration can be laughed at as those participating mutually find a violation funny, the violator can feel corrected or chastised by the experience. Consider the person making a comment 'overheard at the water cooler: 'The boss said that I would get a raise when I earned it. He's crazy if he thinks I'm gonna wait that long!'' What makes that story potentially funny is the person's violation of the social norm to earn more money by being more productive. Such humor has a critical element to it; possibly, it is a verbal attack. Teases, after all, can be fun or mean, depending on the perceptions of receivers. This function of humor points out divergences from the norm as potentially needing correction. Teases still are, however, healthier in relationships than direct criticism in conflicts (Alberts, Kellar-Gunther, & Corman, 1996; Young & Bippus, 2001). It is often more effective to couch criticism in a tease, invoking the clashing norms and violation through humor than it is to directly and forthrightly criticise or complain to someone in a relationship. However, the other party then must decide whether to see the humor in the situation or simply take it seriously as an attack. The more humor is allowed into the relationship, the healthier the relationship is generally found to be.

Different kinds of enforcement humor can solidify and reinforce norms, especially in work organisations (Lynch, 2010). Criticism of norm violations expressed humorously still suggests following them even if all parties can laugh at such violations. Relationships also develop norms that can spark laughter at violations of them, sparked by teases (Young & Bippus, 2001). What is found funny suggests strong values that, when violated, get noticed. The group or couple finds unity in laughing at norm violations, with the clear impression that laughter and notice will continue for those who continue to violate them. Persons can choose to be teased in good fun, but most of us have experienced that awkward feeling of being laughed at and found it to be unpleasant. To avoid constantly being teased, people will conform to the norms. They must be that important, we figure, since violations of them are noticed through humor.

Enforcement can push people or groups apart since it has an inherently critical aspect. If the relationships involved are not strong or cohesive enough, the stress involved in pointing out a norm violation through a tease or cutting comment can build up to damage the dyad or group involved. We start to wonder, 'are they really serious about this?' There is the question of a serious criticism behind the teases or laughter. Taken to extremes of amount or degree, such teasing can hurt emotionally and break up groups or relationships. On the other hand, teasing for many pairs and groups is an essential element showing the relationship solidarity, strength, and unity. Teasing and enforcement humor thus stands on the cusp of potential unity or division through humor use.

Differentiation

Finally, the differentiation function demarcates social boundaries between those who find a particular behaviour expected or acceptable and those who find it laughable—a clear and unbelievable violation of social or group norms. Ridicule, mocking, and sarcasm often enact this function—keying in on the differences as laughable, and perhaps socially unbridgeable. Differentiation as a function of humor does the most dividing, as it 'contrasts dramatically one group with another or one speaker with another' (Meyer, 2015, p. 39). Politicians often invoke this function to criticise and stress distinctions between one political grouping and another (Schutz, 1977). The key point of such humor is to place one social group as better than or superior to another. Through the years, gender differences have proven to be a rich source of differentiation humor, as those of one gender laugh together at odd or pattern-violating behaviour of the other. For instance, it may be asked, 'Why do men like smart women? Answer: Opposites attract.' Another similar question: 'How are husbands like lawn mowers? Answer: They're hard to get started, they emit noxious odours, and half the time they don't work.' Not only do women joke in differentiating from men, but the reverse also occurs; in answer to the question, 'Why do some men have dogs and not wives? Answer: (1) The later you are, the more excited your dogs are to see you. (2) Dogs don't notice if you call them by another dog's name. (3) Dogs like it if you leave a lot of things on the floor. (4) A dog's parents never visit.' The norms and values of one gender are thus mockingly contrasted with some norms and values of the other. Social groups, in these cases by gender, are marked and delineated through pointed or critical humorous statements. Those considered outside of social norms are placed there through mockery. As potentially the most paradoxical function, groups of people may find unity in laughing together at those displaced and differentiated into another social grouping, even if it consists of general norm violators.

This is the kind of humor that involves laughing 'at' another individual or social group. The violation of the expected pattern is dominant in the differentiation function, even as the desired pattern is reinforced as a key for those sharing in appreciation of the humor. This function of humor forthrightly divides social groups and serves as an indicator of who is 'in' and who is 'out,' as well as specifying differing social norms between groups, with laughter at practices or symbols of the others. One widespread email focused on politicians, one of whom had this conversation with a travel agent:

> She called to make reservations and said, "I want to go from Chicago to Rhino, New York." I was at a loss for words. Finally, I said, "are you sure that's the name of the town?" The lady asked, "Yes, what flights do you have?" After some searching, I came back with, "I'm sorry, ma'am, I've looked up every airport code in the country and can't find a Rhino anywhere." The lady retorted, "Oh, don't be silly! Everyone knows where it is. Check your map!" So I scoured a map of the state of New York and finally offered, "You don't mean Buffalo, do you?" The reply was, "Whatever! I knew it was a big animal."

Stories that criticise or ridicule members of contrasting groups are common for differentiation humor. Unpleasant consequences result from frequent use of this humor function, however. An antisocial, bitter attitude and approach to social life may emerge behind the instances of shared humor and laughter with certain people—in-group members only. Scholars find those who regularly participate in or appreciate differentiating humor that disparages groups of people find themselves in groups that typically will have a stronger climate of intolerance of discrimination; the sense of alienation and dislike of that other group becomes normative (Ford & Ferguson, 2004). Persons who have a higher desire for dominance or sense of prejudice show a preference for more aggressive humor (Hodson, MacInnis, & Rush, 2010). Such humor accompanies a quest for power—humor can distinguish those not deserving of power from those who do and clarify in the eyes of those who share it who is (or should be) in control and setting the norms for society. These kinds of social discrimination can be enacted by a differentiating function of humor since such aggressive styles of humor involve putdown humor or superiority humor.

Humor that differentiates can also clearly delineate differences in cultural or artefact status for those seeking certainty in understanding social life and groups. People with a low tolerance for ambiguity in social norms or the social meanings of symbols find solace in laughter at them as 'other,' 'alien,' or simply wrong. Humor use thus strengthens their cultural perceptions and categorisations of social groups. Researchers found that people who are more collectivistic in orientation may appreciate elements of humor that reinforce their unique social or cultural characteristics, as found in advertisements (Lee & Lim, 2008). Such differentiation humor strengthens some people's sense of 'us' versus 'them' in an entertaining way. Social differences—and distances—are maintained through a seemingly pleasant and benign form of humor, which may disguise strong conflict or group distinctions.

Leaders who invoke the differentiation function may reinforce norms and beliefs in their own group, but also reinforce notions of an 'other.' The unity through humor is achieved through (at least perceived) opposition to another that may be harshly teased, ridiculed, or held so ignorant as to be out of social bounds in some way. Such groups where lots of differentiation humor is seen may not be pleasant for interaction or accomplishment, however. In the workplace, managers who use a highly differentiating style of humor, often referred to as an aggressive style, see higher levels of stress and lower morale in their workgroups (Avtgis & Taber, 2006; Evans & Steptoe-Warren, 2018). The group may seem unified, but differentiation humor is invoking the power of one group over another and stressing distinct differences from that other. Such social differences may well lead to conflict; even if they are initially expressed through humor, after further communication, they may not be. Thus, differentiation humor appears on the far end of a continuum which runs from the highly unifying identification function, to the clarification and somewhat divisive enforcement functions, all the way to strong division through the differentiation function.

Next Steps

Whatever function of humor is invoked, much depends on the receiver's or audience's reception of the humorous event or message. One can always choose to acknowledge, experience, or enjoy the humor, yet likewise, one may not choose to do so (Meyer, 2015). A situation that sets up people to perceive and enjoy humor may open people's minds to ideas before strong feelings of threat or anger lead to a serious response. Many have heard a comic performer or actor, for instance, approach and make comments on issues that would gain censure or rejection if taken as serious messages about a situation needing action. People need to be in a mindset willing to discount a need for serious, consequential responses to messages to appreciate humor. The message may be assumed not to contain an immediate, actionable, truth, but merely ideas to think about and play with via words. There is a non-bona-fide characteristic of these playful statements or actions that often lead to humor appreciation (Raskin, 1985). This kind of play setting can set up the situation for an appreciation of humor. The essential qualities and relationships of play and humor in personal interactions merit further exploration—especially of the crucial ways in which they are related. Questions can be asked like: which aspects of communication indicate a state of play? Which indicate humor use? How are play and humor related? Play, for instance, much like humor, involves a suspension of concern for serious consequences, for the sake of a game. The game can be a game of words or a game of actions, involving formal rules or ambiguous, emerging rules.

Rules, in turn, suggest the potential for contradictions and violations of patterns that make humor appreciation possible. If a state of play sets up a situation so that rules exist and are mutually perceived, yet statements made, and actions taken need have no serious, immediate, or long-term consequences for mutual action or survival, one has a non-bona-fide mode of communication where humor appreciation can be enhanced. Studies of play have shown that humorous statements that are made engage social, cognitive, and emotional aspects of interaction during games; these aspects roughly parallel the superiority, incongruity, and relief theories of humor (Dormann & Biddle, 2009). Further study could illuminate how theories of humor apply to communication during play, and vice versa—do theories of play also apply to or shed light on humor? Serious play is broken up in welcome ways by an invocation of humor, and these intervals seem to promote creativity—as well as social bonding. People treasure those times together that involve comfortable, entertaining, unpredictable interactions framed by reasonably shared sets of rules—suggesting both humor and play are essential to such highlights of human interactive experiences. Indeed, even enforcement or differentiation humor, if taken as inconsequential jests, can become part of a group's norm and enhance creativity and a willingness to play with symbols or ideas. Creativity does, indeed, increase with the presence of humor and play (Elkind, 2007). The use of humor seems to both reflect and enhance creativity, as revealed especially by research in the workplace (Chen, Chen, & Roberts, 2019). The play with clashing or contrasting expectations necessary for finding humor leads people to be more open to alternative perspectives and ideas. While play can certainly be quite serious, the chance for humor is often enhanced when we are in a play mode. Additional questions emerge worth asking: How do humor and play relate to, reflect, or affect creativity?

In a playful situation, one can more readily choose to see humor in events, actions, and words. Along with play, there is a lightness, a tentativeness, a flexibility that allows people to run ideas by others and build on them or even put them down in a non-serious manner. Unification can be achieved through the identification and clarification functions readily, as all are comfortable and ready to perceive and enjoy humor. Yet differentiation and enforcement may be 'safely' engaged, as well, as people in a play situation may well refrain from taking such putdowns or corrections seriously and enjoy them as humorous playing with ideas or concepts. Perhaps a play mode can help turn enforcement and differentiation humor into more benign or prosocial communication. Play may be crucial to a non-serious or non-bona-fide response, by reducing the survival urgency of messages and actions—so that patterns and meanings can be observed and shared, but no response is needed for full enactment to improve or preserve the lives of the people and community involved. The only reaction necessary in such situations is one for continued play.

With such a shield against relational or actionable consequences provided by a non-bona-fide communication mode due to play, all kinds of contradictions, clashes, and unexpected ideas can be explored without direct and immediate consequences. People can invoke humor for any of the four major functions, even during serious discourse. Yet, in a play mode, serious consequences may be laid aside for the sake of enjoyment, flexibility, and trial and error. That sort of play situation certainly sounds like a creativity incubator, an aspect of social and group life that is and should be well sought after. Further study and exploration of humor and its relationship to play situations are called for. What leads to humor during play? How can play promote or hinder humor use? Whether we unite using identification humor through similar perspectives to others or clarify views with clarification humor, we enhance a potential play and creative mode. In turn, such a play mode can allow even social discipline through enforcement humor and social division through differentiation humor to be taken less seriously, by the sundered individuals or groups, by playing with creative exploration of ideas rather than the harsh use of humor as a weapon. Future research should illuminate how such seemingly 'anti-social' humor can be made fun, or benign, in play or non-bona-fide communication situations. Through a play mode, all the communicative functions of humor, both unifying and dividing, may, in the end, unite social groups sharing in such humor through play.

References

Airenti, G. (2016). Playing with expectations: A contextual view of humor development. *Frontiers in Psychology, 7*, 1392.

Alberts, J. K., Kellar-Gunther, Y., & Corman, S. R., (1996). That's not funny: Understanding recipients' responses to teasing. *Western Journal of Communication, 60*, 337–357.

Avtgis, T. A., & Taber, K. R. (2006). 'I laughed so hard my side hurts, or is that an ulcer?' The influence of work humor on job stress, job satisfaction, and burnout among print media employees. *Communication Research Reports, 23*, 13–18.

Banas, J. A., Dunbar, N., Rodriguez, D., & Liu, S.-J. (2011). A review of humor in educational settings: Four decades of research. *Communication Education, 60(1)*, 115–144.

Bippus, A. M. (2003). Humor motives, qualities and reactions in recalled conflict episodes. *Western Journal of Communication, 67*, 413–426.

Bolkan, S., & Goodboy, A. K. (2015). Exploratory theoretical tests of the instructor humor–student learning link. *Communication Education, 64(1)*, 45–64.

Chen, C.-H., Chen, H.-C., & Roberts, A. M. (2019). Why humor enhances creativity from theoretical explanations to an empirical humor training program. In S. Luria, J. Baer, & J. Coffman (Eds.), *Creativity and humor* (pp. 83–108). Cambridge, MA: Elsevier.

Chen, C. Y., Joyce, N., Harwood, J., & Xiang, J. (2017). Stereotype reduction through humor and accommodation during imagined communication with older adults. *Communication Monographs, 84(1)*, 94–109.

Daugherty, N. (2019). Directing and increasing traffic: The uses (and abuses) of humor in volunteer organizational meetings. *Atlantic Journal of Communication, 27*, 216–230.

Dormann, C., & Biddle, R. (2009). A review of humor for computer games: Play, laugh and more. *Simulation & Gaming, 40(6)*, 802–824.

Duncan, H. D. (1962). *Communication and social order*. New York: Bedminster.

Elkind, D. (2007). *The hurried child: Growing up too fast too soon* (3rd ed.). Cambridge, MA: Da Capo.

Evans, T. R., & Steptoe-Warren, G. (2018). Humor style clusters: Exploring managerial humor. *International Journal of Business Communication, 55(4)*, 443–454.

Ford, T. E., & Ferguson, M. A. (2004). Social consequences of disparagement humor: A prejudiced norm theory. *Personality and Social Psychology Review, 8(1)*, 79–94.

Goodboy, A. K., Booth-Butterfield, M., Bolkan, S., & Griffin, D. J. (2015). The role of instructor humor and students' educational orientations in student learning, extra effort, participation, and out-of-class communication. *Communication Quarterly, 63(1)*, 44–61.

Graham, E. E., Papa, M. J., & Brooks, G. P. (1992). Functions of humor in conversation: Conceptualization and measurement. *Western Journal of Communication, 56,* 161–183.

Heiss, S. N., & Carmack, H. J. (2012). Knock, knock; Who's there? *Management Communication Quarterly, 26*(1), 106–132.

Hodson, G., MacInnis, C. C., & Rush, J. (2010). Prejudice-relevant correlates of humor temperaments and humor styles. *Personality and Individual Differences, 49*(5), 546–549.

Hu, W., & Luo, J. (2020). Leader humor and employee creativity: A model integrating pragmatic and affective roles. *Asian Business and Management, 1,* 1–20.

Isaksen, J. L. (2017). The power of Obama's racio-rhetorical humor: Rethinking black masculinities. *Howard Journal of Communications, 28*(1), 6–19.

Karakowsky, L., Podolsky, M., & Elangovan, A. R. (2020). Signaling trustworthiness: The effect of leader humor on feedback-seeking behavior. *Journal of Social Psychology, 160*(2), 170–189.

Keyton, J., & Beck, S. J. (2010). Examining laughter functionality in jury deliberations. *Small Group Research, 41,* 386–407.

Lee, Y. H., & Lim, E. A. C. (2008). What's funny and what's not: The moderating role of cultural orientation in ad humor. *Journal of Advertising, 37*(2), 71–84.

Lehmann-Willenbrock, N., & Allen, J. A. (2014). How fun are your meetings? Investigating the relationship between humor patterns in team interactions and team performance. *Journal of Applied Psychology, 99,* 1278–1287.

Lorenz, K. (1963). *On aggression.* New York: Harcourt.

Lynch, O. (2010). Cooking with humor: In-group humor as social organization. *Humor: International Journal of Humor Research, 23,* 127–159.

Martin, R. A. & Ford, T. E. (2018). *The psychology of humor: An integrative approach* (2nd ed.). Boston: Academic Press.

Martin, R. A., Puhlik-Doris, P., Larsen, G., Gray, J., & Weir, K. (2003). Individual differences in the uses of humor and their relation to psychological well-being: Development of the Humor Styles Questionnaire. *Journal of Research in Personality, 37,* 48–75.

McGraw, A. P., & Warren, C. (2010). Benign violations: Making immoral behavior funny. *Psychological Science, 21,* 1141–1149.

McGraw, P., & Warner, J. (2014). *The humor code: A global search for what makes things funny.* New York: Simon & Schuster.

Mesmer-Magnus, J., Glew, D. J., & Viswesvaran, C. (2012). A meta-analysis of positive humor in the workplace. *Journal of Managerial Psychology, 27*(2), 155–190.

Meyer, J. (1997). Humor in member narratives: Uniting and dividing at work. *Western Journal of Communication, 61,* 188–209.

Meyer, J. (2000). Humor as a double-edged sword: Four functions of humor in communication. *Communication Theory, 10,* 310–331.

Meyer, J. C. (2012). Humor as personal relationship enhancer: Positivity for the long term. In Socha, T. J. & Pitts, M. J. (Eds.), *The positive side of interpersonal communication.* New York: Peter Lang.

Meyer, J. C. (2015). *Understanding humor through communication: Why be funny, anyway?* Lanham, MD: Lexington.

Morreall, J. (1983). *Taking laughter seriously.* Albany: State University of New York Press.

Nir, N., & Halperin, E. (2019). Effects of humor on intergroup communication in intractable conflicts: Using humor in an intergroup appeal facilitates stronger agreement between groups and a greater willingness to compromise. *Political Psychology, 40*(3), 467–485.

Raskin, V. (1985). *Semantic mechanisms of humor.* Boston, MA: Reidel.
Robert, C., & Wilbanks, J. E. (2012). The Wheel Model of humor: Humor events and affect in organizations. *Human Relations, 65*(9), 1071–1099.
Romero, E., & Pescosolido, A. (2008). Humor and group effectiveness. *Human Relations, 61*(3), 395–418.
Romero, E. J., & Cruthirds, K. W. (2006). The use of humor in the workplace. *Academy of Management Perspectives, 20,* 58–69.
Schutz, C. E. (1977). *Political humor.* London: Associated Presses.
Veatch, T. C. (1998). A theory of humor. *Humor: International Journal of Humor Research, 11,* 161–216.
Wanzer, M. B., Frymier, A. B., & Irwin, J. (2010). An explanation of the relationship between instructor humor and student learning: Instructional humor processing theory. *Communication Education, 59*(1), 1–18.
Young, S. L., & Bippus, A. M. (2001). Does it make a difference if they hurt you in a funny way? Humorously and non-humorously phrased hurtful messages in personal relationships. *Communication Quarterly, 49,* 35–52.

5
HUMOR AND LONG-TERM ROMANTIC RELATIONSHIPS

Jeffrey Hall

As long as I can remember, I have treasured the feeling of joy emerging from the muddle in my mind when I recognise the kernel of truth hidden in jest or profound absurdity hidden in the mundane. I don't consider myself a particularly funny person. I am a better audience to and collaborator in joking around with others. Making fun is such an appropriate description of humor; it is something new fabricated from ideas, observations, and past points of reference. I find its most potent weight emerges when it is co-constructed in conversation. Humor is a fundamental form of social connection: 'Laughing *with* brings the pleasure of acceptance, in-group feeling, and bonding' (Provine, 2000, p. 43). As I have observed in my own research, romantic partners are probably the single most frequent collaborators in making fun together, eliciting laughter, and in sharing idiomatic humor and inside jokes. This intersection between humor and its influence on romantic relationships has driven my research for 15 years. Although my earliest paper on humor (Hall & Sereno, 2005) never found a publication outlet, my research came full circle when that paper's data was included in my meta-analysis of humor and romantic relationship satisfaction (Hall, 2017). Although I've also published work on humor in the early stages of courtship (i.e., Hall, 2015; Ross & Hall, 2020), in this chapter, I will review my program of research on humor in long-term romantic relationships and highlight the theoretical and empirical contributions of other important scholars.

To organise this chapter, I will start by reviewing four theories and models pertinent to the study of humor in romantic relationships. In the next three sections, I will discuss dimensions of humor I used to organise my meta-analysis: the within-person versus relational dimension, the affective dimension, and the functional/instrumental dimension. In the final paragraph, I will suggest potential next steps in research on humor and relationships.

Section One: Theories and Models of Humor in Relationships

The earliest researchers of humor in long-term romantic relationships (e.g., Lauer, Lauer, & Kerr, 1990; Rust & Goldstein, 1989; Ziv, 1988) noted that people believe that humor is a major contributor to relationship success and reported strong correlations between humor and relationship satisfaction. The strength of this relationship is indeed quite strong: in my meta-analysis, there was a large mean effect size association between relationship satisfaction and perceptions of the quality of a partner's sense of humor, $r = .647$ (Hall, 2017). What does it mean, though, to have a good sense of humor? Without knowing what people are referring to, this particular association tells us very little about how humor functions in relationships. Martin (1998) suggests that saying someone has a good sense of humor reflects an umbrella of positivity about a person but says little about humor as a trait or how it is used in practice. When a person believes their romantic partner has a good sense of humor, she or he may be just saying their partner is a good person, a good spouse, or that the relationship is good. This interpretation is supported by negative evaluations of ex-partners' humor among divorced couples (Saroglou, Lacour, & Demeure, 2010). To understand *why* humor is such a critical contributor to relationship satisfaction, I have found four theoretical perspectives that offer insight and direction.

Theories of Natural Selection

Interpretations guided by theories of natural selection (Darwin, 1859) suggest that humor is advantageous for the survival of primates inasmuch that it enhances pair bonding, eases social interactions, increases group cohesion, and engenders an approach response with other primates (for review see Caron, 2002). Bonding through constructive play is commonplace among many mammals (Caron, 2002; Provine, 2004), and laughter among primates signals playful intent (Provine, 2004). Laughter and play for the sake of bonding likely preceded what could be called humor in humans. For humans, humor's primary value as a trait, skill, or resource is within the social realm (Caron, 2002; Craik & Ware, 1998), with the notable exception of coping or self-enhancing humor. In the social world, a sense of humor is valuable because it is a 'potent instrument for at once forging indispensable social bonds and permitting the individual a great deal of (self-serving) manoeuvrability within them' (Storey, 2003, p. 323). When a sense of humor refers to an individual's ability to produce humor, its strongest benefits are held by that individual (Craik & Ware, 1998). Interpretations of humor that are guided by the evolutionary perspective affirm that humor is a valuable social trait that may have offered several adaptive benefits to our human ancestors.

Perspectives guided by theories of sexual selection, particularly those advanced by Miller (2000, 2001), have taken a distinct view that focuses on humor's link to creativity and intelligence and its role in mate selection and honest signalling.

Importantly, perspectives guided by theories of natural selection tend to focus on different characteristics and benefits of humor than perspectives guided by theories of sexual selection. Consequently, each area of research focuses on different properties and processes.

Self-Expansion Theory

Considering how intimacy is promoted within romantic couples, Reis, de Jong, Lee, O'Keefe, and Peters (2016) suggest that humor can be understood in terms of the appetitive system, which refers to the psychological systems that seek to increase favourable experiences and relationships and decrease unfavourable ones. Specifically, Reis and colleagues (2016) argue that self-expansion motivation leads people to form close relationships and incorporate aspects of their partners' identity into their own sense of self. Along with other self-expanding activities, *fun* is named as one way to expand the self and include one's partner in one's own sense of self. They argue that 'fun might be a quintessentially appetitive process,' but note that research on how exactly fun brings couples together is lacking (Reis et al., 2016, p. 13). Although they draw from different domains of research, Reis et al. (2016) suggest similar pathways proposed by Betcher (1981) regarding how humor facilitates the inclusion of the other in the self: increasing cheer and promoting inclusion and acceptance. Noting other useful theoretical explanations, Reis et al. (2016) also suggest that humor could broaden and build relationships through conflict resolution and relationship maintenance.

Emotion Regulation Model

The role of humor as a coping mechanism with health benefits has its own history and empirical support (see Gonot-Schoupinsky, Garip, & Sheffield, 2020). Sometimes called self-enhancing humor (Martin, Puhlik-Doris, Larsen, Gray, & Weir, 2003), people who score high in this style of humor reframe negative events, accept life's absurdity and vicissitudes, and to find joy in the mundane. Although thought of as primarily self-focused or even *intra*-personal communication, this same facility could be offered to one's romantic partner to help them reframe troubles and cope with life. However, research on this effect is mixed. When used on any given day, self-enhancing humor appears to promote one's own relationship satisfaction, beyond its trait characteristics (Caird & Martin, 2014). My meta-analysis (Hall, 2017) only showed a weak association, $r = .121$, between one's own self-enhancing humor and relationship satisfaction. When directed at one's partner, however, several theorists have suggested that humor may play an important *interpersonal* role as partners help each other cope and regulate each other's emotions (Shiota, Campos, Keltner, & Hertenstein, 2004).

One recent innovative article offered compelling evidence that humor can help couples regulate emotions and cope together. Horn, Samson, DeBrot, and Perrez (2018) suggest that humor can be a distraction from negative emotions and can alter one's point of view through *extrinsic interpersonal emotional regulation,* which is focused not on one's own emotions, but the emotions of one's partner. Using a dyadic experience sampling framework, Horn et al. (2018) explored whether 'bringing good humor' when talking with one's partner helped to promote positive moods. Their results suggest that both romantic partners—the joker and their audience—are benefited affectively after one partner brings good humor to an interaction. In my meta-analysis (Hall, 2017), the partner effect for self-enhancing or coping humor showed a weak mean effect size association, $r = .089$, with relationship satisfaction (Hall, 2017), but a stronger association when perceived in one's partner, $r = .228$. This supports Horn et al. (2018) conclusion that humor helps to regulate mood, partly because of the way it promotes intimacy in relationships. Although the wording of Horn et al.'s (2018) particular item (i.e., 'when dealing with my partner's current mood, I tried to bring good humor,' p. 2378) was ambiguous as to what mood state and what good humor looked like in practice, their evidence speaks to the value of humor for what it does for the relationship—it builds intimacy. The results of Horn et al. (2018) suggest that the interpersonal function of promoting bonding and intimacy, proposed in both evolutionary and self-expansion frameworks, may be *the central* mechanism for explaining why humor is so valuable for relationships.

Relational-Functional Models of Humor

To identify the roots of a distinctly relational perspective, I traced the arguments about why humor might be valuable to long-term romantic relationships to Betcher (1981). Although Ziv (1988; Ziv & Gadish, 1989) was a pioneer in the study of humor in romantic relationships, I found that Betcher (1981) appears to be the first to link the evolutionary concept of humor-as-play to *relational humor,* which is humor jointly created within intimate relationships. Betcher (1981) offered three interpersonal benefits of humor for couples. The first is intrinsic to the value of laughter and mirth itself: humor enhances relationships by magnifying the enjoyment of shared interactions. This value of humor has theoretical and empirical support (e.g., Bazzini, Stack, Martincin, & Davis, 2007). Miller (2000) also suggested that beyond its role in mate selection, humor is a potent anti-boredom device because of the pleasure of novelty and introduction of fun in the mundane. Among humor's functions in romantic relationships, humor used to bring about good cheer is the one function most consistently associated with relationship satisfaction (Hall, 2013). Laughter, particularly shared laughter, is associated with social bonding (Caron, 2002), attraction (Hall, 2015), and relationship satisfaction (Kurtz & Algoe, 2015). The frequency of shared laughter during a couple's interaction may be a potent predictor of their overall relationship satisfaction and ongoing interest in one another.

Secondly, private jokes and playfulness create a shared space; a home where risks can be taken and departures from the mundane are welcomed (Betcher, 1981). Ziv and Gadish (1989) similarly argued that through the expression of taboo or inappropriate thoughts or emotions, humor could help partners build trust and intimacy. Engaging in co-constructed silliness and humorous banter reaffirms the safety and intimacy of the relationship—partners can let their guard down (Bippus, 2000; Ziv, 1988). This function can be seen as distinct from good cheer or fun, and, importantly, Betcher (1981) suggests it engages safety and security processes in the relationship. Although some degree of security in the relationship may be necessary to joke around in general (Caron, 2002), when thoughts and feelings expressed through humor are met without negative evaluation, it builds security between partners.

Third, shared humor affirms each partner's values and perspective (Betcher, 1981). Martin (1998) concurs: 'people tend to enjoy and laugh at humor that reflects themes and attitudes that are in agreement with their own attitudes, interests, and behaviors' (p. 56). The feeling that someone *gets* your jokes means they *get* you too, even when those jokes are in poor taste (Hall & Sereno, 2010). Intriguingly, this perspective suggests that humor, particularly when shared, is a quick and accurate way to judge the underlying similarity of attitudes and values more broadly (Curry & Dunbar, 2013). The benefit of feeling that someone shares your perspective could offer its own boost to romantic relationships (de Koning & Weiss, 2002; Hall & Sereno, 2010; Rust & Goldstein, 1989), perhaps independently of its bonding and security processes.

Section Two: Summary of Hall (2017) Meta-Analysis

Two observations are noteworthy here: (1) most theoretical perspectives about how and why humor affects relationships were developed *after* a great deal of research on humor in long-term romantic relationships had already been conducted, and (2) the most common measures of humor were not built for the theories and models presented above. As I noted in my meta-analysis (Hall, 2017), the association between humor and relationship satisfaction is highly dependent upon the way it is conceptualized and operationalized, and the lack of consensus about what should be measured when studying humor has long vexed attempts to summarize this area of research. Consider the most common measures that I included in my meta-analysis: 29.5% used the Humor Styles Questionnaire (HSQ) (Martin et al., 2003), 11.4% of manuscripts used the Relational Humor Inventory (RHI) (de Koning & Weiss, 2002), 9.1% of manuscripts used humor orientation (HO) (Booth-Butterfield & Booth-Butterfield, 1991), and 6.8% of manuscripts used the Multidimensional Sense of Humor Scale (MSHS) (Thorson & Powell, 1993). Thus, 43.2% of research studies used some idiosyncratic measure of humor! Although a handful of extant measures conceptualise humor in the context of a romantic relationship (e.g., RHI), the majority view humor as a trait of the individual (e.g., HSQ). This presents a further challenge to understanding humor's role in romantic relationships.

To organise all these various measures, but also to offer guidance for future research on humor in relationships, I offered a model (see Figure 5.1). The X-axis represents the affective dimension (i.e., positive vs. negative), which is a widely

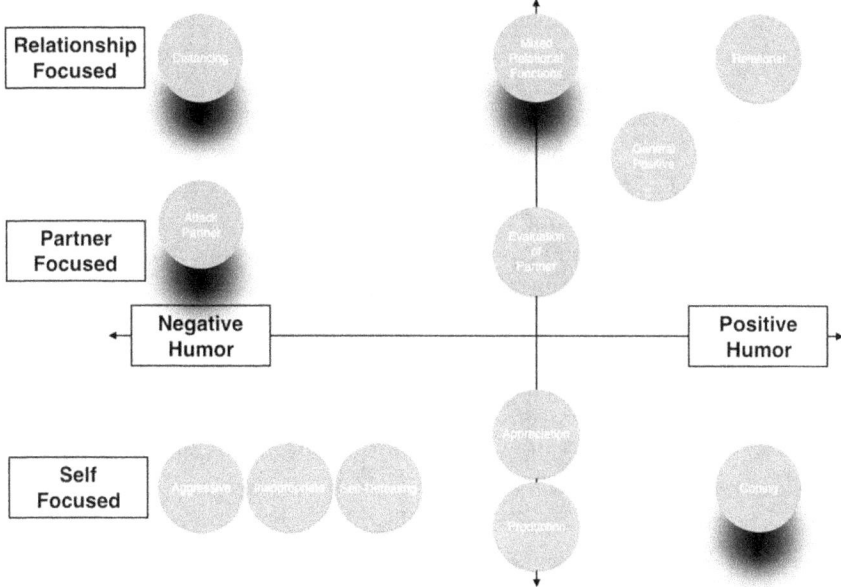

FIGURE 5.1 Three Dimensional Model of humor in romantic relationships

acknowledged dimension of humor (Craik & Ware, 1998; Martin, 1998; Martin et al., 2003). The within-person versus relational dimension is illustrated on the Y-axis. This dimension considers the trait dimension (i.e., the value of humor for the individual) in contrast to the value of humor being seen in a relationship partner or created in conjunction with a relationship partner. The third axis is illustrated by shadowing the complex instrumental/ functional dimension (i.e., type, style, goal, purpose, content) (Craik & Ware, 1998; Martin, 1998).

I included empirical research results from 39 manuscripts, reporting on 43 distinct samples. The final sample included 15,177 participants (54.7% female). Participants were, on average, 34.0 years of age ($M_{samplerange}$ = 18.6–58 yrs.). Sample race/ethnicity was reported in 28 samples, and 31.4% of participants were non-white. Six samples recruited participants from countries exclusively or primarily outside of the US. The average length of relationship was reported in 32 samples and was 11.44 yrs. ($M_{samplerange}$ = 1–33 yrs.). All studies required participants to report on romantic relationship partners, and of the 40 samples reporting the marital status of participants, 82.8% of participants were married to their romantic partners.

Humor as a Within-Person Trait

There are several reasons why individuals who see themselves as able to produce and appreciate humor might be more satisfied with relationships. These measures likely tap into an underlying social facility (Storey, 2003), ability to connect or develop intimacy with others (Caron, 2002), or cheerful trait disposition (Kohler

& Ruch, 1996). It is reasonable that individuals who can create and appreciate humor are more likely to find relationships more pleasant and satisfying in general. Yet, I found the overall mean effect sizes between humor as a trait and romantic relationship satisfaction were small.

Humor production is the ability to produce humorous communication or actions, to make jokes, tell funny stories, and make others laugh (Thorson & Powell, 1993). Items measuring production refer to an ability to create or produce humor or elicit laughter, and related concepts, such as the perception that others think one is funny or witty (e.g., HO, MHSH), being expected to produce humor by friends (e.g., HO), and being someone who enjoys producing humor (e.g., HSQ). By contrast, humor appreciation is someone who enjoys laughing, laughs easily, likes jokes, and is generally a good and receptive audience to others' jokes (Thorson & Powell, 1993; Ziv & Gadish, 1989). Humor appreciation is strongly associated with trait cheerfulness and positive affect. Behavioural measures of production and appreciation suggest they are distinct concepts (Kohler & Ruch, 1996), yet when comparing their mean effect sizes with relationship satisfaction, the value of producing humor, $r = .234$, and appreciating humor, $r = .227$ were nearly identical. These results suggest being funny or laughing easily both have weak positive correlations with being satisfied with one's romantic relationship.

Measured at the trait level, there was a small negative association between relationship satisfaction and the two negative forms of humor (i.e., aggressive humor; $r = -.159$; self-defeating, $r = -.114$) and no association with earthy humor or inappropriate humor, $r = .049$. When measured as a trait of the individual, my meta-analysis confirmed Barelds and Barelds-Dijkstra's (2010) claim that 'humor plays a limited role in intimate, long-term relationships' (p. 458) (see also Cann, Zapata, & Davis, 2011).

Section Three: Humor as Perceived in Partners and Relational Humor

In my meta-analysis, I suggested that there is an important dimension of humor in relationships that deserved further attention: relational versus within-person. This is the degree to which humor—in production, affect, and function—is about us, about you, or is within me. Along with the affective dimension, I argued that the strength of humor's relationship with satisfaction is dependent upon where the form of humor resides on this relational-within person dimension. I found strong support for this moderation: partner perceived humor production, partner perceived humor appreciation, relational/shared humor, general positive humor, and partner perceived self-enhancing humor were all completely outside of the mean effect size confidence interval for the same types of humor when measured as within-person traits (Hall, 2017). Consider the general positive humor category, which combined elements of production, appreciation, and evaluation; when evaluated in oneself, the mean effect size was medium-sized, $r = .329$, but when evaluated in one's partner the mean effect size was large, $r = .522$. This supports what several past scholars (e.g., La France & Hall, 2012; Rust & Goldstein, 1989; Ziv & Gadish, 1989) have noted; humor perceived in one's partner is a better predictor of one's relationship satisfaction than one's own self-reported humor.

Probably the most consequential form of humor in long-term romantic relationships is what I call *relational humor*, which is the degree to which humor is shared by the couple and laughing together occurs in relationships. The Relational Humor Inventory (RHI) self-positive scale (de Koning & Weiss, 2002) is the most commonly used measure of shared humor, but I found other useful operationalizations in other measures (e.g., Raniseski, 1998) that included sharing funny stories or events, sharing inside jokes, and joking around together. One crucial aspect is when couples who *look for* things that they can laugh about together (Bippus, 2000; Lauer et al., 1990; Ziv, 1988). That is, they intentionally bring humor into their relationship. In my meta-analysis (Hall, 2017), I found a large mean effect size for relational humor and satisfaction, $r = .642$. Although not measured in very many studies and conceptualised inconsistently across studies, this association was nearly as large as perceiving that a partner has a good sense of humor. Given these findings, I strongly recommend that future research both seek to improve the measure of relational humor and collect more empirical evidence about this type of humor in practice, including using observational methods (e.g., Kurtz & Algoe, 2015).

Negative Humor Perceived in or Directed at Partners

Humor can be used to demean, belittle, attack, put-down, tease, or mock, and it can be used to express hostility towards one's partner (Ziv, 1988). The two negative RHI subscales (de Koning & Weiss, 2002) both assess partner-directed attacks (i.e., one partner being made the object of humorous attack or put-down by the other partner). In the context of a romantic relationship, negative humor directed at one's partner is very different from negative humor directed at external targets. When the object of ridicule is not one's partner, but a person or group external to the relationship, it is less relationally consequential, although could be embarrassing to the couple if expressed in public (Hall, 2011). Unsurprisingly, partner-perceived aggressive humor was more negatively associated with relationship satisfaction than self-reported aggressive humor (Hall, 2017). However, my meta-analysis results suggest that, at least in terms of mean effect size, the deleterious effect of attacking one's partner with humor, $r = -.258$, or using humor to distance oneself, $r = -.261$, is indistinguishable from perceiving that one's partner has an aggressive style of humor, $r = -.270$. One interpretation of these findings is that functional uses of humor in relationships may emerge from one's internal humor style—people with an aggressive humor style are more likely to use humor to attack their partners (Betcher, 1981; Hall, 2013).

Section Four: Humor as a Communicative Act

The classic research on humor often documented the instrumentality or functions of humor in romantic relationships. On a broad level, the functions of humor include the various roles it may play and/or the various purposes it may serve. Commonly used measures of instrumental humor often combine various functions into a single measure. Perhaps unsurprisingly, my meta-analysis found no association between these omnibus measures of humor functions and relationship satisfaction, $r = .022$. Unfortunately, I expect that poor measurement, rather than a lack of theoretical value, is what underlies this null association with relationship satisfaction.

All of the four theoretical perspectives that I outlined earlier imply that part of humor's value is due to *how* partners use it. There is some consensus that the primary value of humor in relationships is for promoting intimacy and connection. Limiting humor's value to bonding, however, would diminish the diversity of ways in which it is used communicatively between partners, which can offer clues as to *why* it promotes intimacy. I believe that one of the most important challenges for future research on humor in romantic relationships is to integrate the functional uses of humor with these theoretical explanations. In other words, if we think of humor as an interpersonal communicative act, it becomes a pathway toward a particular and interpersonal goal or purpose (Hall, 2013; La France & Hall, 2012). To organise this diverse literature, below, I will summarise and examine the links between the various communicative functions and the four theoretical perspectives offered earlier.

There have been many attempts to list the functions of humor in long-term romantic relationships (Bippus, 2000; Craik & Ware, 1998; de Koning & Weiss, 2002; Graham, Papa, & Brooks, 1992; Lynch, 2002; Raniseski, 1998; Thorson & Powell, 1993; Ziv, 1988). My co-author Betty La France and I (La France & Hall, 2012) concluded, whether they acknowledge this perspective explicitly, humor researchers 'typically approach the use of humor from a functional perspective' (p. 119). The functional perspective is largely a communicative one; it can be defined as the 'intended use of a humorous message or behavior to achieve a communicative goal specific to the romantic relationship' (Hall, 2013, p. 274). From this perspective, the influence of humor in a romantic relationship depends on its ability to help relational partners communicate an attitude or emotion or achieve a relational goal. In accord with the affective dimension in Figure 5.1, partners can have both positive and negative communicative goals.

Fun, Affection, and Playfulness

The most commonly identified function of humor in romantic relationships is to share positivity, happiness, and levity with a partner (Bippus, 2000; de Koning & Weiss, 2002; Ziv, 1988). The appetitive model (Reis et al., 2016) suggests that the having fun through humor promotes self-expansion, and both Betcher (1981) and

Miller (2000) suggest that laughter and mirth enhance relationships by magnifying the pleasure of shared interactions and breaks from the mundane. A similar but distinct function is the expression of affection through humor. The complimentary and affectionate functions of humor can be found in idiomatic humorous communication, including pet names, good-natured teasing, and even sexual play (Bippus, 2000; La France & Hall, 2012; Raniseski, 1998).

Coping and Stress Reduction

Most relevant to the emotion regulation model (Horn et al., 2018), humor can be used to help couples cope with stressful situations and reframe life's challenges (Graham et al., 1992; Martin, 1998; Ziv, 1988). Because this function of humor is typically thought to be a self-focused activity (Caird & Martin, 2014; Thorson & Powell, 1993), no commonly used measure focuses on coping in conjunction with one's partner, which points to an opportunity for future research. A related function is how humor can be used to release stress and tension both internally and interpersonally (Bippus, 2003; Cann et al., 2011; Lynch, 2002; Thorson & Powell, 1993). These two functions are related but distinct: coping utilises humor's ability to reframe information and events cognitively, and humor's ability to generate positive emotion can be used to reduce stress or tension.

Expressing Attitudes

From a communication perspective, a functional approach to humor considers what purpose the attitude and its expression serve for the individual (La France & Hall, 2012). Two of the three benefits of humor in Betcher's (1981) relational-functional model engage the issue of building security and sharing perspectives or values. The perception of a shared perspective is particularly important when humor is used to express taboo thoughts or emotions (Bippus, 2000; Ziv & Gadish, 1989), or to express dark or inappropriate humor (Hall & Sereno, 2010; Hall, 2011). Perceived similarity is important in the expression of such thoughts or beliefs and may indirectly help partners build trust and intimacy. This is also relevant in the domain of sexual communication (La France & Hall, 2012; Ziv, 1988). The degree to which this function contributes positively to the relationship, however, has been called into question (e.g., Hall, 2013; Raniseski, 1998). Yet, this may be due to several theoretical disconnects among commonly explored relational outcomes (e.g., relationship satisfaction), the measurement of functional humor, and a lack of focus on security and shared perspective proposed by Betcher (1981).

Apologizing

Humor can convey a message of apology or an admission of wrongdoing (Graham et al., 1992). Ziv (1988) suggests that when humor is used to apologise, it may make it easier to convey messages that otherwise might not be easily expressed. In a related fashion, Hay (2000) suggested that humor is often used defensively (i.e., to beat someone else to the punch), which is similar to the self-defeating style of humor (Martin et al., 2003). By calling attention to personal flaws or showing oneself to be unable to behave appropriately, the self-deprecator attempts to achieve solidarity and closeness with others through humor (Sharkey, Park, & Kim, 2004). Used in this way, the communicator can admit to mistakes before others point them out or can elicit comfort or reassurance from others.

Humor in Conflict

Both researchers and married couples agree that one important function of humor is to manage conflict (Alberts, 1990; Bippus, 2003; Bippus, Young, & Dunbar, 2011; Campbell, Martin, & Ward, 2008). Alberts (1990) reports that one-third of romantic couples use humor to manage interpersonal conflict. Bippus (2003) found one attempt at humor every 49 seconds of recorded interaction among couples in conflict (p. 297). In observational studies of conflict between romantic partners, individuals who use more affiliative and less aggressive styles of humor were more satisfied with their relationship and reported more conflict resolution (Bippus et al., 2011; Campbell et al., 2008). Cann et al. (2011) also found that possessing a self-enhancing (or coping) sense of humor was related to less conflict in a relationship. However, using humor to manage conflict may be a poor indicator of a satisfying relationship; rather, it could be a sign that conflict needs to be managed (Campbell et al., 2008). Paradoxically, partners who used humor during conflict conversations reported a de-escalation of conflict, but when they perceived their partner using more humor during conflict, they reported less relationship satisfaction (Bippus et al., 2011). Both Campbell and colleagues (2008) and Bippus et al. (2011) suggest that humor is quite difficult to use productively in conflict conversations.

Creating Distance and Attacking a Partner

Attacking, belittling, or making fun of one's partner is a relational use of humor, albeit a negative one (Bippus, 2003; Graham et al., 1992; Ziv, 1988). Another negative use of humor is to create distance (i.e., to push relational partners apart, to avoid one's partner, or to deflect conversations about the relationship) (Raniseski, 1998). The joker often perceives that making light of something, changing the subject, or avoiding a distressing topic is an effective means to mitigate conflict (Bippus et al., 2011). Yet, from the perspective of the joker's partner, such behaviour can be as hurtful as a direct attack (Bippus, 2003). Given the negative relational implications of this function of humor, it may be surprising that the mean effect sizes for both attacking and distancing humor were small (Hall, 2017). This may be explained by Campbell and colleague's (2008) observation that during a conflict conversation, those who used affiliative styles of humor also use more aggressive styles of humor. Joking through conflicts may be a stylistic go-to for someone who uses humor across the diversity of marital experiences (Hall, 2013).

Next Steps

Trait-based approaches to humor have helped to map the range of humorous styles (i.e., affiliative, self-enhancing, self-deprecating, aggressive, earthy/inappropriate) (Hall & Sereno, 2010; Martin et al., 2003), and distinctions among humor production, reception, and appreciation (Kohler & Ruch, 1996; Thorson & Powell, 1993). As several researchers have suggested (Barelds & Barelds-Dijkstra, 2010; Cann et al., 2011), saying a person has whichever humorous style or ability says little about whether it benefits or diminishes the quality of their relationship. Similarly, if an individual perceives that they use humor in a wide variety of ways, this too provides little explanatory power in explaining whether humor promotes their relationship (Hall, 2017). The questions, *why* and *when* does humor benefit the relationship, requires a theoretical mechanism that specifies the link between process and outcome. To advance the research on humor in relationships, more rigorous use of theory is needed.

Theoretical Integration

The four theories and models that I outlined in this chapter are evidence of the maturation of humor research. Each examines slightly different aspects of humor, and each offers slightly different relational outcomes to explore. As my meta-analysis (Hall, 2017) revealed, there has been extensive research on relationship satisfaction as an outcome, yet it is time to explore other outcomes more extensively. Research on humor in conflict (Bippus, 2003; Bippus et al., 2011; Campbell et al., 2008) has shown such diversity of outcomes and tend to focus on the goal of the conversation itself. This diversity and conversational focus, along with the use of observational methods, offers a robust approach to the future study of humor. In addition to conflict management, I believe there are five other possible theoretically supported pathways that may explain why humor promotes intimacy. (1) Humor promotes self-expansion (Reis et al., 2016) through recognition of shared perspective (Curry & Dunbar, 2013; Martin, 1998), through a sense of feeling understood (Betcher, 1981), and through perceived similarity (Hall & Sereno, 2010; Hall, 2011). (2) The appetitive system may be engaged (Reis et al., 2016) through a magnification of positive experiences (Bazzini et al., 2007; Betcher, 1981) or through breaks from the mundane (Miller, 2000) or through a release from unpleasant emotions (Provine, 2004). (3) This is similar to the pathway of mood management and coping (Horn et al., 2018), wherein couples help one another cope through humor. Yet, it is distinct in that the communicative goal is emotion management in response to a particular stressor, rather than joking around for its own sake. (4) The final two pathways that I see have less empirical support. Both Betcher (1981) and Ziv (1988) suggested that expressing taboo or inappropriate thoughts or feelings through humor, especially in conjunction with the feeling of not being judged, may be a pathway toward relational security. Both researchers saw this as a product of the dynamics of the dyad and recommended that it was an important way to build the relationship. (5) Finally, Reis et al. (2016) recommend broaden and build perspectives to explain how humor promotes bonding. The theory of resilience and relational load (Afifi, Merrill, & Davis, 2016) suggests that relational maintenance behaviours create a bank of resources that couples can draw from during times of stress, which can mitigate wear and tear on the relationship. Is shared humor one such resource that helps couples weather hardship? Lauer et al. (1990) report that couples certainly feel that it is a necessary component of a long, successful relationship. As theoretical approaches are better distinguished and developed, competing explanations for why and when humor is helpful (or not) should be tested. Such work can bridge contemporary theory and the classic approaches of the past.

Methodological Diversity

I would also like to celebrate the diversity of methods seen in contemporary scholarship. Observational methods (e.g., Alberts, Yoshimura, Rabby, & Loschiavo, 2005; Bippus et al., 2011; Campbell et al., 2008; Kurtz & Algoe, 2015) and repeated measures longitudinal methods (Caird & Martin, 2014) and dyadic designs (Horn et al., 2018) all provide valuable information on the unique role of humor in explaining within the conversation or end of day changes in relationship satisfaction. I would also like to commend researchers of humor for taking early advantage of the actor-partner interdependence model (Kenny, Kashy, & Cook, 2006) as it shows a recognition of the inherently dyadic nature of both romantic relationships and humor. In my meta-analysis (Hall, 2017), 26% of the studies collected data from both partners. Such dyadic approaches will be critical in testing the theoretical approaches I outlined earlier. Along with longitudinal and dyadic designs, experimental and observational designs should be explored in new research on humor.

Areas of Improvement

Heteronormativity

There is a long history of studying humor in marriage, and only recently have gay and lesbian couples been allowed to legally marry in the US. As such, it is unsurprising that only one study included in my meta-analysis (i.e., St. Germaine, 2010) examined the role of humor in same-sex romantic relationships. This highlights the heteronormative bias of research on humor in romantic relationships—both in committed relationships and in relationship development and partner selection.

Sex Differences

There is also a great deal of interest in sex differences in humor in courtship due to arguments developed from theories of sexual selection. However, I (Hall, 2019) conducted a meta-analysis of ten studies to examine sex differences in actor and partner effects of humor production on relationship satisfaction. For heterosexual couples, the partner effect of women's humor production on men's satisfaction, $r = .231$, was greater than the partner effect for men's production of humor on women's satisfaction, $r = .077$. When humor was perceived in one's partner, no such sex difference was present. This moderation could be interpreted as men stand to benefit more than women in terms of relationship satisfaction by having partners who produce more humor. I offer (Hall, 2019) several untested possibilities of why this might be and contrast these explanations with predictions derived from sexual selection theories (see also, Ross & Hall, 2020). Additionally, a recent meta-analysis of humor production (Greengross, Silva, & Nusbaum, 2020) suggests a medium mean effect size difference, $r = .321$, in humor production favouring men. Sex differences and the role of gender and gender ideology in understanding humor in long-term heterosexual relationships deserve further exploration.

Humor across the Lifespan

In my meta-analysis (Hall, 2017), I found there was a stronger association between humor production and satisfaction found in young, unmarried samples compared to older, married samples. This could be interpreted as the role of humor production diminishing in long-lasting married relationships and among older adults. This seems to stand in contrast to classic research suggesting how important humor is for relationship success (e.g., Lauer et al., 1990). By contrast, I found that evaluating a partner's humor positively becomes a stronger predictor of satisfaction for older adults in longer relationships, compared to younger adults in shorter relationships. I speculated that the value of different aspects of humor might change across the lifespan: in youth, humor for building relationships with one's social network, and for older adults, interpersonal appreciation of each other's sense of humor. To explain why the benefits of two different types of humor (i.e., production, evaluated in partners) differ by age and/or relationship longevity, developmental and lifespan approaches should be engaged in future research. One such study (Verstaen, Haase, Lwi, & Levenson, 2018) demonstrated that couples who stay together longer show an increase in expressions of humor in conversation, but this study was unable to disentangle age-related effects from cohort effects. That is, higher rates of positive humor were expressed by the middle-aged compared to the older-adult cohort. Such robust studies in contrast to a finer-tuned assessment of types of humor may yet clarify the role of humor over couples' relationships.

Measurement

There is a great diversity in measures of humor, and these measures are often out of sync with contemporary theories and models. For example, the lack of association between functional uses of humor in relationship and satisfaction was likely due to conceptually inconsistent measures of function, rather than evidence that the way humor is used in relationships is not important. Along with the function of humor, the measure of relational humor needs further refinement, as it is one of the strongest correlates of satisfaction and is more conceptually rich than rating a partner as having a 'good sense of humor.'

Future research must use measures of humor that are not self-reported. Kohler and Ruch (1996) point out that the distinction between production and appreciation is best differentiated in behavioural rather than self-reported measures. Behavioural indicators of humor production have been used extensively (Greengross, Silvia, & Nusbaum, 2020). There are two observational studies in the context of conflict (Bippus et al., 2011; Campbell et al., 2008) and two in conversation (e.g., Kurtz & Algoe, 2015; Verstaen et al., 2018) that measured humor production objectively. Yet, I found no other studies that used behavioural, non-self-reported measures of humor production or appreciation in the context of romantic relationship initiation, development, or longevity. This means we do not have an objective answer to the question, is humor production or appreciation associated with relationship satisfaction? As a cautionary note, if researchers endeavour to measure humor using these objective measures, they should anticipate a small effect size correlation with self and partner satisfaction and adjust sampling accordingly.

Finally, future research may also wish to disentangle the role of humor from the role of personality. Although it is widely understood that humor is a cluster of behaviours and traits (Kohler & Ruch, 1996; Martin, 1998), it is not well understood if positive humor is merely a signal of underlying traits or characteristics that are profitable in relationships or whether humor itself has a unique value. Similarly, it is possible that types of humor negatively associated with satisfaction (i.e., aggressive, distancing) are not in themselves diminishing satisfaction, but are instead indicative of personality traits that tend to result in less satisfying relationships (e.g., emotional stability) (Martin et al., 2003). Clues about this association are provided by Caird and Martin (2014) who disentangle the daily use of humor from a person's mean level of humor across days. They found that affiliative humor use is associated with relationship satisfaction both within and between days, but for other forms of humor, this daily effect was not detected. Aggressive humor, by contrast, was negatively associated with satisfaction when measured between-participants but did not have such an association on any given day. This suggests that the trait effects of humor may be distinct from its benefits or harms on any given day and that these effects may be dependent on the style of humor.

All in all, I am optimistic and cheerful about the future of humor in romantic relationships, which shouldn't be too surprising since I would rate myself high on humor appreciation (Kohler & Ruch, 1996). The innovation, creativity, and rigour of a community of international scholars and thinkers have continued to enhance our understanding of humor, adding nuance and clarity to this fascinating and important aspect of human behaviour.

References

Afifi, T. D., Merrill, A. F., & Davis, S. (2016). The theory of resilience and relational load. *Personal Relationships*, *23*, 663–683.

Alberts, J. K. (1990). The use of humor in managing couples' conflict interactions. In D. D. Cahn (Ed.), *Intimates in conflict: A communication perspective* (pp. 105–120). Hillsdale, NJ: Erlbaum.

Alberts, J. K., Yoshimura, C. G., Rabby, M., & Loschiavo. (2005). Mapping the topography of couples' daily conversation. *Journal of Social and Personal Relationships*, *22*, 299–322.

Barelds, D. P. H., & Barelds-Dijkstra, P. (2010). Humor in intimate relationships: Ties among sense of humor, similarity in humor, and relationship quality. *Humor*, *23*, 447–465.

Bazzini, D. G., Stack, E. R., Martincin, P. D., & Davis, C. P. (2007). The effect of reminiscing about laughter on relationship satisfaction. *Motivation and emotion*, *31*, 25–34.

Betcher, R. W. (1981). Intimate play and marital adaptation. *Psychiatry*, *44*, 13–33.

Bippus, A. M. (2000). Making sense of humor in young romantic relationships: Understanding partners' perceptions. *Humor*, *13*, 395–417.

Bippus, A. M. (2003). Humor motives, qualities, and reactions in recalled conflict episodes. *Western Journal of Communication*, *67*, 413–430.

Bippus, A. M., Young, S. L., & Dunbar, N. E. (2011). Humor in conflict discussions: Comparing partners' perceptions. *Humor*, *24*, 287–303.

Booth-Butterfield, S., & Booth-Butterfield, M. (1991). The communication of humor in everyday life: The use of humorous messages. *Southern Communication Journal*, *56*, 205–218.

Caird, S., & Martin, R. A. (2014). Relationship-focused humor styles and relationship satisfaction in dating couples: A repeated-measures design. *Humor*, *27*, 227–247.

Campbell, L., Martin, R. A., & Ward, J. R. (2008). An observational study of humor use while resolving conflict in dating couples. *Personal Relationships*, *15*, 41–55.

Cann, A., Zapata, C. L., & Davis, H. B. (2011). Humor style and relationship satisfaction in dating couples: Perceived versus self-reported humor styles as predictors of satisfaction. *Humor*, *24*, 1–20.

Caron, J. E. (2002). From ethology to aesthetics: Evolution as a theoretical paradigm for research on laughter, humor, and other comic phenomenon. *Humor*, *15*, 245–281.

Craik, K. H., & Ware, A. P. (1998). Humor and personality in everyday life. In W. Ruch (Ed.), *The sense of humor: Explorations of a personality characteristic* (pp. 63–94). New York, NY: Mouton de Gruyter.

Curry, O. S., & Dunbar, R. I. M. (2013). Sharing a joke: The effects of a similar sense of humor on affiliation and altruism. *Evolution and Human Behavior*, *34*, 125–129.

Darwin, C. (1859). *On the origin of species*. London, UK: Murray.

de Koning, E., & Weiss, R. L. (2002). The relational humor inventory: Functions of humor in close relationships. *American Journal of Family Therapy*, *30*, 1–18.

Gonot-Schoupinsky, F. N., Garip, G., & Sheffield, D. (2020). Laughter and humour for personal development: A systematic scoping review of the evidence. *European Journal of Integrative Medicine*, *37*, 101144.

Graham, E. E., Papa, M. J., & Brooks, G. P. (1992). Functions of humor in conversation: Conceptualization and measurement. *Western Journal of Communication, 56,* 161–183.

Greengross, G., Silvia, P. J., & Nusbaum, E. C. (2020). Sex differences in humor production ability: A meta-analysis. *Journal of Research in Personality, 84,* 103886.

Hall, J. A. (2011). Is it something I said? Sense of humor and partner embarrassment. *Journal of Social and Personal Relationships, 28,* 383–405.

Hall, J. A. (2013). Humor in long-term romantic relationships: The association of general humor styles and relationship-specific functions with relationship satisfaction. *Western Journal of Communication, 77,* 272–292.

Hall, J. A. (2015). Sexual selection and humor in courtship: A case for warmth and extraversion. *Evolutionary Psychology, 13,* 1–10.

Hall, J. A. (2017). Humor in romantic relationships: A meta-analysis. *Personal Relationships, 24,* 306–322.

Hall, J. A. (2019). Humor production in long-term romantic relationships: What the lack of moderation by sex reveals about humor's role in mating. *Humor, 32,* 343–359.

Hall, J. A., & Sereno, K. (Nov. 2005). *Couples who laugh together: A coorientation approach to positive humor use in relationships.* Paper presented at the National Communication Association Conference at Boston, MA. Open source: http://hdl.handle.net/1808/9919.

Hall, J. A., & Sereno, K. (2010). Offensive jokes: How do they impact long-term relationships? *Humor, 23,* 351–373.

Hay, J. (2000). Functions of humor in the conversations of men and women. *Journal of Pragmatics, 32,* 709–743.

Horn, A. B., Samson, A. C., DeBrot, A., & Perrez, M. (2018). Positive humor in couples as interpersonal emotion regulation: A dyadic study in everyday life on the mediating role of psychological intimacy. *Journal of Social and Personal Relationships, 36,* 2376–2396.

Kenny, D. A., Kashy, D. A., & Cook, W. L. (2006). *Dyadic data analysis.* New York, NY: Guilford.

Kohler, G., & Ruch, W. (1996). Sources of variance in current sense of humor inventories: How much substance, how much method variance. *Humor, 9,* 363–397.

Kurtz, L. E., & Algoe, S. B. (2015). Putting laughter in context: Shared laughter as behavioral indicator of relationship well-being. *Personal Relationships, 22,* 573–590.

La France, B. H., & Hall, J. A. (2012). Sex, humor, and intimacy: An examination of sexual humor use in close relationships. In J. Meyer & R. L. DiCioccio (Eds.), *Humor communication: Theory, impact, and outcomes* (pp. 119–140). Dubuque, IA: Kendall Hunt.

Lauer, R. H., Lauer, J. C., & Kerr, S. T. (1990). The long-term marriage: Perception of stability and satisfaction. *International Journal on Aging and Human Development, 31,* 189–195.

Lynch, O. H. (2002). Humorous communication: Finding a place for humor in communication research. *Communication Theory, 12,* 423–445.

Martin, R. A. (1998). Approaches to the sense of humor: A history review. In W. Ruch (Ed.), *The sense of humor: Explorations of a personality characteristic* (pp. 15–62). NYC, NY: Mouton de Gruyter.

Martin, R. A., Puhlik-Doris, P., Larsen, G., Gray, J., & Weir, K. (2003). Individual differences in uses of humor and their relation to psychological well-being: Development of the Humor Styles Questionnaire. *Journal of Research in Personality, 37,* 48–75.

Miller, G. (2000). *The mating mind: How sexual choices shaped the evolution of human nature.* London, UK: Heinemann Press.

Miller, G. (2001). Mental traits as fitness indicators: Expanding evolutionary psychology's adaptationism. In D. LeCroy & P. Moller (Eds.), *Evolutionary perspectives on human reproductive behavior, 907,* 50–62.

Provine, R. R. (2000). *Laughter: A scientific investigation.* NYC, NY: Viking.
Provine, R. R. (2004). Laughing, tickling, and the evolution of speech and self. *Current Directions in Psychological Science, 13,* 215–218.
Raniseski, J. M. A. (1998). Exploring the relationships between humor and marital well-being. *Dissertation Abstracts International, 59,* 3124.
Reis, H. T., de Jong, D. C., Lee, K. Y., O'Keefe, S. D., & Peters, B. J. (2016). Promoting intimacy: Strategies suggested by the appetitive side. In C. R. Knee & H. T. Reis (Eds.), *Positive approaches to optimal relationship development* (pp. 3–29). Cambridge, UK: Cambridge University Press.
Ross, E. M., & Hall, J. A. (2020). The traditional sexual script and humor in courtship. *Humor, 33,* 197–218.
Rust, J., & Goldstein, J. (1989). Humor in marital adjustment. *Humor, 2,* 217–224.
Saroglou, V., Lacour, C., & Demeure, M.-E. (2010). Bad humor, bad marriage: Humor styles in divorced and married couples. *Europe's Journal of Psychology, 6,* 94–121.
Sharkey, W. F., Park, H. S., & Kim, R. (2004). Intentional self-embarrassment. *Communication Studies, 55,* 379–399.
Shiota, M. N., Campos, B., Keltner, D., & Hertenstein, M. J. (2004). Positive emotion and the regulation of interpersonal relationships. In P. Philippot & R. S. Feldman (Eds.), *The regulation of emotion* (pp. 127–156). Mahwah, NJ: Erlbaum.
St. Germaine, C. (2010). Predicting relationship satisfaction: An analysis of romantic partners' perceptions (AAI3417158). Available from PsycINFO. (862786982; 2011-99040-437).
Storey, R. (2003). Humor and sexual selection. *Human Nature, 14,* 319–336.
Thorson, J., & Powell, F. (1993). Development and validation of a multidimensional sense of humor scale. *Journal of Clinical Psychology, 49,* 13–23.
Verstaen, A., Haase, C. M., Lwi, S. J., & Levenson, R. W. (2018). Age-related changes in emotional behavior: Evidence from a 13-year longitudinal study of long-term married couples. *Emotion (Washington, D.C.), 20,* 149–164.
Ziv, A. (1988). Humor's role in married life. *Humor, 1,* 223–230.
Ziv, A., & Gadish, O. (1989). Humor and marital satisfaction. *The Journal of Social Psychology, 129,* 759–768.

6

HUMOR AND FIGURATIVE LANGUAGE

Good for a laugh, and more

Herbert L. Colston

Please consider the following true story:

> A man and his daughter are in their dining room, where they typically keep at least two big bowls of fruit. The man is thumbing around in the orange bowl when he finds an orange with a pretty under-blanket of light green fluffy mold on it. He doesn't often eat oranges, so he utters the requisite, "eeewwwww" and holds the orange out for the daughter to dispose of (she being the big fruit eater in the family). He considered this an enormous favor to her, having saved her from the inevitable discovery herself and possibly increasing the longevity of the ill-fated orange's neighbors. The daughter gives him a powerful, flat affect glare, humbling him in his tracks, but nonetheless takes the fouled fruit into the kitchen for disposal.
>
> When she returns (she had been reaching for the apple bowl before the man's discovery) he asks her the completely normal and expected question,
>
> "Did you play Fruit Taps?"
>
> [*'Taps' refers to the bugle call played during military funerals by United States Armed Forces*]
>
> First nothing. So he repeats the question. She may not have heard him. Then, she emits the barest of, 'why me....?' eye flutters, but continues with her apple rooting. She then herself finds an apple in similar shape as the fated bearded orange, and has her own 'eeewwww' moment, extracting the apple from the bowl. She then looks at her father begrudgingly and turns again to head into the kitchen.

The father follows her this time. His thoughts had moved onto something else. Coffee, most likely. The daughter then pulls the trash bin from under the sink while the man opens the refrigerator to retrieve the coffee. Just as the man has his head buried into the deepest recesses of the refrigerator, doing some rooting of his own for the hiding coffee tin, suddenly, from nowhere, the daughter loudly trumpets right behind him,

"DA TA TADAAAAAAAAAAAAAAA",

forcing him to slam his head into the top of the fridge cavity, still not having retrieved the desired coffee.

He emerges to see his triumphant daughter, arms in a sarcastic 'voila' pose, sporting a superior smirk, standing over the discarded apple in the trash bin, with an eye twinkle and a raised eyebrow as she says matter-of-factly,

"Fruit Taps."

"Are you happy?"

This anecdote exhibits at once, both of the broad demonstrations sought in the present work. It first shows the complex ways in which figurative language and related forms of language play can interact with humor—how particular figurative forms can both directly cause humor, but how humor can also cause the figurative forms to get used, and how the two in tandem can be caused by and can cause other things.

But the anecdote also shows some of the often stealthy social motivations backgrounding much of figurative language's usage in humorous and other conversational contexts. The anecdote shows how figurative language and what it accomplishes is aligned surprisingly well with deeply seated (i.e., neutrally-driven) social motivations of people interacting with one another (i.e., both the father and the daughter using figurative language and language play as a means of having fun together, to confirm and strengthen their social bonds).

This paper will review both of these phenomena, beginning with the complex causal relationships between figurative language and humor. Initially covering some traditional ways these two phenomena have been linked, and ending with a more nuanced contemporary view motivated in part by a dynamical systems approach to figurative language and its meaningful outcomes. Then the deeper motivations for the humor-figurative language relationship will be discussed. These motivations, inherently social in nature, have been shown by recent advances in socio-cognitive neuroscience to form a fundamental driver in who we are and how we act among one another in a socio-material world.

Humor and Figurative Language—Some Examples

Rhetorical Questions

Many kinds of figurative language can give rise to humor. Consider the relatively simple figurative form of a rhetorical question. Imagine two parents are sitting at their kitchen table after a day's work. Their teenage son is home after school, but he's running around anxiously preparing for after-school events. Suddenly, the son tells the dad that he and his friends need a lift to soccer practice right away, because their normal ride was homesick, something he tells them he'd learned that morning. The dad then responds to the son,

"And why are you telling me this just now?!"

As the father says this, the mother smiles, taking amusement in the all too well-known frustration of teenagers' occasionally lax levels of consideration and her husband's technique of highlighting it, humorously.

Metaphor

Or imagine an aptly used metaphor. Consider a line from a recent sequel film to the American television series, *Breaking Bad*, entitled, *El Camino* (Gilligan & Gilligan, 2019). In the scene, a man wanted by the police is talking with two friends who are helping him make an escape. One of the friends offers his car to the pursued man, earnestly in friendship, but also reluctantly due to his love for the car. The other friend smirks and says,

"That right there's a clown car. No self-respecting outlaw would ever

be caught dead in that thing. That's why it's perfect, yo. Deep cover."

The scene is actually very tense and serious, but the viewer cannot help but feel some bit of mirth as the one friend makes fun of the other friend's car. Especially since these two friend characters had a history in the series of exchanging teasing, bantering, yet affectionate insults, many of which were figurative (i.e., in an earlier scene, the friend saying the '…clown car' line had called the other friend 'Sasquach,' due to his large and burly physique).

Verbal Irony

Many instances of verbal irony are intertwined with humor. Consider the following authentic comment made by a lead university administrator. Members of the faculty had been discussing a proposed policy at a meeting, lamenting at the degree to which the policy would require communication, coordination and cooperation between academic departments. To this, the administrator quipped ironically,

"Oh, no, we can't have *that*!"

Each of these instances of figurative language is capable of conjuring humor, but they do so arguably in somewhat different ways—depending on the core processes of the figure. Putting aside the variety of possible humor theories for the moment to just focus the discussion on discontinuity,[1] rhetorical questions achieve humor by forcing consideration of some state of affairs. This state is not something genuinely being inquired about by the asker. Rather the interrogative construction is just used to bring the state of affairs into the mind of the addressees, usually to serve some purpose (Colston, 2019). For instance, the father in the example above isn't genuinely asking the son to tell him why the son is delivering the need-a-ride news so late. The father is instead *pointing out* or *demonstrating* that the son is asking for a ride extremely late, by getting the son to consider the lateness of the request, without really being expected to report on it (Colston & Gibbs, submitted). This illuminates a discontinuity which can lead to humor—the son *should be considerate* and ask for a favour with plenty of lead time, and instead, the son *fails to be considerate* by not mentioning the favour until the very last second.

For metaphor, humor can arise by the juxtaposition of two domains to invite correspondences between them. An actual 'clown car' for instance, is usually one that is very small, often such that a clown, with exaggerated body parts (i.e., long feet, protruding hair, large nose, etc.) barely fits in the car when driving it, to great comic effect. Clown cars also sometimes have some silly looking features (e.g., jaunty paint jobs, external air horns, etc.). Clown cars are also just generally associated with childlike silliness and naiveté, or perhaps ineptitude, rather than other features like danger or machismo. All these features correspond to the actual car in the movie scene in several ways, making the '…clown car…' metaphor have several related and apt meanings. One concerns the actual car's size, which is tiny by American car standards (being a two-seater). This, coupled with the owner's large stature, conjure the contrast in actual clown cars where an artificially large person is seen driving a disproportionately small car. A second meaning is the term 'clown car' itself, often serving as a generic source domain for anything deemed silly, ridiculous, dysfunctional, inept, etc. (e.g., 'I'm not backing that candidate, his campaign is a clown car'). A third meaning is the one actually making the car well-suited as a getaway vehicle, the car would never be associated with something like an outlaw driver.

Each of these meanings can leverage humor, through their individual forms of discontinuity (i.e., big driver in a little car; something that should be adept is actually off-kilter; and something associated with danger is coupled with something associated with silliness). But the multiple meanings themselves, all residing in one host term, 'clown car,' can also contribute to humor. The very coincidence that these multiple overlapping related meanings (e.g., as in puns or multiple-entendre) can all arise from a single core utterance itself can be funny through discontinuity—it is relatively rare for so many related and relevant meanings to inhabit one construction.[2]

Verbal irony is the perhaps most straightforward of the few figures considered here, in its relationship with humor. In verbal irony, the discontinuity, again according to one theory of humor, is built right into the structure of the form. A particular state of affairs (e.g., an expected, desired, preferred or otherwise similar situation) is purported to be the actual case in reality (e.g., a person proclaims the current weather is 'beautiful'), when the actual situation at hand is contradictory to the purported one (e.g., the weather is actually terrible). The speaker is transparent, however, at least usually, in only purporting their proclamation—they let their pretence be obvious (Clark & Gerrig, 1984). Hearers/readers, etc., can then see the speaker's genuine position to mock the naïve perspective that expectations were met and to belittle or deride the reality around them. So, the discontinuity is built into the form.

Causation, Figurative Language, and Humor

The causal arrangements among figurative language forms and their mechanisms for driving humor, have also undergone a complex evolution. Traditional views had it that first a figurative form was encountered in its contest, then at some point in the processing of the figurative form humor would (or would not) get triggered (Dynel, 2012; 2013; Forabosco, 2008). Then a humorous experience or feeling would ensue, which might be expressed via facial expression or through light to heavy laughter (Gibbs, Bryant, & Colston, 2014). Such a view fits well with traditional humor theories like discontinuity or tension reduction in that those views needed a discontinuity or tension to exist initially for a humor response to arise. Figurative language, on this view, provided that means of discontinuity or tension. Indeed, the way the three forms of figurative language were discussed above was intentionally designed to demonstrate this pattern.

But nuances to this essentially unidirectional causal chain allow other causal components to intervene. For instance, consider certain pragmatic effects. Pragmatic effects are meaningful bits of experience that arise in, from, and alongside language processing proper. They can be things like emotional reactions, humor responses, attitude adjustments (i.e., liking or believing in something to greater or lesser degrees), and many others. They interact with language processing, but can also bring in bits of meaning somewhat independently—coming from other physiological, sensory, perceptual, cognitive, emotional, or other processes going on in parallel to language. These pragmatic effects could intercede in the causal chain between encountering a figurative utterance and the humor. These pragmatic effects could also cascade a bit such that a figurative utterance produces one or more pragmatic effects, which in turn give rise to other pragmatic effects, all or some of which then play a role in humor happening. For instance, imagine a speaker spontaneously composes a clever spoken pun, where both meanings have rich import on some situation (i.e., saying, 'A good pun is its own reword'). Here the speaker might trigger some admiration in a hearer, who recognizes the cleverness of the speaker. This, in turn, could then lead to a humorous reaction. And that humorous reaction could also be of multiple sorts, including mixtures of them (e.g., humor *at* the cleverness recognition, humor *with* the cleverness recognition, humor that the person is finding humor [i.e., *I am finding it funny that I am laughing at this, I never laugh at silly puns like this…*, etc.).

But the causal complexity chain can go much further than this (Gibbs et al., 2014). It can reverse itself. Interlocutors could be finding humor in some situation, which spurs them to use more figurative language. This could be due to some sort of priming or just an ice-breaking taking place such that speakers are now more comfortable being figurative. Many related affective, cognitive, and other reactions can also be involved in this mix, either as participants in different causal chains, as co-causes or co-effects, or as enhancers or catalyzers. Things such as appreciation of quality, ingratiation, identification, and particularized pragmatic effects (i.e., satisfaction over some form of justice being achieved) could all be players in these processes.

Indeed, perhaps the best way of capturing all the swirling and cascading complexity is to view the entire process through a dynamical systems approach. Multiple interacting input parameters (i.e., type of figurative language, contextual input, the relationships and shared knowledge in the interlocutors, the social and cultural factors in the participants and the setting, the immediate and less recent history of the local discourse, affect, humor, other pragmatic effects, and multiple others), all self-organizing according to interacting and cascading influence vectors (Gibbs et al., 2014; Gibbs & Colston, 2012).

Humor, Figurative Language, and Social Interaction

No matter how humor arises in interaction with figurative language—whether in a simple unidirectional causal path or via more dynamic interactivity, humor, along with a suite of related pragmatic effects, are closely related to and often occur alongside figurative language. This thus begs the question of what is it that humor, along with figurative language and its pragmatic effects, is doing for people? Why is this all even there? Is it just present as an artefact of how figurative language, humor, and our minds work? Or is it serving some other possible purpose, perhaps something major, maybe something we cannot live without?

I wish to propose an argument for the latter possibility—figurative language exists along with the pragmatic effects and humor it can produce because it helps people meet their suite of unique and powerful social motivations. To make this argument, we'll first need to depart from direct scrutiny of humor, pragmatic effects and figurative language for a moment, and consider some background information about human and other animals' social interaction and social motivations in general.

People are driven to be social. *Being* social means having more social connections. But being social also means greater potential for social *conflict* (i.e., simply having more toes around means more toes will get stomped, intentionally or not). So social drives are usually accompanied by certain social tools and pressure valves. In many primates, who are extremely social in general, grooming serves as a primary such social navigation and relief system. Primates groom for very fundamental and functional purposes—keeping their often matt-prone fur coats healthy in environments where fur gets dirty, where parasites are present, etc. But grooming is additionally and perhaps primarily used to form bonds, to demonstrate attachment or devotion, to offset tension inevitably produced by the drives to be social. In other words, a basic housekeeping chore serves a much more fundamental function in primates—to enable their needs for social connection and social interaction, as well as to mediate negativity also arising from all those social drives and all that social activity.

In humans, our capacity for language greatly enhanced our social drives. And it also accordingly produced much more opportunity for social conflict. So what then became *our* means of managing complex social situations? According to Robin Dunbar (1996; see also Dunbar, Marriott, & Duncan, 1997), the social content of language, which he estimated to be approximately 70% of all we talk about, is this means of relief. We simply talk about our social issues to work through our social tensions. Or, as Dunbar cleverly put it, we 'gossip'—not so much in the sense of delivering secret information about people, but rather in just talking through social issues.

No issue is taken with this general assertion. But the way language services humans' social needs very likely has more nuance than this. Yes, language is inherently social, in usually taking place between people. And yes, that language can contain social content. And language can perform social acts. Language can even achieve the latter by containing the former (i.e., We can *do a favour* for someone by giving them some *social information* about a person—telling a restaurant manager about the superb skillset of a for-hire short-order cook, or warning a friend about a back-stabbing colleague). Language also requires certain social skills (e.g., mind-reading, comprehension-monitoring, audience-assessment for audience-design, etc.).

But language is also highly social in ways we've not given as much attention. And it is here that we re-encounter figurative language. It has recently been claimed that figurative language, along with other related linguistic and related mechanisms, is doing a great deal of the necessary social work for us (Colston, 2019). To begin to lay out this argument, let's first return to those original social drives briefly mentioned above, and consider them in greater detail. These lay the ground for how figurative language enables us to be the social humans we are.

Warm Embraces and Cold Shoulders

Recent research in socio-cognitive neuroscience suggests that people are driven to be highly social by multiple brain systems (Lieberman, 2013). For example, formerly independent pleasure and pain processing systems in the brain were usurped evolutionarily to create *motivations* for forming social bonds. Animals for which strong pair-bond or group-bond connections were advantageous, for instance, evolved responses of feeling pain when they'd lose social connection, and experiencing pleasure when they'd gain it (Baumeister & Leary, 1995; Dunbar, 1998; Eisenberger & Cole, 2012; Lieberman & Eisenberger, 2009; Stravynski & Boyer, 2001).

This body of work was recently distilled into three primary social needs/motivations people must meet (Colston, 2019). The first is the just-mentioned need to get and stay socially connected. This need is driven by the social-connection pain/pleasure system just-described. This system is not unique to humans, primates or even mammals. Many animal species have evolutionarily worked out how emotionally-driven social bonds among individuals can serve many goals of survival/reproduction.

The second need/motivation is to maintain and/or improve one's position in social networks and hierarchies. The drive to *form* social groups as well as to maintain or improve one's status within them is enabled by a powerful and determined mind-reading ability, along with the more basic collective drive to connect socially. The brain system underlying this motivation, the 'default network' according to Lieberman (see also Mckiernan 2003), is essentially the primary cognitive activity the brain undertakes. For periods of time, the brain can focus on other cognitive work. But once that work is completed, or even in the midst of doing that other work, activity will return to the default network, in much the same way an automobile engine will revert to an idle state after some period of engine-racing. The activity of the default network is essentially social cognition, thinking about the minds of others and what they're thinking (Dunbar, 1998; Spunt & Lieberman, 2012), considering the internal states of others, pondering what other people are feeling or desiring or intending, etc. It involves working on social problems (i.e., how do I handle my accidentally having slighted a friend), planning social activity (i.e., I'm going to apologize, but not until I explain the dilemma I was in, but I don't want it to look like I'm making excuses…). Essentially, it is attempting to navigate through our myriad of complex social networks/hierarchies, toward the goal of at least holding position, and perhaps even gaining ground (i.e., going from being liked by a few others to being liked by many others). Or put very simply, we're thinking about our social status in our social environment. This system is also not unique to humans, but is highly advanced in us, largely due to our abilities with language.

The last social need/motivation is to form a sense-of-self which adheres to socially derived expectations (Colston, 2019; Denny, Kober, Wager, & Ochsner, 2012; Lieberman, 2013). The socially derived sense-of-self system does appear to be unique to humans (only other primates have the brain region that controls this function [Brodmann area 10, or BA10]), but it is significantly bigger in humans (Lieberman, 2010; 2013; Semendeferi et al., 2011).[3] It is also possible this system co-evolved with language. This system appears to allow us to construct a sense-of-self, an idea of what kind of person we are. But we essentially derive this idea by *plagiarizing* it from other people. We are what we think other people think we are. We become what *they* expect us to be. We conform to social expectations, often with the illusion that we've built our sense-of-self on our own. Lieberman calls this the 'harmonizing system,' or the 'Trojan Horse self.' It is essentially a way to get us all (or nearly all of us) to work and play well with others. If a person becomes the sort of person others expect and want that person to be, then they'll simply get along better with others, as will everyone else. The person won't violate people's expectations in negative ways, nor will they behave in ways other people don't like (Nowak and Highfield, 2012).

It helps to understand the evolution of this system in humans by considering an analogy, that of roads. This need for this third neural system has been likened to the major upgrading that road and related systems had to undergo as a result of the advent of motorized transportation (Colston, 2019). Prior to our having motor vehicles, roads were essentially just dirt or perhaps at best stone, brick or plank paths. They hadn't really changed much since the invention of the wheel. And the rules for using them were pretty simple. Don't walk or drive your cart into something or someone else. Don't hog the road (two people walking abreast should revert to single file if another person wants past), etc. This situation is analogous to social interaction in human species (and perhaps other higher primates) prior to having language.

But once motor vehicles appeared, roads changed drastically. Traffic speed and volume increased so much that we needed much greater coordination so that everyone could move around. We needed rules for traversing roads, whose courses and intersections got much more complicated. These rules created the need for education so people could learn the rules, for periodic testing of people's memory of the rules, and for training on the actual vehicle operation. We created licensing systems to keep untrained or unlawful people off the roads. Signage and active signalling were needed to know what rules applied at which times and on which parts of the road, as well as to know when to move your vehicle versus staying put. Signage and maps were needed to indicate which destinations were in which directions, reachable by what routes. We needed monitoring and law enforcement systems. We needed new court and damage financing systems to address the inevitable mishaps, and so on. Essentially, *transportation* complexity grew so much that a much more sophisticated means of traffic *coordination* was needed.

The same was the case for human social interaction. With the appearance of language, our *social interaction* complexity grew so much that a more sophisticated means of social *coordination* was also needed. Hence we evolved a system whereby we all absorb collective expectations from other people, of how people ought to be, and how we especially ought to be (incorporating other self-knowledge we possess). We then use those expectations to create a belief of what we are like. And that belief, and what we indeed *are* like, will align better with other people's expectations of us or human behaviour in general. If we all tend to conform to what others expect us to be like, we'll all get along better.

So all of these mechanisms working in humans end up driving us to be social like no other species we know. This means we need both means to meet the social needs as well as pretty powerful navigation and release valve systems to counterbalance all the social pressure and the inevitable conflicts and tensions the social drives will produce. Let's now see how language in general, and figurative language specifically, working along with humor, deliver this system for us.[4]

Over the Top and Under the Table

We think of language as a system with an *about-ness* quality to it—language is *about* something and what a given instance of language *is* about is essentially infinite in scope. This essentially, call it semantic, ability of language means one person can think about essentially anything[5]. And that person can usually get another person to form those same thoughts or experiences essentially via language. A construction worker can talk about mixing cement. A pearl diver can talk about breath-holding. A laundromat employee can talk about bleach. A physicist can talk about string theory. A toddler can talk about yucky mashed yams. A psycholinguist can talk about talk. And all their addressees can more-or-less come to share those same thoughts. This immensely powerful ability of language steals the show when we think about what language is, what it does and how it works. But we often overlook how this semantic quality of language really serves and indeed probably in part evolved because *it* serves the *social needs* of our species. The evolution of language gave us the powerful ability to exchange *information about anything* between people. But it did so to allow us to exchange information about anything *between people*. The semantic power was just a bonus.

When we share information with someone, it is not just a data transfer. We have *given* something to another person. When we explain something to another person, we have not just increased their knowledge inventory. We have *helped them out*. They might *like us* for doing this. We might *feel good* toward them for having helped them and/or because of their gratitude. All of us might *strengthen our social bond* over this exchange or simply because *we now share something*. These are social processes serving our social needs.

So language is social also in that, even when it seems to just be about the information being imparted by some usage or piece of language, there is usually a social underpinning to that negotiation of information (i.e., a speaker helping a hearer, a writer wooing a reader, a rapper wowing a listener, a politician persuading an audience, a signer making a watcher feel inferior, etc.). But all these ways, some essentially obvious, others more stealthy, that language is social have probably still greatly underestimated the extent to which language, and especially figurative language, is social.

Figurative language is also social because: (1) it has the power to leverage enriched, enhanced and nuanced meaning, (2) much of this rich meaning is delivered 'off record' in the form of pragmatic effects, and (3) figurative language itself enables a social bond between interlocutors. The enriched, enhanced, etc., meaning of figurative language coming by way of pragmatic effects (Colston 2015; 2019; Gibbs, 1992; 1994; Gibbs & Colston, 2012; Gibbs, Strom, & Spivey-Knowlton, 1997; Hamblin & Gibbs, 1999; Kövecses, 2005) has been described as meaningful 'baggage' that often accompanies figurative language (i.e., meaning enhancement, negativity and compliance management, humor, mastery display, emotional leveraging and many others). For instance, an apt metaphor such as, 'Twitter icons are Martian hieroglyphics,' said frustratingly about unlabeled social media website buttons, delivers its rich metaphorical meaning, but it might also impress the hearer, it might achieve affiliation among the interlocutors (their realising they share membership in the category of *frustrated user*), or it might achieve other pragmatic effects.[6] But note how none of these meaningful experiences is generally encoded in the utterance. They instead arise in the perceptual, cognitive, emotional, embodied, as well as socio-cognitive work people engage in when encountering the language.[7] As such, there is no evidence that the interlocutors negotiated these meanings. In much the same way that indirectness as a general interaction strategy can enhance compliance (i.e., as in saying to a slovenly housemate, 'Are those your dirty dishes?'), figurative language, by delivering much of its meaningful social work, under the table, off the books, off-camera, etc., through pragmatic effects, enhances the success of that work (i.e., forming connections, raising one's status, etc.). So figurative language has a lot of bang for its buck. But it gets that bang partly by not handling the money.

Still, we have another way in which figurative language is powerfully social. Termed ingratiation, the mere usage of figurative language (or any form of figurativity for that matter), can achieve a social bond between meaning-maker and meaning-taker, a bond enhanced through the operation of cognitive dissonance. Using figurativity with another person delivers the implicit compliment that the speaker expects the hearer will get the meaning. And especially if the language is novel or clever, the work the meaning-taker puts into getting the meaning will amplify its value in their mind, which in turn can inflate the ingratiation process (Colston, 2019).

Viewing figurative language this way, as leveraging significant 'over the top' extra meaning, but delivering that meaning in a stealthy, 'under the table' fashion, is still only part of the story about how figurative language does its social work. We also can look at patterns in what figurative language does. These will show us another inherent social characteristic of this and related forms of communicating.

Taking Apart and Putting Together

If we take a look at a range of figurative types and distil them into their most basic forms (i.e., the number of domains invoked by a figure, how the domains are invoked, and what the figure does with the domains), something interesting emerges. We are essentially able to see why we have the range of figures we do, why some of them are more prominent than others, why two or so of them are the most prominent, and most interestingly, why what figures do is inherently social.[8]

For this exercise, we'll briefly consider metaphor, verbal irony, hyperbole, idioms, proverbs, simile, metonymy, rhetorical questions, tautologies, a set of antonymic figures, a range of reversal figures and puns. Put in the simplest possible terms, **metaphor** essentially invokes two domains (source and target domains) and invites correspondences between them. This is usually to serve the purpose of enhancing the understanding of the target domain. **Verbal irony** also invokes two domains (expected situations and the actual situation at hand) and nullifies one of them (the expected situation), often for the purpose of casting a negative attitude that that expected situation did not arise. **Hyperbole** invokes just one domain (a discrepancy between expectations and reality) but then inflates it, often to draw attention to the discrepancy, usually because the speaker is not happy about the existence of the discrepancy. **Idioms and proverbs** are similarly structured, and both resemble metaphors—they invoke two domains and invite correspondences between them. But both figures can also contain other figures, and proverbs at least are used usually for the purposes of advocating some state or action. **Simile** also acts a lot like metaphor, invoking two domains and inviting correspondences. But simile makes explicit the fact it is comparing those two domains. **Metonymy** also appears to invoke two parts within a larger main domain but mainly for the sake of substitution (i.e., substituting container for contained as in, 'Yum, I really like that *dish*').[9] **Rhetorical questions** use an interrogative construction to activate just one domain, likely for the purpose of inviting consideration of that domain. **Tautologies** also invoke just one domain, but they present the domain in a kind of circular format (i.e., 'A toaster is a toaster'). Oxymora and other types of **antonymic figures** (e.g., antimony, autoantonyms, apophasis, etc.) also just invoke a single domain, but they present a seeming contradiction in that domain (e.g., 'Her silence was deafening'). **Reversal figures** (e.g., antimetabole, antithesis and others) also invoke only one domain, but they give it a reversal quality (e.g., 'Work to live, live to work'). And finally, **puns** are interesting in that they often invoke two domains (i.e., the domains containing the two coincidental meanings that the utterance invoked).[10] But puns can also invoke more than two domains in the case of multiple entendre.

If we now look at what the different figures do with their domains, a pattern starts to emerge. Several figures invoke two domains to invite correspondences, mappings, substitutions, etc., between them (e.g., metaphor, metonymy-at least in a way, idioms, proverbs, and similes). We'll refer to this as **domain crossing**. Irony (which may also be considered a family of ironic figures itself), invokes two domains but then nullifies one of them through a form of contradiction, or **domain nullification**. Several figures invoke just a single domain, but they do different things with it. Hyperbole inflates its domain—**domain inflation**. Rhetorical questions invoke one domain for consideration—**domain consideration**. Tautologies invoke one domain and give it a circular quality—**domain circularity**. The reversal figures lend a reversing quality to their one domain—**domain reversal**. Several figures invoke a single domain but lend it a contradictory quality—**domain contradiction**. Puns invoke two or more domains that are united by the unitary lexical or phrasal unit—**domain multiplicity**. So most figures invoke only one domain. Two collections of figures invoke two domains. Only puns can invoke more than two domains, but usually, only invoke two.

This pattern of domain invocations, and what figures do with those domains, bears a strong resemblance to what we can do manually with physical objects[11]. If you don't have an object in hand, you can get it (domain consideration). If you hold an object, you can get rid of it (domain nullification). If you hold an object, you can do things with it. You can stretch or squeeze it (domain inflation). You can toggle it back and forth between states (domain reversal). You can turn an object over and over (domain circularity). If you have two objects available, you can grab both at the same time (domain multiplication). You can also put them together (domain crossing). We can even do complex things that figures do with domains involving contradictions (domain contradiction), in our manual manipulation of objects. We can bounce objects off of something. We throw the object away, but it bounces back to us. We can also throw it skyward, to have it fall back toward us. We can also turn the object inside out and then back again.

More interestingly, the two actions done on domains which have the largest number of figures doing them are **domain crossing** (e.g., metaphor, metonymy, idioms, proverbs, and similes) and **domain nullification/contradiction** (verbal irony, oxymora, antimony, autoantonyms, apophasis, antithesis). These two operations resemble very closely two of the most fundamental cognitive abilities (and manual abilities) we have. We see things that are apart as if they are together, and we see things that are together as if they are apart. We *cleave*—we *combine,* and we *divide*.

But when we manipulate physical objects, although we might do so occasionally with other people, most of the time arguably, we do so just by ourselves. When we use figurative language, though, we're almost always attempting to accomplish these domain invocations and manipulations *in other people*. So the existence and operation of figurativity itself are inherently social in this way as well. It extends the very same range of things we typically do manually and by ourselves with objects, into what we do cognitively, linguistically *and socially*, in and for other people. It is as if the range of forms of figurative language inherently accounts for what we know other people can do—they can manipulate things pretty much the same way as we do.

So it is likely not an accident that we have the figures we do, that figures doing the combining and dividing are the most prevalent (i.e., metaphor and verbal irony), and that almost all figures invoke only one or two domains—juggling three objects/figures is just too hard. But we have all these figures because they aid us in socially connecting, managing status, etc. They serve our social needs.[12] It is also clearer now how figurative forms are so closely related to humor. The invocation of various domains by different figurative forms all afford strong and varied means by which discontinuities among the activated domains, or between an activated domain and its context, are possible. Such discontinuities can produce tensions, either of which readily can give rise to humor.

Next Steps

This chapter has taken a look outside of the processes involved in figurative language and its pragmatic effects, including humor. It has tried to imagine what larger frame might explain the presence of figurative language and humor, why they often appear together and what role they might play in broader human needs and functioning. We have seen that the extent to which figurative language, figurative meaning, and figurative pragmatic effects like humor serve people's core social motivations has very likely been greatly underestimated. Figurative language, pragmatic effects, and humor aren't just decorative things that we enjoy and can enjoy together, they instead or additionally, are necessary to serve intense human neurological drives; to get and stay socially connected, to navigate the complex social networks and hierarchies these social drives create, and to form a sense of self that aligns who we think we are, with socially derived expectations. They also afford a means of managing negativity that can arise as a perhaps unintended, but inevitable side-effect of such powerful social drives. This is why people will often use figurative language and humor to get socially connected, to manage social status, to reduce social tension, to break social ice, and to repair social wounds. We use it to be social and to preserve that sociality via social mending.

Future research on figurative language would benefit by greater recognition of this framework—that by leveraging extra meaning through pragmatic effects, via a system that is 'under the table,' a great deal of social work can be accomplished between interlocutors. If we look past the semantic meaning of figurative and other forms of language, or if instead, we consider the semantic meaning alongside the social work being conducted, it can open whole new hypotheses to test (i.e., do people use more or less of different kinds of figurative language when under varying social motivations?). Indeed, adding in the social component could lead to an entirely new sub-discipline—socio-psycholinguistics.

Notes

1 Discontinuity is the view that deviances from well-established expectations are the underlying source of humor. It can be applied to very simple forms of humor (e.g., slapstick—finding humor in a person falling down) to more sophisticated sorts (e.g., jokes with ending punchlines that force alterations to the interpretation that was built up in hearing the joke, as in, 'The woman, upon the birth of her tenth child, was running out of names for her, husband').
2 The sensation of humor can also be catalyzed by an appreciation of the cleverness of the multi-layered comment, and concomitantly, its speaker.
3 BA10 is one of a few brain areas known to be disproportionately larger in humans versus other primates (Lieberman, 2013).
4 Figurative language along with other partner forms of communicating (i.e., deviance, omission, etc.).
5 Or at least anything a human mind is capable of thinking.
6 And the humor available in the use of this utterance can catalyze these effects.
7 And it should be noted, much of this work takes place in parallel to or in interaction with language processing proper, sometimes at the earliest stages of processing.

8   A similar distillation may be found in Colston, 2019, but it makes less of the point that the results demonstrate the sociality of figurativity. See also Colston & Rasse (in press).
9   One could argue that just one domain is invoked in some synecdoche and other types of metonymy, where only one thing is invoked but we substitute a part of the thing for the entirety of the thing, as in, 'all hands on deck.'
10 To illustrate with a personal anecdote, we use one pun regularly in our department. When we have a student successfully complete one of their graduate examinations, we host a 'finish ceremony' to toast the person's success. This phrase arose the first time when one of our faculty members used it for one of his students, one of two faculty members from Finland.
11 The distilled figure structures also align closely with our attentional and memory capacities and other very basic cognitive operational limits.
12 Bertrand Russell argued that four 'desires' drive all human behaviour, acquisitiveness, rivalry, vanity and power—all social aspirations at the core (Draugsvold, 2011).

References

Baumeister, R. F., & Leary, M. R. (1995). The need to belong: Desire for interpersonal attachments as a fundamental human motivation. *Psychological Bulletin*, *117*(3), 497.

Clark, H. H., & Gerrig, R. J. (1984). On the pretense theory of irony. *Journal of Experimental Psychology: General*, *113*(1), 121–126.

Colston, H. L. (2015). *Using figurative language*. New York, NY: Cambridge University Press.

Colston, H. L. (2019). *How language makes meaning: Embodiment and conjoined antonymy*. New York, NY: Cambridge University Press.

Colston, H. L., & Gibbs, R. W. (submitted). A fresh look inside and outside of figurativity: Precise vagueness and flexible conformity. *Canadian Journal of Experimental Psychology*.

Colston, H. L., & Katz, A. (Eds.). (2005). *Figurative language comprehension: Social and cultural influences*. Hillsdale, NJ: Erlbaum.

Colston, H. L., & Rasse, C. (in press). Figurativity: Cognitive, because it's social. In H. Colston, T. Matlock, & G. Steen (Eds.), *Dynamism in metaphor and beyond*, Amsterdam: Benjamins.

Denny, B. T., Kober, H., Wager, T. D., & Ochsner, K. N. (2012). A meta-analysis of functional neuroimaging studies of self and other judgments reveals a spatial gradient for mentalizing in medial prefrontal cortex. *Journal of Cognitive Neuroscience*, *24*(8), 1742–1752.

Draugsvold, O. G. (Ed.), (2011). *Nobel writers on writing*. Jefferson, NC, U.S.: McFarland Publishing.

Dunbar, R. (1996). *Grooming, gossip, and the evolution of language*. Boston, MA: Harvard University Press.

Dunbar, R. (1998). The social brain hypothesis. *Evolutionary Anthropology*, *6*, 178–190.

Dunbar, R., Marriott, A., & Duncan, N. D. (1997). Human conversational behavior. *Human Nature*, *8*(3), 231–246.

Dynel, M. (2012). Garden paths, red lights, and crossroads: On finding our way to understanding the cognitive mechanism underlying jokes. *Israeli Journal of Humor Research*, *1*, 6–28.

Dynel, M. (2013). When does irony tickle the hearer? Toward capturing the characteristics of humorous irony. In M. Dynel (Ed.), *Developments in linguistic humor theory* (pp. 289–320). Amsterdam, NL: Benjamins.

Eigenberger, N. I., Lieberman, M. D., & Williams, K. D. (2003). Does rejection hurt? An fMRI study of social exclusion. *Science, 302*, 290–292.

Eisenberger, N. I., & Cole, S. W. (2012). Social neuroscience and health: Neuropsychological mechanisms linking social ties with physical health. *Nature Neuroscience, 15*, 669–674.

Forabosco, G. (2008). Is the concept of incongruity still a useful construct for the advancement of humor research? *Lodz Papers in Pragmatics, 4*, 45–62.

Gibbs, R. (1992). What do idioms really mean? *Journal of Memory and Language, 31*, 485–506.

Gibbs, R. (1994). *The poetics of mind: Figurative thought, language, and understanding.* New York, NY: Cambridge University Press.

Gibbs, R., Strom, L., & Spivey-Knowlton, M. (1997). Conceptual metaphor in mental imagery for proverbs. *Journal of Mental Imagery, 21*, 83–110.

Gibbs, R. W., & Colston, H. L. (2012). *Interpreting figurative meaning.* New York, NY: Cambridge University Press.

Gibbs, R. W., Bryant, G. A., & Colston, H. L. (2014). Where is the humor in verbal irony? *International Journal of Humor Research, 27*(4), 575–596.

Gilligan, V. (writer), & Gilligan, V. (director). (2019). *El Camino.* Television series episode. In M. Bernstein (producer), *Breaking bad.* Los Gatos, CA: Netflix.

Hamblin, J., & Gibbs, R. (1999). Why you can't kick the bucket as you slowly die: Verbs in idiom understanding. *Journal of Psycholinguistic Research, 39*, 25–39.

Kövecses, Z. (2005). *Metaphor and emotion.* New York, NY: Cambridge University Press.

Lieberman, M. D. (2010). Social cognitive neuroscience. In S. T. Fiske, D. T. Gilbert, & G. Lindsey (Eds.), *Handbook of social psychology* (5th ed., pp. 143–193). New York, NY: McGraw-Hill.

Lieberman, M. D. (2013). *Social: Why our brains are wired to connect.* New York, NY: Broadway Books.

Lieberman, M. D., & Eisenberger, N. I. (2009). Pains and pleasures of social life. *Science, 323*, 890–891.

McKiernan, K. A., Kaufman, J. N., Kucera-Thompson, J., & Binder, J. R. (2003). A parametric manipulation of factors affecting task-induced deactivation in functional neuroimaging. *Journal of Cognitive Neuroscience, 15*(3), 394–408.

Nowak, M., & Highfield, R. (2012). *SuperCooperators: Altruism, evolution, and why we need each other to succeed.* New York, NY: Free Press.

Semendeferi, K., Teffer, K., Buxhoeveden, D. P.l, Park, M. S., Bludau, S., Amunts, K. ... & Buckwalter, J. (2011). Spatial organization of neurons in the frontal pole sets humans apart from great apes. *Cerebral Cortex, 21*(7), 1485–1497.

Spunt, R. P., & Lieberman, M. D. (2012). Dissociating modality-specific and supramodal neural systems for action understanding. *Journal of Neuroscience, 32*, 3575–3583.

Stravynski, A., & Boyer, R. (2001). Lonliness in relation to suicide ideation and parasuicide: A population-wide study. *Suicide and Life-Threatening Behavior, 31*(1), 32–40.

PART III
Group processes

7

WORKPLACE HUMOR

The good, the bad, and the non-existent

Barbara Plester

Humor is a key component of working life for most people and has a significant role in group processes. Drawing from a program spanning 17 years of workplace humor research, this chapter emphasises the complexity of successfully creating, managing, and participating in workplace humor. While there are a variety of functional benefits arising from workplace humor, there are also dark, confronting elements in some humor that may threaten group harmony and performance. In short, workplace humor can be wonderful and appalling sometimes at the same time, which can have multiple impacts on workgroups.

Workplace humor has changed and is continuing to change. Modern influences and movements such as #metoo combined with increasingly diverse workgroups, combine to make workplace humor a more problematic and risky activity. Workgroups develop their own humor protocols that influence what may be perceived as funny and what might be considered offensive. My ethnographic research shows that groups of people mostly navigate workplace humor successfully so that humor offers relief from pressurised work situations. However, while workgroups take care not to offend others through humor, this raises questions for the future about whether humor is becoming overly 'politically correct' and is humor at risk of disappearing from work environments, or only existing in its most insipid form? This chapter reviews the complexity of workgroup humor dynamics, offers examples taken from actual workplaces and speculates on the changing nature of humor at work.

Why Workplace Humor is an Important Topic of Investigation

Workplaces are sites where people work for themselves, or an employer and workplaces can range from home-based businesses to corporate offices, production factories or open fields and natural surrounds. Workplaces usually have rules, policies, procedures, codes, safety requirements and they comprise all sorts of people. Workplaces are hotbeds of high-intensity activity, economic considerations, environmental and strategic issues, and compliance with governmental regulations. Most significantly, workplaces contain people who need to communicate and socially interact and humor is an integral part of workplace interactions that remains somewhat under-researched and overlooked in organisational studies.

The most important dynamic of humor is that it involves people, and most people engage in humor of some form regardless of race, ethnicity, religion, gender, age, or ability (Radcliffe-Brown, 1940). Researching workplace humor is intense, complex, it is frequently interdisciplinary, it's difficult, it can be scary, but most of all it is fascinating with many aspects of humor that is still not well understood. What is known is that workplace humor offers a multitude of benefits to lubricate the social interactions necessary at work. It can adopt an ice-breaking function for people who do not know each other well but need to work together, can offer relief from tension when workplace demands accumulate and can alleviate the boredom of some jobs (Roy, 1959). Workplace humor can decrease hierarchical differences by offering a safe way of challenging directives (Holmes, 2000; Marra, 2007) and can enhance and maintain organisational culture by uniting workgroups and teams (Cooper, 2005, 2008). Office banter is one way of recognising and appreciating differences and similarities of colleagues in a lighthearted, inclusive way (Plester & Sayers, 2007).

As an organisational humor scholar, one of my first literature discoveries was that there were three groups of well-established theories: *release/relief* (mostly attributed to Freud, 1905); *superiority theories* (dating back to Hobbes, 1640); and *incongruity theories* (Berger, 1976). Freud's (1905) psychological influence and theories on why people laugh has particularly influenced all of my workplace humor research. Freud theorises that humor allows people to say the 'unsayable' which explains aspects such as hierarchical humor in organisations in situations where a subordinate employee may be able to safely challenge a managerial directive using a joke frame—a technique that Freud (1905) calls 'joke work' (see also Holmes, 2000; Holmes & Marra, 2002a; Plester & Inkson, 2019). Freud's (1927) work also accounts for the commonly discussed 'gallows' humor where dire circumstances are coped with and relieved through joking. In workplace scenarios, for example, an employee who has been laid off may make a quip about the event, offering relief from tension through shared laughter, while notably, their still-employed workmates are very unlikely to use any humor at all. Such functional aspects of workplace humor assist people in navigating the travails and pitfalls of working life, offering an important rationale for further investigations into workplace humor. Functional and positive aspects of sharing humor at work currently dominate workplace humor research and are discussed next, followed by a subsequent recognition of the less researched aspects of workplace humor.

Literature Review

Relationship Functions-

The functional aspects of workplace humor have been well-researched in recent times (Cooper, 2008; Fine & De Soucey, 2005; Holmes, 2006; Lang & Lee, 2010; Plester, 2009a; Romero & Cruthirds, 2006; Sanders, 2004) to the extent where humor at work is considered to be 'endemic' (Marra, 2007). Even the most serious workplace meetings average a humor instance every six minutes (Holmes & Schnurr 2005). One of the most significant functions of humor at work is the construction and maintenance of positive workplace relationships. Humor is a social lubricant (Duncan & Feisal, 1990) that can stimulate high-quality workplace interactions through relationship building, cooperation and the development and affirmation of positive workplace identities (Cooper & Sosik, 2012; Tracy, Myers, & Scott, 2006). Cooper's (2008) in-depth investigation into the social processes of workplace humor exchanges found that humor can create, maintain, impede, or even destroy workplace relationships. Cooper (2008) identified four social processes through which workplace humor operates: (1) *affect-reinforcement* whereby people are attracted to each other by the degree of positive affect elicited; (2) *similarity-attraction* where shared appreciation of humor makes people feel closer to each other; (3) *self-disclosure* where humor operates as a form of self-disclosure revealing peoples' characters; and (4) *hierarchical salience* where humor either reinforces workplace hierarchy or breaks down barriers between people of different status. Through integrating these four processes, Cooper developed the 'relational process model' of humor, which explains how humor influences relationship quality through the four different interrelated humor processes. Her model accounts for the multifaceted aspects of humor that makes it equally enjoyable or offensive depending on perceptions and feelings towards the source. As well as enhancing relationships, humor has been found to offer relief from stress and boredom, which is an important function in modern workplaces.

Stress Relief

Humor has long been associated with wellbeing benefits such as the alleviation of stress, reduction of anxiety and depression, and mood enhancement (Lefcourt, 2001; Martin, 1996; McGhee, 2000). Positive workplace humor has been linked with outcomes such as employee health, performance, and job satisfaction, and positive humor is argued to mitigate effects of stress and burnout upon employees (Mesmer-Magnus, Glew, & Viswesvaran, 2012). Researchers have explored links between humor and workplace effectiveness (Decker, 1987; Duncan, 1982; Malone, 1980) as well as humor's impact on increasing morale (Clouse & Spurgeon, 1995; Duncan, Smeltzer, & Leap, 1990; Holmes & Marra, 2002a; Romero & Cruthirds 2006) and humor that alleviates boredom and frustration (Fine, 1988; Roy, 1959). Roy's (1959) *Banana Time* is a seminal paper that presents an ethnographic study identifying humor as a coping mechanism for factory workers. Roy explores factory floor pranks played with a banana and other fruit, highlighting micro-practices in humor interactions that relieve boredom in a factory shop floor. More recently, Sanders (2004) analysed humor as a coping strategy for sex workers and found that humor helped to manage client interactions and establish support networks with colleagues—showing that humor is a defence mechanism that helps protect emotional wellbeing. Humor is increasingly seen as a coping mechanism that alleviates workplace stress and strain (Plester, 2009a) and in their extensive review of workplace humor research, Mesmer-Magnus 2012 argue that positive workplace humor promotes good physical and mental health, alleviates stress effects which in turn promotes improved workplace functioning. They conclude that positive humor should be cultivated in workplaces but concede that this is not easily accomplished due to the inherent ambiguity and perceptive aspects of sharing humor at work, as well as contextual workplace elements such as hierarchy, power and leadership.

Leadership and Performance

Hierarchy, managerialism, and leadership are significant facets within work organisations, and humor researchers have begun investigating these aspects in recent studies. Much of the workplace humor research focuses on leaders' humor (Cooper 2005, 2008; Cooper & Sosik, 2012; Duncan et al., 1990; Robert & Wilbanks, 2012; Romero & Cruthirds, 2006). In a significant study, Romero and Cruthirds (2006) position workplace humor as a 'multifunctional management tool' that can help to enhance leadership, group cohesiveness and organisational culture while simultaneously reducing stress. They argue that different humor styles can achieve a variety of positive workplace outcomes and that managers can learn to tailor their humor to increase positive results at work. Cooper, Kong, and Crossley (2018) further argue that leader humor can encourage organisational citizenship behaviour from subordinate employees and they posit that leader humor is an 'overlooked but important socioemotional resource for social exchange' (p. 769).

A further functional benefit attributed to workplace humor is in mitigating or diminishing differences between employees and managers within hierarchical relationships. While creating bonds among employees, and between managers and employees, humor can lower status differentials between those from different hierarchical levels (Vinton, 1989) which can open up alternative communication pathways between workers and their managers/supervisors. In a linguistic analysis of humor in workplace meetings, Marra notes that although 'dominance is organisationally sanctioned' (2007, p. 141) in workplaces, humor allows subordinates to challenge or criticise those superior in the hierarchy and the use of humor mitigates the effect offering the challenger a safety shield from censure. Contrastingly, a recent study undertaken in South Korean workplaces identified how humor was used to *reinforce* hierarchy which was necessary to maintain traditional Confucian values of harmony at work. Some of this humor was affiliative and positive, but some were also aggressive and threatened workers' wellbeing (Kim & Plester, 2019). With such contrasts in the literature, there appears to be a need for further in-depth investigations into hierarchical effects in humor from both subordinate and managerial perspectives and these could be undertaken in a variety of cultural (workplace) contexts.

Humor is also linked with improved workplace performance especially in enhancing workplace creativity (O'Quin 1997) and liberating humor positively impacts workplace creativity while controlling humor has a negative impact (Lang & Lee, 2010). In line with earlier arguments of humor's positive impact on workplace relationships, humor is also associated with enhanced performance in workgroups (Robert & Wilbanks, 2012). The wheel model of humor identifies humor events as significant drivers of employee well-being and happiness. This causes positive affect that transmits to social groups, creating a climate for humor use that subsequently fosters further humor events, in a circular repeated pattern (Robert & Wilbanks, 2012). The wheel model can influence in different contexts such as in groups and teams, and in leadership and mentoring interactions. The relationship between workplace humor, leadership, and hierarchy is complex, and this complexity increases further when gender factors are considered and explored.

Gender Functions

Gender is an ambiguous and complex topic (Butler, 1990), is significant in workplace contexts (Hearn, 2019), and this is further complicated in humor use due to the ambiguity and unknown intentions in joking interactions. Humor is a 'significant linguistic tool' used as part of a discursive strategy to construct gender (Schnurr & Holmes, 2009, p. 102). Research has identified gendered elements in the performance and delivery of workplace humor as well as gendered variations in the types and styles of humor used at work (Hay, 2000; Holmes, 2006). Women use more supportive, encouraging, and self-denigrating humor styles at work, whereas men use more combative, challenging humor (Schnurr & Holmes, 2009). Furthermore, gender may become the focus of humor (Decker & Rotondo, 2001; Evans, Slaughter, Ellis, & Rivin, 2019; Holmes, 2006) and gendered, sexist humor can become part of the office joking repertoire (see Plester, 2015).

Most early workplace studies of gendered humor focus on stereotypical and aggressive masculinity (Collinson, 1988; Linstead, 1985; Vinton, 1989) where humor is used to reinforce 'masculine norms' (Schnurr & Holmes, 2009, p. 103). Plester (2015) also found that humor was used extensively to express hegemonic masculinity in one idiosyncratic organisation and that women in this company also felt compelled to perform this specific form of masculinity in contestive humor interactions where they became 'one of the boys.' Humorous exchanges are used to regulate masculinities and to negotiate gendered identity and sexual hierarchies although there may be 'oppressive dynamics' in these humor exchanges (Kehily & Nayak, 1997, p. 69). Gendered humor exchanges may create joking cultures where the group has a repertoire of joking references that separates them from outsiders (Fine & De Soucey, 2005) and maintaining this type of culture may involve gendered joking that mocks and derides femininities and alternative masculinities (see Plester, 2015). This type of workplace humor may proceed even further to become sexual harassment—wrapped up in a joke frame to protect the perpetrators (Collinson & Collinson, 1996) and thus, this review now turns towards the 'dark side' of humor which is much less researched and explored in workplace humor research.

Dark Side of Humor

Social psychologist Michael Billig (2005) argues that humor research ascribes a benevolence and positivity to humor that is reflected in most humor research throughout different disciplines. Billig calls for more studies that recognise, acknowledge, and explore the dark side of humor. Key questions are posed by Cooper and Sosik (2012) as worthy of further research investigation including: What comprises the dark side of humor in organisations and what are some of the negative consequences of humor in organisations? Can well-intentioned humor be misinterpreted and can humor detract from workplace performance?

Warren and Fineman (2007) explore the notion that workplace humor is not as straightforward as it may appear. They reference the 'mini-industry' of fun at work where fun is prescribed and reveal a workplace 'morality' governing the type of fun that employees *should* enjoy. They note that fun and humor are never free from the social context in which they reside and argue that the workplace is a complex example of this. Modern western workplaces are coming under increasing pressure to offer aesthetic, exciting workplaces where fun and humor are encouraged to the extent that structured fun programmes are created for this purpose (Fleming, 2005). Positive humor experiences at work are believed to create hedonistic work experiences where employees experience engagement, flow and happiness in the quest for the modern feel-good factor at work.

Critical researchers refute the 'forced fun' movement and Warren and Fineman (2007) analyse one organisation that prescribed fun through displaying playful artefacts—Russian dolls of diverse ethnicities, ages and genders and wearing business dress. The dolls were displayed in reception and after some initial dismay employees started to play with the dolls, arranging them in unexpected places and positions. This angered management, as this type of fun was considered unacceptable, and employees were ordered to desist. After this directive, one of the dolls was punched in the face leaving a notable indentation and management deemed this to be malicious damage of company property. The dolls created cynicism and a gulf between management and employees, and Warren and Fineman conclude that prescribed fun can seriously misfire, create subversion and cynicism and result in increased control from management. Fleming (2005, 2009) found similar results in his call centre research where fun and humor were prescribed, encouraged and rewarded while employees became cynical and disenfranchised with such practices. Plester and Hutchison (2016) also found that 'managed fun' was employees' least favoured form of workplace fun and that they preferred fun to be either 'organically' developed or an inherent part of workplace tasks and organisational culture.

Manufacturing and shop floor studies by David Collinson (1988, 2002) and Steven Linstead (1985) offer rich ethnographic theorisations of workplace dynamics and focus on critical power and control elements. Collinson (2002) who investigated the critical relationship between humor, power and management, found that management control may be perpetuated through joking relations. Paradoxically, he found that suppressing humor may increase its resurgence while trying to artificially manufacture humor can suppress it. One of the few studies regarding *responses* to humor concerns the notion of 'unlaughter' and is beautifully debated by Nick Butler (2015) as he pinpoints responses to humor that 'goes wrong,' falls flat, or even offends. Unlaughter is defined by Billig (2005) as 'a display of not laughing when laughter might otherwise be expected, hoped for or demanded' (p. 192). Butler argues that 'unlaughter' is a useful workplace response to humor that causes displeasure and upsets people.

Rodrigues and Collinson (1995) questioned the universality of the 'safety valve' theory of humor. They found that humor can be an effective method whereby employees can express dissatisfaction in preference to using overt forms of resistance. Taylor and Bain (2003) further highlight the subversive elements of workplace humor, finding that subversive satire can align with the collective organisation to create countercultures conflicting with managerial objectives and priorities. Building on this, Westwood and Johnston (2012) theorise that workplace humor is 'double edged' because the ambiguous nature of humor contributes to maintaining the status quo and power relations at work while also offering the potential for resistance and subversion of managerial processes.

Although the risk inherent in all humor gives it its edge and makes it exciting and even irresistible, work contexts are increasingly diverse, risk-averse, careful, and even litigious. Therefore, the dark side of humor needs further investigation, and the complexity of the workplace context has a significant influence on when and why humor may occur, what types of humor are permitted, who can joke, and what is and is not, funny at work. This offers significant potential for future workplace humor research undertaken in actual functioning workplaces to explore the key contextual elements of workplace humor through an everyday, lived approach.

Ethnography as an Optimal Method for Organizational Research

I made an early decision that I would not study humor in a vacuum, and that laboratory studies were not for me, nor were cartoon analyses, or experimental designs. These are all respected and valid approaches, and I have frequently discussed and followed the fascinating research work of David Cheng and his experimental humor research (see Cheng, Amarnani, Le, & Restubog, 2019; Cheng, Jackson, & Lee, 2015; Cheng & Wang, 2015). My fascination in humor comes from people and their complex interactions and more specifically, people in their everyday context. I am fascinated by the minutiae of humor interactions and focus on the micro-moments and the surrounding influences that can either make or break the humor. My focus on the context can be a difficult aspect to research requiring background, history and information about the people, place, positions, and events. In the words of French philosopher Henri Bergson: 'To understand laughter, we must put it back in its natural environment' (1911, p. 12).

The context for my humor research is work organisations, and in particular, I focus on organisational culture with its professional and social interactions, behavioural norms, espoused values, and embedded organisational assumptions (see Schein, 1985/2004, 1991). All of my empirical research has been conducted from an ethnographic frame whereby I have spent lengths of time inside actual workplaces, usually a time span of one full-time month. I have interacted with participants, questioned them, made notes about what I see and experience, and taken detailed notes of the surroundings, including wall hangings and decorations, cartoons, and light-hearted paraphernalia. I have recorded verbatim corridor conversations, big (sometimes critical) incidents, small everyday interactions, banter, and teasing. I have attended events and parties to experience first-hand workplace fun, frivolity and celebration. I have achieved this inside a variety of organisations in different industries, talking to people at all levels of workplace hierarchy—from the mailroom to the CEO. This gives me a rich, insider view to workplace humor and its contextual elements.

As I am implicitly involved in my own research and become part of the very context that I research, I need to be carefully reflexive about the impact that I might have on the research. I also need to reflect upon my own world view and interpretive position as these influences what, and how, I research (see Alvesson, 2010; Alvesson & Sköldberg, 2000). My world view embraces social constructionism that sees knowledge as constructed through socio-cultural processes which influence our understandings of the world (Allen, 2005). Berger & Luckmann, (1967) argue that socially constructed knowledge guides everyday conduct and behaviour, and they emphasise the importance of human interactions in the social construction process. As social constructionism assumes that all knowledge is socially and culturally specific and heavily influenced by social, historical, and political factors sustained within various contexts, especially through language, this underpins my imperative that I conduct my humor research on-site and in context. In other words, I become part of the social construction of humor and fun in the studied organisations taking careful measures not to create humor artificially but to offer organisational participants opportunities to describe, discuss, interact, and deconstruct interactions and events as we collaboratively engage in the sensemaking process (see Weick, 1995, 2000) during my short tenure.

I position myself as an interpretive researcher, whereby I seek interpretations of the meaning of interactions, behaviours, and discourse. Interpretations are in the first instance, gleaned from participants and usually presented as either verbatim quotes or constructed as a narrative derived from in-depth interviews and interchanges. This allows multi-voiced interpretations where participant voices permeate the work and offer a rich authenticity to reported humor interactions (Cunliffe, 2004). Multiple voices present in research analyses are known as 'polyphony' (Cunliffe & Coupland, 2012). Once I have captured participants' interpretations, the analysis process focuses on collating, understanding, exploring, and creating a combined interpretation of organisational life through humor dynamics and behaviour. I influence these overarching interpretations as a researcher and through my prior theoretical knowledge. However, as I frequently collaborate with other scholars, a synthesis of interpretations can extend analyses through wider expert knowledge on specific aspects of humor. For example, I collaborate with discourse and linguistic scholars in some interpretations of humor narratives (see Plester, Carroll, & Kim, 2018; Schnurr & Plester, 2017). Collaborations help build multi-voiced theoretical and empirical knowledge about humor in organisational contexts. Understanding how we 'constitute our realities and identities in relational ways' (Cunliffe, 2004, p. 407) underpins this process of collective social knowledge that offers a unique, nuanced and complex understanding of workplace humor.

My Research Program: Boundaries, Roles, Complexity, and the Dark Side

Humor is increasingly appearing in management and workplace research programs. One of the most significant influences on my work came from a long-term workplace study carried out by a group of linguistic scholars based at Victoria University in Wellington, New Zealand (Language in the Workplace Project). This eminent group has conducted multiple different projects exploring linguistic structures at work and openly admits that they had not considered humor at the outset but found it a significant part of linguistic interaction at work. Not only has this team of researchers developed many publications that have influenced my thinking and my work (see Angouri, Marra, & Holmes, 2017; Holmes, 2000, 2007; Holmes & Marra, 2002a, 2002b, 2006; Holmes, Marra, & Burns, 2001; Holmes & Stubbe, 2003), but they have become friends and colleagues as we have interacted virtually and in-person at conferences around the world. They have supported and mentored my work, and I highly value on-going collaboration and cross-disciplinary debates with this eminent group of scholars.

Humor Boundaries

In my research programme, I prefer to unpack the concepts of humor and fun as separate yet overlapping concepts, and I work with each concept in different ways depending on my specific research focus. Therefore, my research into workplace fun rationale, and fun initiatives, draws on work from different theorists specifically interested in the concept of fun at work and many of these researchers identify positive functions of workplace fun (see Karl & Peluchette, 2005, 2006, 2008; Peluchette & Karl, 2005; Tews, Michel, & Bartlett, 2012; Tews, Michel, Xu, & Drost, 2015). My own critical analyses of workplace fun align with the research of Peter Fleming (2005, 2009) that questions some of the universally positive assumptions attributed to workplace fun, and my recent research examines whether 'managed' fun is still considered to be fun by employees. I argue that fun can easily disappear when organisationally prescribed or forced and I have found that employees prefer organic forms of spontaneous fun or fun experienced during actual workplace tasks (see Owler, Morrison, & Plester, 2010; Plester, 2009b; Plester, Cooper-Thomas, & Winquist, 2015; Plester & Hutchison, 2016). One of my key findings is that fun at work is highly influenced by normative boundaries which are assumed and known by socialised employees within the prevailing organisational culture (see Plester, 2009b).

In all of the organisations I have studied, there were discernible, metaphorical boundaries that influenced workplace humor and fun. The notion of boundary is becoming increasingly important as organisations become more diverse and globally connected, creating greater opportunities for miscommunications, cultural misunderstandings, and a variety of different behavioural standards and expectations. Although humor is ubiquitous, it is (as already argued) both contextual and cultural, and humor creates risks for boundary violation. Boundary violation can be deliberate or unintentional because of differing normative and cultural expectations concerning perceptions of what is funny and what is not. Organisations are becoming increasingly careful in their social behaviour and humor may be perceived as risky and even expendable, and I once had the misfortune to work in a company where laughter was banned.

The importance of norms in workplace culture underpins the social construction of humor boundaries at work. As humor and fun are social activities and/or interactions shared between people, there are many influences on what humor can and cannot be shared in a work situation. Within organisations, I have found that this is most significantly influenced by the prevailing organisational culture and the associated norms, values, and behavioural expectations. Organisational culture is co-created by organisational founders, employees, customers, stakeholders, and the wider industry within which the organisation operates (Parker, 2000). The organisational culture guides social and professional behaviour and therefore, also determines the boundaries for humor and fun. Through my ethnographic analyses I have found that although humor boundaries are dynamic and somewhat fluid, in highly formal organisations the boundaries are tighter, more constrained, and more carefully controlled (sometimes by HR or senior managers), whilst in smaller more informal organisations, boundaries are looser which fosters humor that is less constrained. Although freer humor might seem desirable and livelier, it also carries some risks for the organisation, especially when new non-socialised employees join the group (see Plester, 2015, 2016). When discussing humor boundaries, organisational participants used phrases such as:

'crossed the line' and identified humor that 'goes too far.' Many humor incidents were described, observed, and experienced first-hand during different phases of my research program.

In one corporate organisation, Pete[1] described a prank where he hid in the office wheelie bin and jumped out when his manager walked past. He claimed that he was attempting to liven up a dull day, but his manager had a visitor with him, and both got a big fright. Pete was hauled into HR for a disciplinary meeting and reprimand. His intentions seemed benign, but the resulting fallout was not. The context for this prank was a highly formal organisation that did not encourage pranks and physical humor. Context is defined by the industry, the type of work, the organisational culture, and political dynamics perpetuated by senior power-holders. Pete's prank was considered to have 'gone too far' and overstepped the metaphorical boundary in this organisation, resulting in a formal response from HR and management. In most of the smaller, less formal organisations this would have been simply laughed at, and indeed many more extreme pranks were viewed in the less formal organisations (see Plester, 2016). This clearly demonstrates the importance of contextual elements and their influence on humor boundaries.

Socialised employees and managers have to carefully navigate their way through communication with groups of people of different demographics and sensibilities. Pleasant, light-hearted social interaction, including joking, is part of organisational actors' communicative repertoire but is significantly bounded by workplace propriety, professionalism, and normative behavioural expectations. The relationship between fun, humor and worker well-being and the emergence of new boundaries will be the focus of future studies (discussed in the final section).

In the aforementioned example of Pete, the wheelie bin prankster, Pete considered himself to be a 'joker' in his workplace and thus entitled to create a prank. People enact humor in different ways at work, some taking the lead as 'joker' (Plester & Orams, 2008) while others simply respond and interact. There are also 'gatekeepers' which task themselves with limiting or constraining humor within acceptable boundaries (Plester, 2016). I continue to explore roles adopted by organisational actors in regard to the creating, encouraging, appreciation, and constraint of humor. Further research work is underway analysing jokers, gate-keepers, humor targets and successful and unsuccessful workplace humor interactions. Workplace humor can reveal much about individual attitudes, feelings, moods, stereotypes, and biases but also is indicative of relational dynamics (Cooper, 2008; Romero & Pescosolido, 2008) and in-groups versus out-groups (Terrion & Ashforth, 2002). Such complexity and variety are presented and analysed throughout my research program.

Complexity and Intentions

My research program has generated a variety of findings of both workplace humor and fun. Overarching findings have indicated the complexity and ambiguity of humor and fun at work. My data includes a wide variety of interactions, events, stories, reactions and non-reactions. My studies have identified that workplace *banter* is the most prevalent form of workplace humor and I define this as (mostly) good-natured teasing interchanges between colleagues—although it can also be barbed, biting, and even rather cruel in some instances (see Plester & Sayers, 2007). Banter is shared almost constantly in some organisations—as colleagues quip back and forth, tease, and enjoy the repartee as a micro-break from work and associated tensions. The most difficult aspect of analysing banter (and other forms of workplace humor) is discerning participants' intentions.

My analyses have attempted to interpret the intentions behind humor, but it is very difficult to discern intention and sometimes even the humor protagonists themselves, may have mixed motives. Most jokers (those who create humor) ascribe only the noblest of intentions to their enactments—usually declaiming that a joke is simply 'fun,' intended to cause collegial laughter, and dispel workplace tensions. However, even with the very best of intentions, humor can damage others and cause significant disruption to a workplace unit, group, or in some of my examples—the entire company. In a prestigious law firm, I observed as they suffered considerable embarrassment and reputational damage when an innocuous humorous email decrying 'political correctness' was extended into political and homophobic comments and was published in a national newspaper. The law firm CEO sent a reprimand to the entire firm, and the HR director was deputised to speak to the perceived offenders (in Plester, 2016). This had the effect of eliminating most overt humor exchanges in the company for quite some time—especially in group emails. As this demonstrates, humor can and does go horribly wrong even though the original intention in this email was reported to be 'light-relief.'

It is very unlikely that anyone creating a joke or prank would admit to less than honourable intentions and the 'just a joke' defence is often used to excuse inappropriate workplace behaviour such as banter that is sexist, sexual, racist, and/or barbed. I have experienced all types of humor (some that I'd rather forget) in my studied workplaces and all protagonists fervently claim that their comments and actions were 'harmless fun' and 'just in jest.' I once observed a small company where a photograph of the boss's naked buttocks was uploaded to a female administrator's computer while she was away from her desk—causing her to scream loudly and laugh—creating hilarity for the rest of the staff and CEO (see Plester, 2015). Many readers will be appalled and calling for a sexual harassment complaint, while others might be chuckling or smiling. The victim of the joke laughed heartily, claimed to enjoy the prank, and was happily plotting a revenge jape for the future. However, although she laughed merrily, my analysis questions whether she *had* to accept the joke with apparent humor as this was perpetuated by her boss—the most powerful person in the small company. The buttocks prank was indicative of everyday behaviour in this small, idiosyncratic company, but there are very few organisations that would condone such a prank, and, in most organisations, this would become a disciplinary matter, inciting wrath in groups such as those aligned with the 2017 #metoo movement. This example illustrates the complexity and ambiguity inherent in humor research—one person's lighthearted joke may cause deep outrage and upset in a different person or in a different context. Additionally, workplaces are complicated, steeped in power, control, and organisational politics and joking intentions may have multiple conflicting aspects.

Work contexts steeped in power relations, diversity and economic imperatives exacerbate the complexity of humor, as the ambiguous nature of humor can leave people questioning meaning and motives from different organisational actors. I have published a critical paper on gendered performance and sexual harassment (Plester, 2015), am investigating bullying through humor (forthcoming) and an entire chapter is devoted to the dark side of humor in my (2016) book, *The Complexity of Workplace Humor*. Dark side analyses have prompted me to unpack key workplace dimensions such as power, control, and organisational politics and this has balanced my research program and offered a more nuanced and realistic perspective that recognises times when humor is used destructively, reactively, or even dangerously alongside positive functional uses of humor.

My recent work has invoked psychological research (Freud, 1905; Martin, 2007; Martin & Ford, 2018; Martin, Kuiper, Olinger, & Dance, 2009; Martin, Puhlik-Doris, Larsen, Gray, & Weir, 2003) to theorise a recent publication in *Frontiers of Psychology* that identifies how hierarchical power differentials in South Korean workplaces control employee responses to humor. My colleague and I explore psychological distress experienced by subordinate (mainly young) employees forced to respond positively to humor that they found offensive or upsetting (Kim & Plester, 2019).

Since beginning my research, I have had a copy of Rod Martin's (2007) book—*The Psychology of Humor* close at hand on my shelf—constituting a type of theoretical bible for my studies. It was, therefore, a great honour and privilege when Thomas Ford contacted me regarding the update of this beloved tome in 2018 (Martin & Ford, 2018) and the updated version includes an interview about my workplace humor research. This collaboration highlights the variety of perspectives offered by different research disciplines, recognizes the potential of alternative lenses, and successfully brings together psychological work with management and workplace implications. Such collaborative exercises can only enhance humor research and should be considered for future studies.

Next Steps

I plan to continue investigating workplace humor and fun in a nuanced, holistic, and authentic way, which, for me, involves ethnographic cultural studies in organisations. My next project is under development and will constitute an ethnographic study in a number of New Zealand and Australian organisations where I will investigate humor and fun in the social spaces of work. In response to recent global events, I will explore the impact of the Covid-19 pandemic on workplace humor and question how and if, fun activities and social events have changed significantly through this crisis. Worker well-being will be a focus of this new project, and the lighter side of working from home may offer some rich examples and encourage further analyses on boundary spanning, new ways of working and sharing humor. I will investigate how the Covid-19 pandemic has reduced, increased and/or changed collegial humor interactions. I will also explore whether or not Zoom and other virtual meetings platforms facilitate, hinder, or alter humor and fun in workplace communications.

Boundaries for fun, humor and collegial interaction are being more closely examined, and some activities are even curtailed or becoming highly controlled in the attempt to eliminate behaviours and interactions that could be viewed as harassment, bullying, or simply inappropriate. I am frequently asked: 'has political correctness gone too far?' This emerging sanitisation of work needs further investigation, and I plan to investigate whether fun and humor are disappearing from work contexts.

Future projects are also planned to explore gendered performances of workplace humor more deeply, and I will ensure that gender is conceptualised in a way that includes non-binary gender presentations and gender fluidity. In such studies, I hope to incorporate perspectives from the #metoo movement and question how humor plays a role in discrimination and harassment at work.

The roles of organisational actors in workplace humor continue to fascinate me, and a forthcoming analysis extends my earlier investigation of jokers and gatekeepers by considering other roles adopted by humor participants. I am currently analysing the *targets* of workplace banter and using bystander theory to question the implications and outcomes for those affected by workplace humor and fun.

An on-going thread of my research program concerns cultural interpretations of workplace humor, and through working with research students from different ethnicities and cultural backgrounds, this aspect can be extended. I aspire to have a team of researchers investigating cultural differences in humor in both multicultural and monocultural workplaces. Questions for exploration include the relevance and appropriateness of workplace humor in different cultural contexts, and how hierarchy, power, and politics influence humor interactions between work colleagues from different cultural backgrounds. I have had two PhD students complete very fine workplace humor analyses in South Korean (see Kim & Plester, 2019) and Nepalese organisations and their diligence and success offer a blueprint for future cultural work and publications.

My lifelong interest and fascination with humor sustain me through the complexities and difficulties in analysing workplace humor interactions, helps me endure situations that I personally find unfunny or distasteful, while also allowing me to enjoy some really good laughs in my work. It will always fascinate me as to how people construct and create humor, the roles they play, the performances they give, and the ways they justify their humor. Humor is important in helping people cope and endure work in the best of times and even more so right now, in a global pandemic—the worst of times. I am just starting to investigate the dynamics of workplace humor in this crisis but have started to collect some wonderful stories of humor experienced during virtual online meetings conducted from workers' homes. Children and pets have featured significantly in these warmly funny narratives showing a lighter side of the global crisis. I have some concern that humor may be disappearing or becoming heavily diluted in cautious organisations worried about reputation and public scrutiny, and I would be very distressed if humor becomes 'too risky' for modern workplaces. Humor is important to people in their social dynamics and for their health, well-being and happiness. I hope that my on-going work reflects the value of workplace humor in all its mystery, ambiguity, darkness, complexity, and joyous laughter.

Note

1 Not his real name.

References

Allen, B. J. (2005). Social constructionism. In S. May & D. K. Mumby (Eds.), *Engaging organizational communication theory and research: Multiple perspectives* (pp. 35–53). Sage Publications, Inc.
Alvesson, M. (2010). *Interpreting interviews*. London, UK: Sage.
Alvesson, M., & Sköldberg, K. (2000). *Reflexive methodology. New vistas for qualitative research*. London, UK: Sage.
Angouri, J., Marra, M., & Holmes, J. (2017). *Negotiating boundaries at work*. Edinburgh: Edinburgh University Press.
Berger, A. A. (1976). Anatomy of the joke. *Journal of Communication, 26*(3), 113–115.
Berger, P. L., & Luckmann, T. (1967). *The social construction of reality: A treatise in the sociology of knowledge*. London, UK: Penguin.
Bergson, H. L. (1911). *Laughter, an essay on the meaning of the comic*. (C. Brereton & F. Rothwell, Trans., 1935). London, UK: MacMillan & Co.
Billig, M. (2005). *Laughter and ridicule. Towards a social critique of humor*. London: Sage.
Butler, J. (1990). *Gender trouble: Feminism and the subversion of identity*. New York, NY: Routledge.
Butler, N. (2015). Joking aside: Theorizing laughter in organizations. *Culture and Organization, 21*(1), 42–58.
Cheng, D., & Wang, L. (2015). Examining the energizing effects of humor: The influence of humor on persistence behavior. *Journal of Business and Psychology, 30*, 759–772.
Cheng, D., Amarnani, R., Le, T., & Restubog, S., (2019). Laughter is (powerful) medicine: The effects of humor exposure on the well-being of victims of aggression. *Journal of Business and Psychology, 34*, 389–402.
Cheng, D. C. M., Jackson, C. J., & Lee, I. (2015). Does laughing at yourself help you work? Self-deprecating humor and performance. In *Academy of Management Proceedings* (Vol. 2015, No. 1, pp. 13992). Briarcliff Manor, NY: Academy of Management.
Clouse, R., & Spurgeon, K. (1995). Corporate analysis of humor. *Psychology, 32*, 124.
Collinson, D. (1988). 'Engineering humor': Joking and conflict in shop-floor relations. *Organization Studies, 9*, 181–199.
Collinson, D. (2002). Managing humor. *Journal of Management Studies, 39*(3), 269–289.

Collinson, M., & Collinson, D. (1996). 'It's only Dick': The sexual harassment of women managers in insurance sales. *Work, Employment and Society, 10*(1), 29–56.

Cooper, C. (2005). Just joking around? Employee humor expression as an ingratiatory behaviour. *The Academy of Management Review, 30*(4), 765–776.

Cooper, C. (2008). Elucidating the bonds of workplace humor: A relational process model. *Human Relations, 61*(8), 1087–1115.

Cooper, C., & Sosik, J. J. (2012). The laughter advantage: Cultivating high-quality connections and workplace outcomes through humor. In K. Cameron & G. Spreitzer, *The Oxford handbook of positive organizational scholarship.* New York, NY: Oxford University Press, 474–501.

Cooper, C. D., Kong, D. T., & Crossley, C. D. (2018). Leader humor as an interpersonal resource: Integrating three theoretical perspectives. *Academy of Management Journal, 61*(2), 769–796.

Cunliffe, A., & Coupland, C. (2012). From hero to villain to hero: Making experience sensible through embodied narrative sensemaking. *Human Relations, 65*(1), 63–88.

Cunliffe, A. L. (2004). On becoming a critically reflexive practitioner. *Journal of Management Education, 28*(4), 407–426.

Decker, W. H. (1987). Managerial humor and subordinate satisfaction. *Social Behavior and Personality: An International Journal, 15*(2), 225–232.

Decker, W. H., & Rotondo, D. M. (2001). Relationships among gender, type of humor, and perceived leader effectiveness. *Journal of Managerial Issues, 13*(4), 450–465.

Duncan, J. W. (1982). Humor in management: Prospects for administrative practice and research. *Academy of Management Review, 7*(1), 136–142.

Duncan, J. W., & Feisal, P. J. (1990). No laughing matter: Patterns of humor in the workplace. *Organisational Dynamics, 17,* 18–30.

Duncan, J. W., Smeltzer, L. R., & Leap, T. L. (1990). Humor and work: Applications of joking behaviour to management. *Journal of Management, 16*(2), 255–279.

Evans, J. B., Slaughter, J. E., Ellis, A. P., & Rivin, J. M. (2019). Gender and the evaluation of humor at work. *Journal of Applied Psychology, 104*(8), 1077.

Fine, G. A. (1988). Dying for a laugh: Negotiating risk and creating personas in the humor of mushroom collectors. *Western Folklore, 47*(3), 177–194.

Fine, G. A., & De Soucey, M. (2005). Joking cultures: Humor themes as social regulation in group life. *Humor, 18*(1), 1–22.

Fleming, P. (2005). Worker's playtime? Boundaries and cynicism in a 'Culture of fun' program. *The Journal of Applied Behavioral Science, 41*(3), 285–303.

Fleming, P. (2009). *Authenticity and the cultural politics of work.* Oxford, UK: Oxford Unity Press.

Freud, S. (1905). *Jokes and their relation to the unconscious.* (A. Richards, Trans., 1991). London, UK: Penguin.

Freud, S. (1927). *Humor.* Retrieved from https://www.scribd.com/doc/34515345/Sigmund-Freud-Humor-1927.

Hay, J. (2000). Functions of humor in the conversations of men and women. *Journal of Pragmatics, 32*(6), 709–742.

Hearn, J. (2019). Gender, work and organization: A gender–work–organization analysis. *Gender, Work & Organization, 26*(1), 31–39.

Hobbes, T. (1640). Hobbes tripos in three discourses: Human nature. *The English works of Thomas Hobbes of Malmesbury* (Vol. 4, pp. 183–945). London: John Bohn.

Holmes, J. (2000). Politeness, power and provocation: How humor functions in the workplace. *Discourse Studies, 2*(2), 159–185.

Holmes, J. (2006). Sharing a laugh: Pragmatic aspects of humor and gender in the workplace. *Journal of Pragmatics*, *38*(1), 26–50.
Holmes, J. (2007). Humor and the construction of Maori leadership at work. *Leadership*, *3*(1), 527.
Holmes, J., & Marra, M. (2002a). Having a laugh at work: How humor contributes to workplace culture. *Journal of Pragmatics*, *34*(12), 1683–1710.
Holmes, J., & Marra, M. (2002b). Over the edge? Subversive humor between colleagues and friends. *Humor, International Journal of Humor Research*, *15*(1), 65–87.
Holmes, J., & Marra, M. (2006). Humor and leadership style. *Humor, International Journal of Humor Research*, *19*(2), 119–138.
Holmes, J., & Schnurr, S. (2005). Politeness, humor and gender in the workplace: Negotiating norms and identifying contestation. *Journal of Politeness Research*, *1*(1), 121–149.
Holmes, J., & Stubbe, M. (2003). *Power and politeness in the workplace: A sociolinguistic analysis of talk at work*. London, UK: Longman.
Holmes, J., Marra, M., & Burns, L. (2001). Women's humor in the workplace. A quantitative analysis. *Australian Journal of Communication*, *28*(1), 83–108.
Karl, K., & Peluchette, J. (2005). How does workplace fun influence employee perceptions of customer service quality? *Journal of Leadership & Organizational Studies*, *13*(2), 2–13.
Karl, K., & Peluchette, J. (2006). Does workplace fun buffer the impact of emotional exhaustion on job dissatisfaction? A study of health care workers, *Journal of Behavioral and Applied Management*, *7*(2), 128–141.
Karl, K., & Peluchette, J. (2008). Give them something to smile about: A marketing strategy for recruiting and retaining volunteers. *Journal of Non-profit & Public Sector Marketing*, *20*, 91–96.
Kehily, M. J., & Nayak, A. (1997). 'Lads and Laughter': Humor and the production of heterosexual hierarchies. *Gender and Education*, *9*(1), 69–88.
Kim, H. S., & Plester, B. A. (2019). Harmony and distress: Humor, culture, and psychological well-being in south Korean organizations. *Frontiers in Psychology*, *9*, 2643.
Lang, J. C., & Lee, C. H. (2010). Workplace humor and organizational creativity. *The International Journal of Human Resource Management*, *21*(1), 46–60.
Lefcourt, H. M. (2001). The humor solution. In C. R. Snyder (Ed.), *Coping with stress: Effective people and processes* (pp. 68–92). Oxford, UK: Oxford University Press.
Linstead, S. (1985). Jokers wild: The importance of humor in the maintenance of organizational culture. *Sociological Review*, *13*(3), 741–767.
Malone, P. B. (1980). Humor: A double-edged tool for today's managers? *Academy of Management Review*, *5*(3), 357–361.
Marra, M. (2007). Humor in workplace meetings: Challenging hierarchies. In R. Westwood & C. Rhodes (Eds.), *Humor, work and organization* (pp. 139–157). London, UK: Routledge.
Martin, R., & Ford, T. E. (2018). *The psychology of humor. An integrative approach* (2nd ed.). London, UK: Academic press.
Martin, R. A. (1996). The situational humor response questionnaire (SHRQ) and coping humor scale (CHS): A decade of research findings. *Humor*, *9*, 251–272.
Martin, R. A. (2007). *The psychology of humor. An integrative approach*. Burlington, MA: Elsevier.
Martin, R. A., Puhlik-Doris, P., Larsen, G., Gray, J., & Weir, K. (2003). Individual differences in uses of humor and their relation to psychological well-being: Development of the humor styles questionnaire. *Journal of Research in Personality*, *37*(1), 48–75.

Martin, R. A., Kuiper, N. A., Olinger, L. J., & Dance, K. A. (2009). Humor, coping with stress, self-concept, and psychological well-being. *Humor International Journal of Humor Research, 6*, 89–104.

McGhee, P. (2000). The key to stress management, retention, and profitability? More workplace fun. *HR Focus, 77*(9), 5–6.

Mesmer-Magnus, J., Glew, D. J., & Viswesvaran, C. (2012). A meta-analysis of positive humor in the workplace. *Journal of Managerial Psychology, 27*(2), 155–190.

Owler, K., Morrison, R., & Plester, B. (2010). Does fun work? The complexity of promoting fun at work. *Journal of Management and Organization, 16*(3), 338–352.

O'Quin, K., & Derks, P. (1997). Humor and creativity: A review of the empirical literature. *Creativity Research Handbook* (Vol. 1, pp. 223–252). Cresskill NJ: Hampton Press.

Parker, M. (2000). *Organisational culture and identity*. London, UK: Sage.

Peluchette, J., & Karl, K. A. (2005). Attitudes toward incorporating fun into the health care workplace. *The Health Care Manager, 24*(3), 268–275.

Plester, B., & Hutchison, A. (2016). Fun times: The relationship between fun and engagement. *Employee Relations, 38*(3), 332–350.

Plester, B., & Inkson, K. (2019). *Laugh out loud: A user's guide to workplace humor*. Cham, Switzerland: Springer.

Plester, B. A. (2009a). Healthy humor: Using humor to cope at work. *Kotuitui: New Zealand Journal of Social Sciences Online, 4*(1), 89–102.

Plester, B. A. (2009b). Crossing the line: Boundaries of workplace humor and fun. *Employee Relations, 31*(6), 584–599.

Plester, B. A. (2015). Take it like a man! Performing hegemonic masculinity through organizational humor. *Ephemera, 15*(3), 537–559.

Plester, B. A. (2016). *The complexity of workplace humor: Laughter, jokers and the dark side*. Dordrecht: Springer.

Plester, B. A., & Orams, M. B. (2008). Send in the clowns: The role of the joker in three New Zealand IT companies. *Humor: International Journal of Humor Research, 21*(3), 253–281.

Plester, B. A., & Sayers, J. G. (2007). Taking the piss: The functions of banter in three IT companies. *Humor: International Journal of Humor Research, 20*(2), 157 -187.

Plester, B. A., Cooper-Thomas, H., & Winquist, J. (2015). The fun paradox. *Employee Relations, 37*(3), 380–398.

Plester, B. A., Carroll, B., & Kim, H. (2018). Body Joking: The aesthetics and creativity of organizational humor. In J. Kaufmann, J. Bauer, & Sara Luria (Eds), *Creativity and humor* (pp. 129–142). San Diego, CA: Elsevier.

Radcliffe-Brown, A. R. (1940). On joking relationships. *Africa: Journal of the International African Institute, 13*(3), 195–210.

Robert, C., & Wilbanks, J. E. (2012). The wheel model of humor: Humor events and affect in organizations. *Human Relations, 65*(9), 1071–1099.

Rodrigues, S. B., & Collinson, D. L. (1995). 'Having fun'? Humor as resistance in Brazil. *Organization Studies, 16*(5), 739–768.

Romero, E. J.; & Cruthirds, K. W. (2006). The use of humor in the workplace. *Academy of Management Perspectives, 20*(2), 58–70.

Romero, E. J., & Pescosolido, A. (2008). Humor and group effectiveness. *Human Relations, 61*(3), 395–418.

Roy, D. (1959). 'Banana Time': Job satisfaction and informal interaction. *Human Organization Studies, 18*, 158–168.

Sanders, T. (2004). Controllable laughter: Managing sex work through humor. *Sociology*, *38*(2), 273–291.

Schein, E. (1991). 'What is culture?' In P. Frost, L. Moore, M. Louis, C. Lundberg, & J. Martin (Eds.), *Reframing organizational culture* (pp. 243–253). Newbury Park, CA: Sage.

Schein, E. H. (1985/2004). *Organizational culture and leadership*. San Francisco, CA: Jossey Bass.

Schnurr, S., & Holmes, J. (2009). Using humor to do masculinity at work. *Humor in Interaction*, *182*, 101.

Schnurr, S., & Plester, B. (2017). Functionalist discourse analysis of humor. In S. Attardo (Ed.). *Routledge handbook of language and humor* (pp. 309–321). New York, NY & London, UK: Routledge.

Taylor, P., & Bain, P. (2003). 'Subterranean worksick blues': Humor as subversion in two call centres. *Organization Studies*, *24*(9), 1487–1509.

Terrion, J. L., & Ashforth, B. E. (2002). From 'I' to 'we': The role of putdown humor and identity in the development of a temporary group. *Human Relations*, *55*(1), 55–87.

Tews, M. J., Michel, J. W., & Bartlett, A. (2012). The Fundamental role of workplace fun in applicant attraction. *Journal of Leadership & Organizational Studies*, *19*(1), 105–114.

Tews, M. J., Michel, J., Xu, S., & Drost, A. J. (2015). Workplace fun matters … but what else? *Employee Relations*, *37*(2), 248–267.

Tracy, S. J., Myers, K. K., & Scott, W. (2006). Cracking jokes and crafting selves: Sensemaking and identity management among human service workers. *Communication Monographs*, *73*(3), 283–308.

Victoria University of Wellington. (1996). Language in the workplace project. *School of linguistics and applied language studies*. Retrieved 11 August 2020 from https://www.wgtn.ac.nz/lals/centres-and-institutes/language-in-the-workplace/about-us/people.

Vinton, K. L. (1989). Humor in the workplace: It is more than telling jokes. *Small Group Behavior*, *20*(2), 151–166.

Warren, S., & Fineman, S. (2007). 'Don't get me wrong, it's fun here, but…' Ambivalence and paradox in a 'fun' work environment. In R. Westwood & C. Rhodes (Eds.), *Humor, work and organization* (pp. 92–110). London, UK: Routledge.

Weick, K. (1995). *Sensemaking in organizations*. Thousand Oaks, CA: Sage.

Weick, K. (2000). *Making sense of the organization*. Oxford, UK: Blackwell.

Westwood, R., & Johnston, A. (2012). Reclaiming authentic selves: Control, resistive humor and identity work in the office. *Organization*, *19*(6), 787–808.

Westwood, R., & Rhodes, C. (Eds.). (2007). *Humor, work and organization*. London, UK: Routledge.

8
HUMOR COMPETENCE IN THE CLASSROOM

Ann B. Frymier and Melissa B. Wanzer

Dr. Smith is lecturing on how individuals use avoidance as a consistent way to manage conflict in relationships and the problems with this approach. She shares the following story with her class to illustrate the course material:

> "When my grandparents would disagree on something and this would escalate into a heated argument, my grandfather would often say, 'I am not going to talk about this anymore.' Next, he would go to their bedroom, pack all of his socks in a suitcase, and leave, usually for a few hours. He always returned with his socks in tow; however, the issues that resulted in his socks-only-exit were never discussed."

A student in the class asks, 'Why did he only pack socks?' The rest of the class laughs and Dr. Smith proceeds to have a conversation about the utility of socks as well as the benefits and drawbacks of conflict avoidance as a means of managing conflict. Importantly, students recall the 'sock story' on the exam and use it to illustrate the problems with conflict avoidance.

How do we go about evaluating this example of instructional humor to determine its value? Does it make students laugh? Does it help students learn? In this chapter, we take a communication competence approach to teacher humor. Teachers use humor in classrooms across grade levels (Tsukawak, Imura, Kojima, Furukaw, & Katsuhiro, 2020), disciplines (Cooper et al., 2018) and cultures (Lui, Sun, & Wu, 2017). For decades, communication scholars have examined the use of humor by teachers as one of several behaviours that affect student motivation and learning outcomes (Banas, Dunbar, Rodriguez, & Liu, 2011). Teacher use of humor is one communication behaviour among many studied by instructional communication scholars. Instructional communication scholars examine communication between teachers and students across disciplines and educational levels.

An underlying principle of this research is that teaching is communication, and to be a competent teacher, one must be a competent communicator (Hurt, Scott, & McCroskey, 1978). In this chapter, we examine teacher use of humor as a form of communication used to facilitate learning. Specifically, we use a communication competence framework for evaluating teacher use of humor in learning environments. We begin by defining communication and communication competence and then in the context of teacher use of humor in the classroom.

A Communication Approach

Communication is the use of verbal and nonverbal messages to stimulate meaning in the mind of another person or persons (McCroskey, Richmond, & Stewart, 1986) and some describe it as the process of 'making meaning.' Message content, how it is delivered (nonverbal behaviours), as well as the context, expectations, and the roles of communicators contribute to the stimulation of meaning and the creation of shared meaning between interactants. Communication is both explicit and implicit. The *explicit* characteristics of communication include what is actually said orally or in writing, but much of the meaning stimulated in any given interaction is based on *implicit* qualities of communication such as social norms, context, and culture. Communication also involves both *relational* and *task* dimensions. In each interaction, face-to-face or otherwise, there is a task goal. We communicate for a reason. For example, we want students to read a particular chapter or engage in an activity. The task goal is communicated explicitly using verbal messages to tell or ask someone to do something. However, all communication also has a relational message component. The relational dimension is often implicit and communicates power, respect, liking, and other emotions. We typically rely on nonverbal behaviour and messages to communicate the relational component of a message. For example, using eye contact and a forward lean to communicate power, or a smile and downward cast glance to show respect. The use of humor illustrates these two dimensions of communication. The task or goal of humor varies; it may be to get attention, to build rapport, to exert control, or to enhance message retention. Both explicit and implicit messages are used to achieve the task while also communicating relational messages about how the source feels about the receiver. As with all communication attempts, humor can be done well or not, or in other words, it can be transmitted competently or incompetently.

Communication Competence

What does it mean to be a competent communicator? Communication competence is defined in numerous ways, but the most common conceptualisation involves the terms *effectiveness* and *appropriateness* (Spitzberg, 2003). Communication is said to be effective when the message source achieves the desired goal. For instance, if my goal is to obtain help from a colleague with organising an event, I am effective if my request for help gains assistance from my colleague.

Effectiveness is viewed as an essential element of competence. However, effectiveness alone is an insufficient definition of competence because communication goals can be achieved through a variety of immoral and unethical means, such as coercion and deception. Therefore, appropriateness is also necessary for communication to be competent. Appropriate communicators avoid violating relational or situational rules and norms. For example, there are social norms against insulting others, being disrespectful, and failing to show appreciation for assistance (Canary & Spitzberg, 1989). Appropriateness can be expressed in a general or specific way in social interactions (Canary & Spitzberg, 1990). For example, if Chris and Pat are discussing an upcoming meeting, Chris might generally engage in appropriate communication behaviour over the course of the entire conversation but make a specific comment, such as a racist joke, which is perceived as inappropriate, and therefore incompetent. To be a competent communicator means using communication (both verbal and nonverbal messages) to achieve our task goals in a manner that avoids violating social norms.

Competent Communication in the Classroom

Competent teaching cannot occur without effective and appropriate communication both inside and outside of the classroom setting. Teachers communicate with students in a variety of ways such as face-to-face, through email, text, and learning management systems, and in a variety of contexts such as in traditional classrooms, online, in academic offices, hallways, and public places such as the local grocery store or coffee shop. A variety of teacher and student communication behaviours have been examined in classrooms across disciplines and primarily in higher education. Several teacher communication messages and behaviours impact student outcomes (see Witt [2016] for a review of several programs of research in instructional communication). Instructional communication research does not examine course content and the best way to teach a concept. Rather instructional communication examines the communication behaviours used to deliver the content and to manage the learning environment. Teacher use of humor is one such behaviour that has received substantial attention and is the focus of this chapter.

Early work on teacher humor focused on the frequency and types of humor used in the classroom. Bryant, Comisky, and Zillmann (1979) and Bryant, Comisky, Crane, and Zillmann (1980) conducted some of the earliest work by observing and classifying the types of humor used by college teachers. This work was followed by others who further examined whether certain types of teacher humor were related or unrelated to course content (Downs, Javidi, & Nussbaum, 1988) and impacted student learning (Gorham & Christophel, 1990). This research resulted in a fairly consistent set of humor types that teachers used (e.g., jokes, stories, physical humor), but tended to assume that most humor was positive and had a similar impact on students. This early work was based on the premise that instructors' humor was prosocial and did not consider that humor could be funny, but not appropriate. This assumption was questioned by Wanzer, Frymier, Wojtaszczyk, and Smith (2006) with the examination of humor appropriateness, introducing a communication competence approach to teacher humor.

In this chapter, we examine the communication competence approach to teacher's use of humor. For teacher humor to be competent, it must be both effective and appropriate. Communicators generally use humor to stimulate mirth and laughter in receivers. Therefore, effective humor is that which achieves the goal of stimulating mirth and laughter, or in other words, being funny. In the following section, we examine major humor theories that explain why a communication act is perceived as funny, which serves as the foundation for defining humor. While there are many humor theories, three serve as foundations for describing humor.

Theoretical Explanations for Competent Humor in the Classroom

Three frequently cited theories attempt to explain why individuals perceive stimuli as humorous (Meyer, 2000). The three seminal theories that established the foundation for subsequent theoretical approaches to humor are incongruity theory (Berlyne, 1960), superiority or disparagement theory (Wolff, Smith, & Murray, 1934) and arousal relief or relief theory (Berlyne, 1960). These classic theories are relevant because they explain why students might perceive certain types of instructional humor as effective and appropriate in the classroom.

Incongruity Theory

Incongruity theory is one of the most frequently cited explanations for why individuals find something funny (Berger, 1976; Berlyne, 1960; McGhee, 1979). The basic premise of this theory is that humorous responses result from exposure to stimuli that are unexpected, surprising, or shocking. Central to this theory is the idea that we enter social situations with a set of specific expectations, and when those expectations are violated, we may perceive humor. Instructional humor may be a type of behaviour that is unexpected in the classroom. Frymier and Weser (2001) observed that students do not necessarily expect their instructors to use humor; thus, even weak instructor attempts at humor may be unexpected and appreciated by students. A recent survey of 1,637 science students indicated that 99% of the respondents appreciated instructor humor and felt that the humor attempts improved student learning experiences and enhanced the classroom environment and instructor-student relationships (Cooper et al., 2018). However, humor must be more than just unexpected to be funny.

Incongruity resolution theory (e.g., LaFave, Haddad, & Maesen, 1996; Suls, 1972) extends incongruity theory and provides a more comprehensive explanation for why something is funny. It is important to note that not all stimuli that are unexpected or surprising are funny. Instructors might share jokes or make humorous comments about historical events that students might not recognise. For example, an 8th-grade science teacher's joke that refers to Eddie Haskell will likely be met with blank stares, unless the students are familiar with the 1950's *Leave it to Beaver* sitcom and the Eddie Haskell character. For incongruity to work there also must be background or context against which to compare the humor (Berlyne,1960; LaFave et al., 1996). Incongruity resolution theory clarifies the incongruity theory by stipulating that the frame or content of the attempted humor is resolved as indeed 'humorous.' If the content isn't understood (as in language, cultural, or age differences) or is not interpreted/resolved as funny (it's amusing if I say it, but not if you say it), then the communication will not be perceived by the receiver as humorous.

Superiority or Disparagement Theory

The second theory included in the big three trifecta is superiority or disparagement theory (Feinberg, 1978; Gruner, 1978). According to this theory, people find stimuli funny when it makes fun of others' shortcomings, mistakes, or failures. According to Gruner (1978), a strong proponent of this theory, humor attempts possess game-like qualities where there is a clear winner and loser. When a source enacts humor targeted at herself or others, and it elicits laughter, she 'wins' the communication event. When teachers use humor that makes fun of themselves or others, they are engaging in this form of humor. However, this form of humor can be risky because targeting oneself may result in a loss of credibility. Targeting students in classroom humor attempts may be perceived as funny and therefore effective but may also be perceived as offensive or verbally aggressive (Frymier, Wanzer, & Wojtaszczyk, 2008) and negatively affect the classroom environment.

An outgrowth of superiority theory is disposition theory (Zillmann & Cantor, 1996). This theory addresses the fact that it really does matter who the target of the intended humor is. Individuals will describe humor as inappropriate when it is aimed at people they like, who they feel are protected or vulnerable, or individuals who are part of their own referent groups (Wanzer et al., 2006). Conversely, we are more likely to view humor attempts favourably when they target individuals we dislike, consider as adversaries, or when the targets are not included in our referent groups. Disposition theory explains why students may label humor attempts that attack individual students, sororities, fraternities, political affiliations, males, or females as inappropriate in the classroom (Frymier et al., 2008). On the other hand, humor that denigrates or makes fun of rival schools or teams is likely to be well-received.

Arousal Relief or Relief Theory

The third and final theory included in the 'big three' is arousal relief or relief theory (Berlyne, 1960; Morreall, 1983). According to relief theory, when receivers are exposed to humorous content, it offers a cathartic release of pent-up emotions through laughter. Humor often triggers laughter, which then leads to a release of negative emotions and positive health outcomes. At the centre of this theory is the notion that laughter is a complex physiological response connected to a number of beneficial physical outcomes such as releasing muscle tension, clearing ventilation, increasing oxygen and improving the body's ability to fight infections (Fry, 1992). A teacher's joke at the beginning of class about the shortage of toilet paper during the coronavirus pandemic offers a type of escape from the stressful situation students face. Such relief may help create a positive classroom climate where students are more comfortable talking to each other and their teacher.

These three theories serve as the foundation for what makes humor effective (funny) and to a lesser extent, appropriate. Incongruity resolution theory provides guidance on what makes something funny and the importance of students 'making sense of the joke' for humor to be effective. Similarly, arousal relief theory illustrates the usefulness of using humor to disperse tension during difficult moments. Teachers' use of humor can serve as a release to the anxiety and challenging moments common in learning environments. Superiority theory explains the effectiveness of humor that puts down our rivals. Disposition theory sheds light on appropriateness by indicating that humor targeted at in-group members is often not perceived as funny. Research conducted from a communication competence framework has focused on students' perceptions of appropriate teacher humor in the college classroom. The following section examines this line of research.

Appropriate Humor in the Classroom

Most people inherently recognise that humor attempts can be perceived as either appropriate or inappropriate and that these determinations are based on many factors. We have all been in situations where someone made a joke or said something funny that was perceived as inappropriate. As discussed previously, competent humor must be both effective (funny) and socially appropriate. Perceived appropriateness varies based on the context, culture, and interaction partners. What makes humor appropriate? This is the question tackled by Wanzer et al. (2006).

In 2006, Wanzer and colleagues formalised our understanding of forms of humor that are considered appropriate or inappropriate. Students were asked to list examples of the appropriate and inappropriate instructor humor they had experienced. Using grounded theory and constant comparative methods, four major categories of appropriate and four major categories of inappropriate humor were identified. See Table 8.1.

The four broad categories of appropriate humor subsumed several subcategories that served to further explain and elucidate the major categories. Related humor where the humor was connected to course content accounted for 47% of appropriate examples generated by students and included eleven sub-categories. The unrelated category accounted for 44% of the examples and consisted of nine subcategories. Just 9% of the examples involved self-disparaging humor and less

TABLE 8.1 Humor Categories from Wanzer et al. (2006)

Appropriate Humor	Inappropriate Humor
Related humor	**Offensive humor**
Humor related to material without a specified tactic	Sexual jokes/comments
Using media or external objects to enhance learning	Vulgar verbal and nonverbal expressions
Jokes	Drinking
Examples	Inappropriate jokes
Stories	Personal life
Critical/cynical	Drugs/illegal activities
College life stereotypes	Morbid humor
Directed towards student/teasing	Sarcasm
Teacher performance	
Role playing/activities	
Creative language usage	
Unrelated humor	**Disparaging student humor**
Stories	Non-specific response
Jokes	Based on intelligence
Critical/cynical	Based on gender
Directed towards student/teasing	Based on appearance
College life stereotypes	Based on student's personal life/opinions/interests
Teacher performance	Based on gender
Creative language usage	Based on religion
Current events/political	
Using media or external objects	
Self-disparaging humor	**Disparaging other humor**
Make fun of himself/herself (non-specific)	Using stereotypes in general
Make fun of personal characteristics	Targeting gender groups
Tell embarrassing stories	Targeting ethnic or racial groups
Make fun of mistakes made in class	Target is university related
Make fun of abilities	Targeting religious groups
	Targeting persons of a given sexual orientation
	Targeting persons of a given appearance
	Political motivation
Unplanned humor	**Self-disparaging humor**

than 1% were unplanned. The most common form of inappropriate humor was disparaging humor targeted at students accounting for 44% of the examples. This category included students being targeted as individuals or as a part of a group. Disparaging humor targeted at non-student groups and individuals accounted for 27% of the examples. Offensive humor, which included sexual and vulgar humor and joking about death, accounted for 30% of the examples. The final category of inappropriate humor was self-disparaging humor which accounted for 1% of the examples. Wanzer et al. (2006) noted overlap in appropriate and inappropriate humor, particularly regarding both unrelated and self-disparaging humor. Inappropriate humor was generally unrelated to the course; however, some unrelated humor was perceived as appropriate and emerged as a category. Inappropriate self-disparaging humor took the same form as appropriate self-disparaging humor but was perceived as inappropriate.

To help clarify these initial inductive findings, Frymier et al. (2008) conducted a follow-up study aimed at understanding why students perceived humor as either appropriate or inappropriate. To explain these findings, they put forth three explanations that were theoretically and conceptually framed. These explanations were based on the following: (1) Incongruity Resolution and Disposition Theories—humor is considered inappropriate if it is not recognised and, in turn, resolved and when it makes fun of others that the students like or perceive as similar; (2) Receiver personality traits/characteristics—perceptions of appropriateness are related to students' humor orientation, verbal aggressiveness, and communication competence; and (3) Teacher traits/characteristics—perceptions of appropriateness are related to teachers' exhibited levels of humor orientation, verbal aggressiveness, and nonverbal immediacy.

After collecting student self and other (teacher) reports of communication-based personality traits and humor use, Frymier et al. (2008) concluded that all three explanations were at least partially valid. First, consistent with disposition theory, students viewed teachers' use of disparaging other humor as inappropriate. Second, students high in verbal aggression and humor orientation generally perceived disparaging humor as more appropriate than students low in verbal aggressiveness and humor orientation, providing support for the notion that individual characteristics influence perceptions of appropriateness. Third, students' perceptions of teachers' verbal aggressiveness, humor orientation, and nonverbal immediacy were related to the appropriateness, suggesting that teacher personality and delivery of the humor influence perceptions of appropriateness. Frymier et al. (2008) concluded that perceptions of appropriateness are influenced by social norms, and student and teacher communication predispositions. While this research enhanced our understanding of students' perceptions of humor and appropriateness, it did not address whether teacher use of humor facilitated learning. The instructional humor processing theory was developed to fill this gap.

Instructional Humor Processing Theory

Drawing on previous research on humor, learning, and social influence, Wanzer, Frymier, and Irwin (2010) advanced the Instructional Humor Processing Theory (IHPT). This theory draws on incongruity resolution theory, disposition theory, and the elaboration likelihood model (Wanzer et al., 2010). IHPT attempts to explain the variability in student perceptions of instructor humor and predict when certain types of humor will affect learning outcomes.

IHPT begins with incongruity resolution theory (LaFave, Haddad, & Marshall, 1974) to address the cognitive element of humor (Martin & Kuiper, 2016). When an instructor uses humor while teaching, students must first recognise and resolve the incongruity in the instructor's message. If the incongruity is not resolved, the student does not 'get the joke', and the student will not perceive humor in the message. From a competence perspective, the humor would not be effective if we presume the instructor's goal was to incite laughter. The student may find the instructor's message confusing, distracting, or both, further indicating ineffective communication by the instructor. If the student resolves the incongruity, he/she may perceive the message as humorous and laughter may result. If students get the humor and find it funny, the humorous communication by the instructor would be considered effective (but not necessarily appropriate).

IHPT also draws on the elaboration likelihood model (ELM; Petty & Cacioppo, 1986) to explain the relationship between humor and learning. (See Chapter 1 in this volume for more on ELM.) A basic premise of ELM is that for messages to be deeply processed, receivers must be both motivated and able to process the message (Cacioppo & Petty, 1984). One factor that influences motivation to process is the perceived personal relevance of the message (Claypool, Mackie, Garcia-Marques, McIntosh, & Udall, 2004; Johnson & Eagly, 1989). Increases in motivation have been associated with students' perceptions of instructional content as relevant to their needs or goals (Frymier & Shulman, 1995; Keller, 1987; Knoster & Goodboy, 2020). Humor is one means of making content relevant. IHPT draws on this previous research on relevance as well as ELM to predict that students who perceive humor as relevant should be more motivated to process the message, which in turn results in greater content understanding and retention. Humor that is related to the course content or that helps students to learn the content in some way is predicted to enhance students' motivation to process the instructional message.

Consistent with ELM, IHPT also predicts that humorous messages that distract students will reduce the ability to process an instructional message, resulting in less learning. Humorous messages may be distracting for two reasons. First, students may be distracted if the humor targets them or liked others and generates negative affect. Creating negative emotions in students often leads to avoidance behaviours (Mottet, Frymier, & Beebe, 2006) and interferes with the cognitive processing of information (Titsworth, Quinlan, & Mazer, 2010). Therefore, inappropriate humor that is offensive may reduce the ability to process because of the negative affect that is generated. A second reason humorous messages may distract students and reduce ability is that the humor may draw students' attention away from the course content. If the humor lacks relevance to course content, it may divert students' attention to unrelated thoughts.

Disposition theory is included in IHPT to address the important role affective responses play in message processing and student learning specifically (Zillmann & Cantor, 1996). Exposure to humorous content often results in both emotional and behavioural responses such as laughing, smiling, and warm feelings. If the instructor's humor is targeted at those who are liked by the student, a negative affective response is generated as indicated by disposition theory (Zillmann &

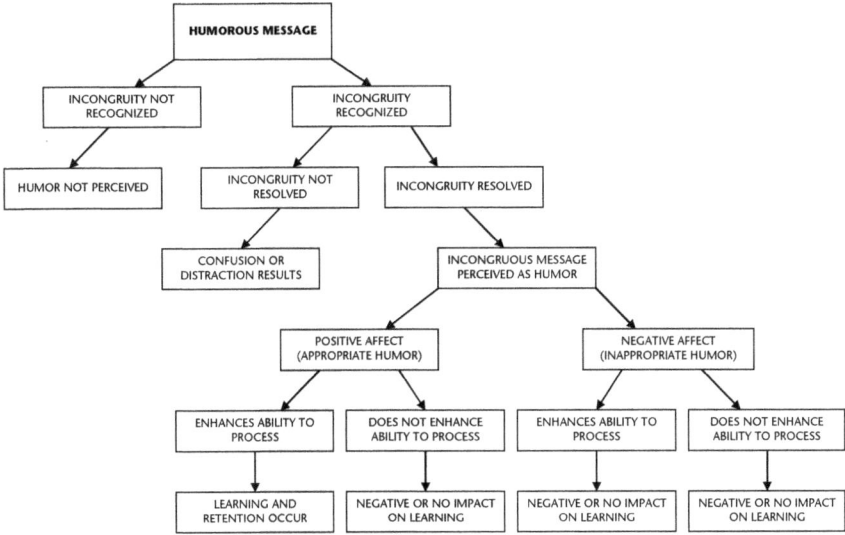

FIGURE 8.1   Instructional humor processing theory

Cantor, 1996), and the expected result is a reduced motivation to process the message. According to disposition theory, any negative humorous message that targets liked or familiar individuals or groups will not be perceived as funny by message recipients. In these instances, the message recipients empathise or relate to the target and experience negative reactions to the humor attempts. Therefore, instructional humor must generate a positive affective response to enhance motivation to process. Humor that targets liked others, in-group members, or that generates a negative affective response will reduce motivation to process the instructional message.

In summary, IHPT predicts that humor must first be understood as humor for it to have a positive effect on student learning outcomes. If humorous messages are not understood, the humor has the potential to be distracting or confusing. Once a humorous message is recognised and resolved as humor, it needs to generate positive affect. Negative affect is predicted to reduce either motivation or the ability to process the instructional message. IHPT also recognises that humor that is perceived as inappropriate may be distracting and reduce students' ability to process the message and therefore reduce learning. Figure 8.1 illustrates the premises of IHPT.

IHPT Research

Wanzer et al. (2010) provided support for the IHPT in a study of 343 college students enrolled in a communication class at either a Midwestern state university or a Northeastern private college. Students reported on the instructor they had immediately before their communication class. This methodology was used to maximise the variability in the types of teachers reported on by students. Students reported on their teachers' use of humor behaviours and self-reported their affective and cognitive learning in that class. As in much instructional communication research, both cognitive and affective learning were measured with self-report measures to allow comparisons across classes, teachers, and disciplines. Wanzer et al. (2010) used Frymier and Houser's (1999) revised learning indicators scale to measure cognitive learning and Mottet and Richmond's (1998) affective learning scale. Wanzer et al. (2010) reported positive correlations between related appropriate humor and both affective and cognitive learning, but no correlation between unrelated humor and either type of learning. Presumably, related humor enhanced both motivation and ability to process instructional messages while unrelated humor did not. These results provide some support for IHPT. Wanzer et al. (2010) reported that offensive and other disparaging humor, two forms of inappropriate humor, were unrelated to affective and cognitive learning.

Other scholars have sought to test IHPT with mixed results. In a recent study of 668 German students (average age 12), IHPT and the control-value theory of achievement emotions were applied to address the effects of instructor's type of humor use on students' positive and negative emotions over time (Bieg, Grassinger, & Dresel, 2019). Students completed online assessments of their instructors' use of different forms of humor (course-related, unrelated, self-disparaging, and aggressive) as well as their positive (enjoyment) and negative emotions (boredom, anger). As predicted by IHPT, instructors' use of course related humor was related to decreased reductions over time in students' positive emotions such as enjoyment; thus, instructors were able to maintain students' positive emotions over time by using more related or appropriate forms of humor. Also, instructors' use of course related humor was related to lower increases over time in student reports of negative emotions such as boredom and anger. Teachers' use of aggressive/offensive humor was related to student reports of less enjoyment and more boredom and anger over time, which is also consistent with IHPT. These findings are consistent with original research on IHPT that points out the benefits of the instructor's use of related humor and drawbacks of offensive humor (Bieg et al., 2019).

A second investigation of instructional humor appropriateness by West and Martin (2019) was framed using a communication competence approach. In addition to arguing that instructors had to be both effective and appropriate to be competent, West and Martin (2019) argued that the relationship between student perceptions of instructors' humor appropriateness might vary based on humor homophily. While West and Martin did not explicitly test IHPT, the results provide some support for the theory. When students perceived their instructors as humorous and indicated that their humor use was like their own, they viewed the humor as more appropriate. 'Students had greater affect for instructors who were appropriate, providing theoretical support for instructional humor processing theory (IHPT)' (West & Martin, 2019, p. 340). Interestingly, the authors note that while the data offer some support for IHPT, the effect of instructor's humor on student affect diminished as perceptions of appropriateness increased. One explanation for this unexpected finding is the use of the Humor Assessment Scale (Wrench & Richmond, 2004), which is a measure of humor frequency and does not distinguish between appropriate and inappropriate forms of instructional humor.

Two other studies on the effects of instructor humor on student outcomes claimed to test IHPT. In the first study, the researchers stated that they 'Implemented instructional humor processing theory (IHPT) to frame the relationships among instructor humor usage, student learning, and communication outcomes' (Goodboy, Booth-Butterfield, Bolkan, & Griffin, 2015, p. 45). Applying some of the tenets of IHPT, the researchers predicted that instructor humor would remain a significant positive predictor of student reported cognitive learning, extra effort, participation and outside of class communication after controlling for students' educational orientations (learning orientation and grade orientation). Goodboy et al. (2015) used a revised version of Booth-Butterfield and Booth-Butterfield's (1991) humor orientation scale (HOS) to measure teacher humor. The HOS measures how often individuals use humor as well as their self-perceived effectiveness in humor production (Booth-Butterfield & Booth-Butterfield, 1991). It is important to note that this measure does not assess different types of instructional humor articulated in IHPT (i.e., related, unrelated, offensive, or self-disparaging); instead, the scale measures global perceptions of classroom humor use. As Goodboy et al. (2015) predicted, instructor humor orientation was a significant predictor of student reports of cognitive learning, extra effort, and outside of class communication after controlling for students' educational orientations. Goodboy and colleagues (2015) concluded that the results were consistent with IHPT because instructor humor positively predicted student outcomes such as cognitive learning and extra effort. Without explicitly measuring specific forms of instructional humor or appropriateness, only the general principle of IHPT and none of the finer points were tested.

To understand how instructor humor drives student motivation and learning in the classroom, Bolkan and Goodboy (2015) tested IHPT against self-determination theory. Self-determination theory proposes that human motivation is a function of three basic psychological needs consisting of competence, autonomy, and relatedness (Ryan & Deci, 2002). The researchers expressed concerns with IHPT and argued that instructor humor facilitated student learning via need fulfilment and not positive affect and that once students' needs of competence, autonomy and relatedness were satisfied, learning increased.

Bolkan and Goodboy (2015) reported positive relationships between instructor humor and perceived cognitive learning, attention, and cognitive engagement, however, they argued that 'the variables did not work together in a causal model in the manner explicated by Wanzer et al., (2010)' (p. 56). They concluded that self-determination theory provided a better explanation for the results. However, their second hypothesis was consistent with IHPT, that is, 'the resolution of incongruity leads to perceptions of humor and that humor must result in positive affect for it to lead to learning,' (p. 56). This study, as well as the one conducted by Goodboy et al. (2015), measured teacher humor with the humor orientation scale (Booth-Butterfield & Booth-Butterfield, 1991), which measures humor frequency, rather than humor appropriateness. The lack of attention to humor appropriateness, a key component of IHPT makes these findings interesting, but not an explicit test of IHPT.

Frymier and Wanzer (2016) tested the IHPT using an experimental method where students (N=413) were exposed to one of five audio recorded lectures on verbal aggression. Two dimensions of humor were manipulated, offensiveness and relatedness to content, creating a 2 × 2 design with a control condition. In each condition, an example was inserted in the middle of the lecture that involved a humorous story/joke. The control condition contained a non-humorous example. Manipulation checks indicated that both relatedness and offensiveness were manipulated; however, unoffensive conditions were perceived as more related to content than offensive conditions. The control condition was perceived to be the least funny and the most related to content. The perceived funniness of the humor conditions was disappointingly low (overall M=39.03 on a 100-point scale).

Frymier and Wanzer (2016) predicted that students in the related/unoffensive condition would have the highest levels of cognitive and affective learning. There were no differences in cognitive learning, which was measured with a seven-question quiz. However, differences were observed in self-reported affective learning, but not quite as predicted. Students in the unrelated/unoffensive condition had the highest level of affective learning, not the students in the related/unoffensive condition as predicted. Students in the unrelated/offensive condition had the lowest level of affective learning, as was expected. This same pattern persisted in students' perceptions of the teacher's credibility. Perceived teacher credibility was significantly greater in the unrelated/unoffensive condition than in the unrelated/offensive condition. No other significant differences were observed.

To further explore how students perceived the study conditions, correlations were examined between cognitive learning, affective learning, credibility, and the manipulation check variables (student perceptions of funniness, relatedness, and offensiveness of the humor in the scenarios). When participants perceived the humor as related to the content, they also reported greater affective learning, performed better on the quiz, and perceived the instructor as being more credible. The same pattern of relationships was observed when participants perceived the manipulation as funny. When participants perceived the manipulation as offensive, participants reported lower levels of affective learning, had lower scores on the quiz and perceived the instructor as less credible. It should also be noted that the condition perceived as the funniest (unrelated/offensive) was perceived as inappropriate and did not result in greater learning. Funny does not trump appropriateness in the classroom. The correlations between the outcome variables and the manipulation checks were consistent with the predictions of IHPT. This discrepancy may be explained by the amount of variance in how students perceived the humor conditions. Examination of the standard deviations in the manipulation check analyses indicate a good deal of variability, suggesting other variables, such as student differences may be occurring.

Wanzer et al. (2010) concluded that humor needed to be related to course content to be appropriate but Frymier and Wanzer (2016) did not find support for relatedness in an experimental study. Perhaps rather than being *related to content*, the humor needs to be *relatable*. Students may perceive instructor humor as more relatable when it is like their own humor. Indeed, research by West and Martin (2019) indicates that when students view their instructors' humor as similar to their own, they viewed it as more appropriate and this resulted in greater affect toward the instructor. Relatable humor may be more memorable or may generate a more positive affect. Relating humor to content is likely a useful strategy but may not be as important as initially thought by Wanzer and her colleagues.

Frymier and Wanzer's (2016) test of IHPT provided support for the proposition that offensive humor is inappropriate in the classroom. Affective learning differed between the condition perceived as being the most offensive (unrelated/offensive) and the condition perceived as the least offensive (unrelated/unoffensive). Appropriateness is necessary for competent humor use, and Frymier and Wanzer's results provide support for the proposition that offensive humor is inappropriate and negatively impacts students' affective responses. Appropriate humor likely takes many forms on an endless number of topics and may be best defined by what it is not. It does not disparage students or others, and it does not address topics that evoke negative emotional responses in students. Humor must be both appropriate and effective to be considered competent in the classroom.

Conclusions About Competent Instructional Humor

Throughout this chapter, we have argued that competent teacher humor must be both effective and appropriate. We have drawn on incongruity theory, disparagement theory, and arousal relief theory to explain why humor may or may not be perceived as effective and appropriate in the classroom. Teacher humor must effectively stimulate mirth and laughter to be effective in the classroom. Perceptions of appropriateness are based on social norms (Canary & Spitzberg, 1989) and so, therefore, are rooted in students' interpretations of teacher humor. Wanzer and Frymier's research indicates that perceptions of appropriateness are influenced by social norms, teacher communication style, and student predispositions (Frymier et al., 2008). Inappropriate humor offends students by being vulgar, violating classroom norms, disparaging students, or disparaging others liked by students. The three major theories of humor discussed provide the basis for understanding what types of messages will be effective at inciting laughter and mirth. Wanzer and Frymier's work provides the basis for understanding the types of humor that students perceive as inappropriate in the classroom.

Next Steps

In this final section, we offer a list of ideas for future research on humor in the classroom. Our suggestions are based on research as well as our anecdotal teaching experience.

Further testing on IHPT is needed. While preliminary results are promising. We need to test the theory and some of its tenets more precisely. First, the extent to which instructional humor leads to message elaboration is still unclear. If students identify and resolve the humor, under what conditions or circumstances does it lead to message elaboration? While related humor has shown some promise in the classroom, the results are equivocal. Does the humor have to be related directly to the course material, or is it more important for it to be 'relatable'? We suggest the use of more experimental designs where researchers test different forms of instructional humor (related/relatable, non-offensive, self-disparaging, offensive, etc.) and compare the effects of these types of humor on student comprehension, motivation, and affect toward the content.

To date, most of the research on instructional humor focuses almost exclusively on what the instructor does or says in the classroom and how those behaviours impact student outcomes such as learning, motivation, and outside-of-class communication. We need to take a closer look at how teachers and students collaborate in producing humor and laughter in the classroom. When students are more involved and co-create the classroom humor, is this 'classroom humor' viewed more favourably by students than when the humor is coming from the teacher only? Does student involvement with classroom humor account for variability in student outcomes? Future studies on instructional humor should measure how students are involved in the process and whether their involvement is related to their perceptions of the appropriateness and effectiveness of the collaboratively produced humor.

While there are several humor scales and competence scales available, none measure humor competence. A humor competence scale needs to be developed that measures humor effectiveness and appropriateness. Scale items might include questions about verbal and nonverbal skills linked with humor production such as the use of incongruity in content, timing in delivery, fluctuations in rate, pitch, and volume to produce humor, and audience considerations in message delivery. A scale that measures humor competence might be used in different contexts to determine whether competent communicators are more successful in delivering content and achieving goals.

Most of the research on teacher humor has framed it as a positive behaviour. Researchers also need to study the disruptive aspects of humor. In addition to laughter, humor may distract students from important content as predicted by IHPT. Similarly, does failed humor negatively impact students? How much risk is involved in a novel humor attempt? Additionally, are there training strategies for helping instructors who are motivated to use humor, but struggle with their content and delivery? Studies would help us determine whether instructors can be trained to use humor competently. Truly understanding the competent use of humor should include an analysis of incompetent humor, including both effectiveness and appropriateness.

In response to Frymier and Wanzer's (2016) findings, future research needs to examine humor that is *related to content* versus humor that is *personally relatable*. Wanzer et al. (2006) identified unrelated humor as a type of appropriate humor, but also observed a general theme of unrelatedness in students' descriptions of inappropriate humor. It appeared that students did not necessarily appreciate humor that was unconnected (unrelated) to the course content. However, Frymier and Wanzer (2016) found no effect on related humor. In that study offensiveness was the only humor factor that mattered. We speculate that for student participants in the Wanzer et al. (2006) study, the concepts of related to content and personally relatable were conflated. Perhaps unrelated humor that was perceived as relatable was perceived as appropriate, where unrelated humor perceived as unrelatable was perceived as inappropriate. This issue is worthy of further investigation.

References

Banas, J., Dunbar, N., Rodriguez, D., & Liu, S. (2011). A review of humor in educational settings: Four decades of research. *Communication Education, 60*, 115–144.

Berger, A. A. (1976). Anatomy of the joke. *Journal of Communication, 26*, 113–115.

Berlyne, D. E. (1960). *Conflict, arousal, and curiosity.* New York, NY: McGraw-Hill.

Bieg, S., Grassinger, R., & Dresel, M. (2019). Teacher humor: Longitudinal effects on students' emotions. *European Journal of Psychology of Education, 34*, 517–534.

Bolkan, S., & Goodboy, A. K. (2015). Exploratory theoretical tests of the instructor humor-student learning link. *Communication Education, 64*, 45–64.

Booth-Butterfield, S., & Booth-Butterfield, M. (1991). Individual differences in the communication of humorous messages. *Southern Communication Journal, 56*, 205–218.

Bryant, J., Comisky, P., & Zillmann, D. (1979). Teachers' humor in the classroom. *Communication Education, 28*, 110–118.

Bryant, J., Comisky, P., Crane, J. S., & Zillmann, D. (1980). Relationship between college teachers' use of humor in the classroom and students' evaluations of their teachers. *Journal of Educational Psychology, 72*, 511–519.

Cacioppo, J. T., & Petty, R. E. (1984). The elaboration likelihood model of persuasion. *Advances in Consumer Research, 11*, 673–675.

Canary, D. J., & Spitzberg, B. H. (1989). A model of the perceived competence of conflict strategies. *Human Communication Research, 15*, 630–649.

Canary, D. J., & Spitzberg, B. H. (1990). Attribution biases and associations between conflict strategies and competence outcomes. *Communication Monographs, 57*, 139–151.

Claypool, H. M., Mackie, D. M., Garcia-Marques, T., McIntosh, A., & Udall, A. (2004). The effects of personal relevance and repetition on persuasive processing. *Social Cognition, 22*, 310–335.

Cooper, K., Hendrix, T., Stephens, M., Cala, J., Mahrer, Kali, K., ... Brownell, S. (2018). To be funny or not to be funny. Gender differences of student perceptions of instructor humor in college science courses. *PLoS One, 13*, 1–24.

Downs, V. C., Javidi, M., & Nussbaum, J. F. (1988). An analysis of teachers' verbal communication within the college classroom: Use of humor, self-disclosure, and narratives. *Communication Education, 37*, 127–141.

Feinberg, L. (1978). *The secret of humor.* Amsterdam: Rodopi.

Fry, W. F., Jr. (1992). The physiologic effects of humor, mirth, and laughter. *Journal of the American Medical Association, 267*, 1857–1858.

Frymier, A. B., & Houser, M. L. (1999). The revised Learning indicators scale. *Communication Studies, 50*, 1–12.

Frymier, A. B., & Shulman, G. M. (1995). "What's in it for me?": Increasing content relevance to enhance students' motivation. *Communication Education, 44*, 40–50.

Frymier, A. B., & Wanzer, M. B. (2016, November). *Testing instructional humor processing theory.* National Communication Association Annual Conference, Philadelphia, PA.

Frymier, A. B., & Weser, B. (2001). The role of student predispositions on student expectations for instructor communication behavior. *Communication Education, 50*, 314–326.

Frymier, A. B., Wanzer, M. B., & Wojtaszczyk, A. (2008). Assessing students' perceptions of inappropriate and appropriate teacher humor. *Communication Education, 57*, 266–288.

Goodboy, A. K., Booth-Butterfield, M., Bolkan, S., & Griffin, D. J. (2015) The role of instructor humor and students' educational orientations in student learning, extra effort, participation, and out-of-class communication. *Communication Quarterly, 63*, 44–61.

Gorham, J., & Christophel, D. M. (1990). The relationship of teachers' use of humor in the classroom to immediacy and student learning. *Communication Education, 39*, 46–62.

Gruner, C. R. (1978). *Understanding laughter: The working of wit and humor.* Chicago, IL: Nelson-Hall.

Hurt, H. T., Scott, M. D., & McCroskey, J. C. (1978). *Communication in the classroom.* Addison-Wesley.

Johnson, B. T., & Eagly, A. H. (1989). Effects of involvement on persuasion: A meta-analysis. *Psychological Bulletin, 106*, 290–314.

Keller, J. M. (1987). Development and use of the ARCS model of instructional design. *Journal of Instructional Development, 10* (3), 2–10.

Knoster, K. C., & Goodboy, A. K. (2020). Making content relevant: A teaching and learning experiment with replication, *Communication Education.* Advance online publication. doi:10.1080/03634523.2020.1788106.

LaFave, L., Haddad, J., & Marshall, N. (1974). Humor judgments as a function of identification classes. *Sociology and Social Research, 58*, 184–194.

LaFave, L., Haddad, J., & Maesen, W. A. (1996). Superiority, enhanced self-esteem, and perceived incongruity humour theory. In A. J. Chapman & H. C. Foot (Eds.), *Humor and laughter: Theory research and applications* (pp. 63–91). New Brunswick, NJ: Transaction Publishers.

Lui, Y. P., Sun, L., Wu, X. F., Yang, Y., Zhang, C. T., Zhou, H. L., & Quan, X. Q. (2017). Use of humor in medical education: A survey of students and teachers in China. *BMJ Open, 7*(11), e018853. doi:10.1136/bmjopen-2017-018853.

Martin, R., & Kuiper, N. A. (2016). Three decades investigating humor and laughter: An interview with Professor Rod Martin. *Europe's Journal of Psychology, 12*, 498–512.

McCroskey, J. C., Richmond, V. P., & Stewart, R. A. (1986). *One on one: The foundations of interpersonal communication.* Englewood Cliffs, NJ: Prentice-Hall.

McGhee, P. E. (1979). *Humor: Its origin and development.* San Francisco: W.H. Freeman.

Meyer, J. (2000). Humor as a double-edged sword: Four functions of humor in communication. *Communication Theory, 10*, 310–331.

Morreall, J. (1983). *Taking laughter seriously*. Albany: State University of New York.
Mottet, T., & Richmond, V. P. (1998). Newer is not necessarily better: A reexamination of affective learning measurement. *Communication Research Reports, 15*, 370–378.
Mottet, T. P., & Beebe, S. A. (2006). Foundations of instructional communication. In T. P. Mottet, V. P. Richmond, & J. C. McCroskey (Eds.), *Handbook of instructional communication: Rhetorical and relational perspectives* (pp. 3–32). London, UK: Pearson Education.
Mottet, T. P., Frymier, A. B., & Beebe, S. A. (2006). Theorizing about instructional communication. In T. P. Mottet, V. P. Richmond, & J. C. McCroskey (Eds.), *Instructional communication: Rhetorical and relational perspectives* (pp. 253–282). Boston, MA: Allyn & Bacon.
Petty, R. E., & Cacioppo, J. T. (1986). *Communication and persuasion: Central and peripheral routes to attitude change*. New York, NY: Springer-Verlag.
Ryan, R. M., & Deci, E. L. (2002). Overview of self-determination theory: An organismic dialectical perspective. In E. L. Deci & R. M. Ryan (Eds.), *Handbook of self-determination research* (pp. 3–36). Rochester, NY: University of Rochester Press.
Spitzberg, B. H. (2003). Methods of interpersonal skill assessment. In J. O. Greene & B. R. Burleson (Eds.), *Handbook of communication and social interaction skills* (pp. 93–134). Mahwah, NJ: Lawrence Erlbaum.
Suls, J. M. (1972). A two-stage model for the appreciation of jokes and cartoons: An information-processing analysis. In J. H. Goldstein & P. E. McGhee (Eds.), *The psychology of humor* (pp. 81–100). New York: Academic.
Titsworth, S., Quinlan, M., & Mazer, J. (2010). Emotion in teaching and learning: Development and validation of the classroom emotions scale. *Communication Education, 59*(4), 431–452.
Tsukawak, R., Imura, T., Kojima, N., Furukaw, Y., & Katsuhiro, I. (2020). The correlation between teachers' humor and class climate: A study targeting primary and secondary school students. *Humor*. Advance online publication. doi:10.1515/humor-2019-0021.
Wanzer, M. B., Frymier, A. B., Wojtaszczyk, A., & Smith, T. (2006). Appropriate and inappropriate uses of humor by teachers. *Communication Education, 55*, 178–196.
Wanzer, M. B., Frymier, A. B., & Irwin, J. (2010). An explanation of the relationship between instructor humor and student learning: Instructional humor processing theory. *Communication Education, 59*, 1–18.
West, M. S., & Martin, M. M. (2019). Students' perceptions of instructor appropriateness and humor homophily. *Communication Education, 68*, 328–349.
Witt, P. L. (Ed.). (2016). *Communication and learning*. Walter de Gruyter, Inc.
Wolff, H. A., Smith, C. E., & Murray, H. A. (1934). The psychology humor. *The Journal of Abnormal and Social Psychology, 28*(4), 341–365.
Wrench, J. S., & Richmond, V. P. (2004). Understanding the psychometric properties of the humor assessment instrument through an analysis of the relationships between teacher humor assessment and instructional communication variables in the college classroom. *Communication Research Reports, 21*, 92–103.
Zillmann, D., & Cantor, J. R. (1996). A disposition theory of humour and mirth. In A. J. Chapman & H. C. Foot (Eds.), *Humor and laughter: Theory, research and applications* (pp. 93–115). New Brunswick, NJ: Transaction Publishers.

PART IV
Intergroup relations

9
DISPARAGEMENT HUMOR AND PREJUDICE

Advances in theory and research

Thomas E. Ford and Andrew R. Olah

> "Humour is ... the all-consoling and ... the all-excusing, grace of life."
> — *C. S. Lewis (1942)*

Efforts to understand humor in intergroup settings have largely focused on disparagement humor: humor that attempts to amuse through the denigration of a social group or individual (Ferguson & Ford, 2008). In the quote above, C.S. Lewis provided an important insight into the nature of disparagement humor. Disparagement humor represents a paradox, simultaneously communicating two conflicting messages. It communicates an explicit, prejudiced message of denigration with an implicit subtext that the denigration is not malicious because it is not real; it is 'just a joke' not *intended* to be taken seriously (Attardo, 1993; Martin & Ford, 2018; Zillmann, 1983). The inherent ambiguity of intention, meaning, and affect gives disparagement humor the appearance of acceptability excusing it from the opposition that more serious communication would incur (Bill & Naus, 1992; Johnson, 1990). Consequently, disparagement humor represents a powerful vehicle for shaping the ways people think about and respond to one another in intergroup settings.

Accordingly, theorists historically have considered the impact of disparagement humor on *prejudice*—a negative attitude or affective disposition toward a social group (e.g., Crandall, Eshleman, & O'Brien, 2002; Dovidio, 2001). Specifically, theorists have argued that disparagement humor reinforces negative stereotypes and prejudice (e.g., Berger, 1993; La Fave & Mannell, 1976; Martineau, 1972; Meyer, 2001; Stephenson, 1951; Zenner, 1970). And, by reinforcing negative stereotypes and prejudice in individuals, disparagement humor is thought to maintain cultural or societal prejudice at a macro-sociological level. Husband (1977), for instance, proposed that racist humor depicted on television reinforces stereotypes and prejudice and thus functions to perpetuate a racist society.

Similarly, Montemurro (2003) argued that sexist humor strengthens a social system that trivialises women and promotes sexism.

Martineau (1972) added that disparagement humor has the power to function in both positive and negative ways in intergroup settings, acting as either a 'lubricant' or an 'abrasive.' He proposed that on the one hand, disparagement humor 'serves as oil pumped from an oil can … to keep the machinery of interaction operating smoothly and freely.' On the other hand, it can constitute a 'measure of sand' that causes interpersonal friction (p. 103). Similarly, Rappoport (2005) proposed that disparagement humor can serve as either a 'sword' or a 'shield' in intergroup settings.

Recent advances in theory and research have expanded upon early conceptualisations demonstrating that disparagement humor relates to prejudice in both negative and positive ways through processes that are unique to humor as a medium for communicating disparagement. Specifically, disparagement humor can have detrimental effects functioning as a sword in intergroup settings in two ways. First, disparagement humor *releases* or disinhibits prejudice by loosening the norms (the 'rules') of a social setting to permit expressions of prejudice. Second, it *legitimises* prejudice by making targeted social groups seem more deserving of prejudice. Disparagement humor also can have beneficial consequences, functioning as a shield in intergroup contexts: it *subverts* prejudice when people use it constructively to expose the ugliness of prejudice.

We review and discuss these recent advances with a particular focus on disparagement humor as a releaser of prejudice because of the amount of research on this function and because Chapter 10 of this volume addresses the processes by which disparagement humor legitimises prejudice. As such, this chapter expands upon and updates previous reviews by Ford, Richardson, and Petit (2015) and Ford, Breeden, O'Connor, and Banos (2017). We conclude the chapter by discussing potential next steps for future research focusing on the detrimental consequences of disparagement humor from the target's perspective.

Disparagement Humor Releases Prejudice: Prejudiced Norm Theory

Ford and Ferguson's (2004) Prejudiced Norm Theory (PNT) proposed that disparagement humor contributes to prejudice through social processes unique to humor as a medium for communicating disparagement. Specifically, disparagement humor can change how people understand the norms or 'rules' of appropriate conduct in a given setting in a way that permits them to express their prejudice against the targeted group. As a result, disparagement humor functions to disinhibit or 'release' prejudice.

The expression of prejudice is constrained by social norms that vary over time and between cultures (e.g., West & Hewstone, 2012). In the United States, the civil rights, gay rights, and women's movements of the 1960s and 1970s contributed to the emergence of new norms that prohibit open expressions of prejudice toward groups historically victimised by institutional discrimination

Disparagement humor and prejudice 153

(Taylor, Sheatsley, & Greeley, 1978). The emergence of these egalitarian norms has changed the way people experience and express prejudice.

Crandall, Ferguson, and Bahns (2013) normative window model of prejudice categorises groups as belonging to one of three adjacent positions in society defined by the degree to which society views prejudice against the group as acceptable. The left-most position, the 'justified prejudice region,' is comprised of groups society consensually defines as deviant or morally reprehensible (e.g., racists, criminals). Because such groups violate our collective values of civility, negative attitudes toward them are not only justified, they are not even viewed as prejudice. The right-most position called the 'unjustified prejudice region' consists of groups that society consensually defines as good or righteous (e.g., firefighters, nurses) against whom prejudice is completely unjustified. In fact, negative sentiments toward such groups are not considered prejudice but rather idiosyncratic views of an irrational person.

The middle position, called the 'normative ambiguity region,' applies to groups society defines as socially disadvantaged (e.g., women, religious minorities, sexual minorities). Groups in this region are characterised by social change or 'shifting acceptability.' With the emergence of egalitarian norms of tolerance and acceptance, prejudice against these groups is shifting from being completely justified to being completely unjustified.

Motivated by external pressure to conform to the increasingly prevalent nonprejudiced norms, or by internal forces (e.g., religious beliefs; humanitarian goals), people attempt to suppress prejudiced thoughts and behaviours against 'normative ambiguity' groups. They express prejudice only when they believe it does not violate prevailing social norms or internalised standards of right conduct (e.g., Crandall & Eshleman, 2003; Dovidio, 2001; Pearson, Dovidio, & Gaertner, 2009). That is, in order to act in a prejudiced manner, people need something in the immediate context to communicate approval to do so. Crandall and Eshleman (2003) referred to contextual events that permit or justify expressions of prejudice as 'releasers' of prejudice.

According to PNT, disparagement humor creates a social norm that communicates permission to behave in a prejudiced manner, thus functioning as a releaser of prejudice. PNT specifies the processes unique to disparagement *humor* related to (a) the interpretation of the disparagement, (b) the emergence of a prejudiced norm, and (c) the role of personal prejudice that jointly functions to permit one to release rather than suppress their prejudice (see Figure 9.1).

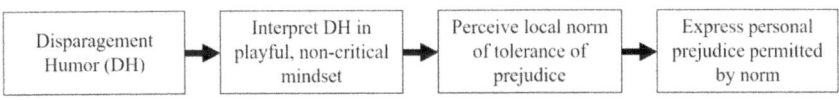

FIGURE 9.1 Prejudiced norm theory: The effect of disparagement humor for people high in prejudice against the targeted group

Interpretation of Disparagement Humor: The 'Humor Mindset'

Humor invites us to think about and respond playfully and non-critically to its underlying message (e.g., Berlyne, 1972; Mannell, 1977; Mulkay, 1988; Ziv & Gadish, 1990). Mulkay (1988) suggested that when people shift to a humor mindset, they loosen the rules of logic and expectations of common sense; they do not apply the information-processing strategies typically required by serious communication. They abandon the usual serious ways of thinking. Raskin (1985) referred to the serious and humorous mindsets as 'bona-fide' and 'non-bona-fide' information processing modes respectively. Apter (1982; 1991) referred to the humor mindset as a paratelic state of mind (contrasted with the serious telic state of mind) and characterised it as a non-goal oriented playful state of mind. McGhee (1972) characterised the serious mindset as 'reality assimilation' and the humor mindset as 'fantasy assimilation.'

Disparagement humor, then, invites us to think about and respond playfully to its underlying expression of prejudice, communicating an implicit 'meta-message' (Attardo, 1993) that, in this context, expressions of prejudice can be treated playfully or light-heartedly rather than seriously or critically (Duchscherer & Dovidio, 2016; Greenwood & Isbell, 2002; Montemurro, 2003). Duchscherer & Dovidio (2016), for instance, found that White participants were less critical of memes disparaging Asians when the memes were presented in a humorous versus serious manner.

The Emergence of a Prejudiced Norm

By approving of disparagement humor (i.e., interpreting it in a playful, non-critical mindset), recipients tacitly assent to a shared agreement with the 'joke teller' and with one another to suspend the usual serious ways of thinking about the underlying derision in the immediate context (Emerson, 1969; Kane, Suls, & Tedeschi, 1977; Khoury, 1985). Emerson (1969) proposed that a joke teller and recipient form an 'implicit contract' to withhold critical ways of thinking about socially unacceptable or 'taboo' topics. Thus, through the initiation and approval of disparagement humor, the joke teller and recipients collectively create a local norm of tolerance of prejudice (i.e., a prejudiced norm) for the immediate social context. They create a rule for the immediate context that it is okay for one another to express their prejudice.

By relaxing the standards of right conduct and creating a prejudiced norm, disparagement humor expands the bounds of acceptable conduct to include responses that would otherwise be considered wrong or inappropriate. In this context of expanded acceptability, people can feel freer to express hostilities in a variety of ways without the risk of violating social norms and facing social reprisals (see Figure 9.2).

The Role of Personal Prejudice

Contemporary superiority theories of humor appreciation (La Fave, Haddad, & Maesen, 1976; Zillman, Cantor, Chapman & Foot, 1976 [1996]) propose that

Disparagement humor and prejudice   **155**

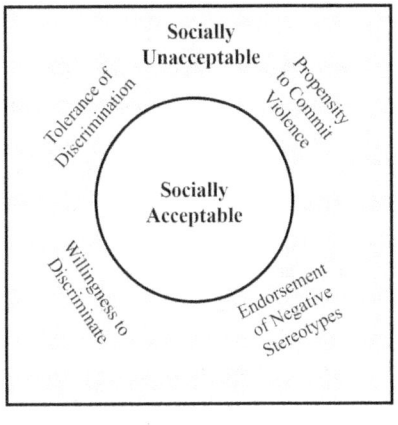
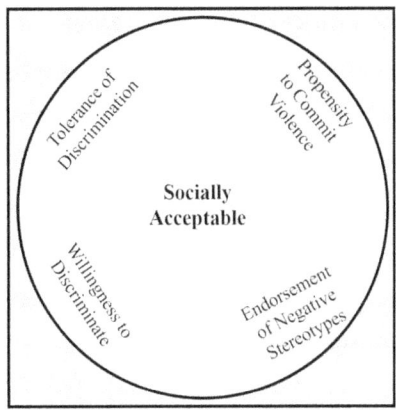

Social Norms of Acceptable Conduct

Effect of Disparagement Humor on Social Norms of Acceptable Conduct

FIGURE 9.2 Disparagement humor expands the bounds of acceptable behaviour to include responses that would otherwise be considered wrong or inappropriate

people interpret disparagement humor in a non-critical humor mindset insofar as they are prejudiced against the targeted group. Supporting this hypothesis, empirical research has shown that people find disparagement humor more amusing and less offensive to the extent they dislike the targeted group (e.g., Greenwood & Isbell, 2002; LaFrance & Woodzicka, 1998; Thomas & Esses, 2004; Zillmann, 1983).

Since prejudiced people are especially inclined to interpret disparagement humor in a non-critical humor mindset, they should be more likely to perceive and assent to an emergent prejudiced norm in the immediate social context, and to use that norm to guide their own responses toward members of the targeted group. That is, upon exposure to disparagement humor, people higher in prejudice are especially likely to assume that others in the immediate context would permit expressions of prejudice thus making them feel more comfortable expressing or 'releasing' their own prejudice.

Empirical Support: The Prejudice-Releasing Effects of Disparagement Humor

Supporting PNT, research has shown that exposure to disparagement humor targeting historically disadvantaged groups (e.g., women, gay men, Muslims) fosters a perceived local norm that allows prejudiced individuals to more freely release their prejudice against the targeted group. Specifically, exposure to disparagement humor has been shown to release prejudice in the form of (a) tolerance of discrimination, (b) willingness to discriminate, (c) endorsement of negative stereotypes, and (d) propensity to commit violence.

Tolerance of Discrimination

Ford (2000, Exp. 1) asked participants, who were either high or low in hostile sexism (Glick & Fiske, 1996)—antagonism against women—to imagine they worked in the distribution department for a newspaper. In the context of their imagined workgroup participants read a number of sexist jokes, serious sexist statements, or neutral jokes. Participants then read a vignette in which a male supervisor treated a new female employee in a patronising manner, using a pet name, which suggests a level of romantic intimacy that is inappropriate and potentially threatening in the workplace. Participants then rated the offensiveness of the supervisor's behaviour.

Participants low in hostile sexism rated the supervisor's behaviour as comparably offensive across the experimental conditions. In contrast, participants high in hostile sexism reported greater tolerance for the supervisor's behaviour in the sexist joke condition compared to the other two. In each of the other two conditions, participants high and low in hostile sexism rated the supervisor's behaviour as comparably offensive; participants high in hostile sexism presumably suppressed their prejudice in those conditions. They felt free to express their prejudice against women only in the sexist humor condition. Ford, Wentzel, and Lorion (2001) further demonstrated that this effect was mediated by an emergent prejudiced norm—the perception that others in the immediate context viewed the sexist event as acceptable.

Demonstrating the importance of interpreting the disparagement humor in a non-critical mindset, Ford (2000. Exp. 2) found that the effect of sexist humor on tolerance of sexism was attenuated when participants were instructed to interpret the humor as they would a serious, non-humorous message. Similarly, Bill and Naus (1992) found that men viewed incidents of sex discrimination as harmless and acceptable insofar as they perceived them as humorous.

In addition, research has demonstrated that exposure to sexist humor affects willingness to express approval for broader sexist ideologies (Wright, DeFrancesco, Hamilton, & Vashist, 2018) and institutional sexism (Ford, Woodzicka, Triplett, & Kochersberger, 2013). Ford et al. (2013), for instance, found that men higher in hostile sexism reported greater tolerance of societal sexism (acceptance of the gender status quo) after reading sexist jokes versus neutral jokes or non-humorous sexist statements.

Recent research has extended this line of research by examining the effects of disparagement humor targeting other social groups. Ford, Woodzicka, Triplett, Kochersberger, and Holden, (2014, Exp. 1), for instance, examined whether exposure to anti-Muslim jokes promotes greater tolerance of discrimination against Muslims. Participants imagined that they were a manager of a retail store, and in that context, they read anti-Muslim jokes, neutral jokes or non-humorous anti-Muslim statements exchanged among employees in their workgroup. Then they read that they discriminated against a new Muslim employee by prohibiting her from waiting on customers because she was wearing a burqa and asking her to, 'please try to dress more American, not so…ethnic.' Participants then reported how badly they would feel about themselves for having behaved this way. The results indicated that participants felt less bad about themselves after reading anti-Muslim jokes versus non-humorous anti-Muslim statements or neutral jokes. Furthermore, this effect was mediated by a perception that others in the immediate context approved of the manager's responses to the Muslim employee.

In addition, Greenwood and Gautam (2020) addressed the prejudice-releasing effects of disparagement humor targeting *overweight* women. Participants high in hostile sexism judged an instance of harassment of an overweight woman as more acceptable after exposure to anti-fat sexist jokes compared to a control condition and compared to participants low in hostile sexism in the anti-fat sexist joke condition.

Willingness to Discriminate

Ford, Boxer, Armstrong, and Edel (2008) examined the effect of sexist humor on men's willingness to discriminate against women. In small groups, participants watched either sexist or neutral comedy skits from popular television shows and movies. The sexist comedy skits depicted women in demeaning, stereotyped roles (e.g., sex objects, angry feminists). Then, participants completed a second, allegedly unrelated project designed to determine how the student population believes the university should allocate budget cuts to student organisations. Their task was to allocate budget cuts across five different organisations as they saw fit. Men higher in hostile sexism cut more money from a women's organisation relative to the other four student organisations upon exposure to sexist comedy skits, but not neutral comedy skits. Further, a perceived norm of approval of funding cuts for the women's organisation among other men in that context mediated the effect; sexist humor created a social norm in which sexist men felt comfortable expressing their prejudice against women.

Endorsement of Negative Stereotypes

Disparagement humor communicates culturally shared stereotypes and prejudiced attitudes. Indeed, in order to 'get' a disparaging joke, one has to be aware of the cultural stereotypes or sentiments communicated in set-up or punchline of the joke. Accordingly, early experiments by Weston and Thomsen (1993) and Ford (1997) revealed that disparagement humor could prime negative stereotypes, making them more accessible and thus more likely to bias social judgment.

Two recent lines of research expand upon those studies supporting the hypothesis that disparagement humor creates a prejudiced norm that allows people to more freely express prejudice by ascribing negative stereotypes to a member of the disparaged group. Frist, Saucier, Strain, Miller, O'Dea, and Till (2018) tested the hypothesis that racial disparagement humor creates a prejudiced norm that allows Whites to more freely express *racial* prejudice. White participants read racist (anti-Black) jokes (e.g., 'Where do you hide your money from a Black thief? In your books.') or neutral jokes (e.g., 'Have you heard about corduroy pillows? They're making headlines.'). Then, they indicated how accurately various positive stereotypical traits (e.g., athletic, entertaining) and negative stereotypical traits (e.g., lazy, aggressive) describe Blacks. As expected, participants attributed negative (but not positive) stereotypes to Blacks to a greater degree after exposure to the racist versus neutral jokes. Saucier et al. concluded that racist humor loosened the norms of appropriate conduct, making expressions of prejudice seem less inappropriate.

Second, Argüello Gutiérrez, Carretero-Dios, Willis, & Moya (2016) examined the effect of disparagement humor on *in-group* stereotyping. They exposed college students either to humor that disparaged their university (in-group disparagement humor), non-humorous disparagement of their university, or neutral humor. Participants then completed a measure of stereotype activation similar to that described in Ford et al. (2001): they listed typical characteristics of students at their university and rated the favourability of each characteristic.

In Experiment 1, participants listed more stereotypical descriptions of their university following exposure to in-group disparagement humor versus non-humorous disparagement of their university or neutral humor. However, participants did not differ across conditions in how favourably they rated the in-group (typical students at their university). Importantly, these findings cannot be easily explained as merely a general priming effect as disparagement humor increased stereotyping relative to non-humorous disparagement. Humor as a medium for communicating disparagement played a critical role above and beyond the content of the disparaging message.

Experiments 2 and 3 identified in-group identification as a moderator for these effects. Specifically, in-group disparagement humor increased stereotyping only among students who weakly identified with their university (low identifiers). Only low-identifiers wrote more stereotypical descriptions of the in-group after exposure to in-group disparagement humor versus non-humorous disparagement or neutral humor.

Propensity to Commit Violence

A growing body of research extends the application of PNT by showing that disparagement humor can stretch the boundaries of acceptable conduct to include not only mild or subtle expressions of prejudice but also the propensity to commit violence against the targeted group. In particular, a number of studies have shown that sexist humor can disinhibit sexist men's expression of antipathy for women and foster sexist responses, even sexual violence, against women (Romero-Sánchez, Carretero-Dios, Megías, Moya, & Ford, 2017; Romero-Sánchez, Duran, Carretero-Dios, Megías, & Moya, 2010; Romero-Sánchez, Megías, & Carretero-Dios, 2019; Ryan & Kanjorski, 1998; Thomae & Pina, 2015; Thomae & Viki, 2013; Viki, Thomae, Cullen, & Fernandez, 2007).

Ryan and Kanjorski (1998) first established a connection between exposure to sexist humor and rape proclivity, men's self-reported inclination to rape a woman under circumstances in which they could not be discovered. Men who enjoyed sexist jokes also reported greater acceptance of rape myths, acceptance of violence against women, and self-reported willingness to rape a woman. Viki et al. (2007) extended these findings showing that exposure to sexist humor increased men's rape proclivity, particularly for acquaintance (versus stranger) rape scenarios.

Building on these findings, Romero-Sánchez, Duran, Carretero-Dios, Megías, and Moya (2010) exposed male participants to either four sexist jokes or four neutral jokes. Participants then completed a measure of rape proclivity consisting of five fictitious scenarios involving a man and a woman that end in rape. For each scenario, participants indicated the degree to which they would have behaved like the male character. Participants exposed to sexist jokes reported greater rape proclivity than those exposed to neutral jokes. This effect was moderated by the perceived aversiveness of the sexist jokes. Participants who expressed less aversion to the sexist jokes reported greater rape proclivity, suggesting that sexist humor functioned as a releaser of prejudice against women to the extent that men interpreted the humor in a non-serious, humor mindset.

Thomae and Viki (2013) further demonstrated that men's level of hostile sexism moderates the effect of sexist jokes on self-reported rape proclivity. Thomae and Viki found that exposure to sexist (versus neutral) jokes increased rape proclivity among men high but not low in hostile sexism. In keeping with prejudiced norm theory, Thomae and Viki suggested that a local norm implied by sexist jokes made sexist men feel comfortable expressing their antipathy toward women in the form of sexual aggression.

Finally, Romero-Sánchez et al. (2017) found that exposure to sexist humor affects, not only sexist men's self-reported willingness to rape a woman in a hypothetical scenario, but also how acceptable they view sexual violence perpetrated against women as a whole. This finding suggests that sexist humor might contribute to a broader culture of rape and sexual violence against women.

Group Status Moderates the Prejudice-releasing Effects of Disparagement Humor

Research has demonstrated that social groups are differentially vulnerable to the prejudice-releasing effects of disparagement humor depending on the position they occupy in society as described by Crandall et al.'s (2013) normative window theory of prejudice (Ford et al., 2014, Mendiburo-Seguel & Ford, 2019). Ford et al. (2014) demonstrated that disparagement humor fosters a willingness to discriminate against groups that occupy the normative ambiguity position of shifting acceptability (i.e., gay men, Muslims), but not groups for whom prejudice is already socially acceptable or justified (i.e., racists, terrorists). Prejudice against 'justified prejudice' groups is already acceptable; people do not need disparagement humor to justify or permit prejudice against them.

Mendiburo-Seguel and Ford (2019) conceptually replicated and extended these findings with a representative sample of residents of Santiago, Chile. First, they demonstrated that in Santiago, Chile, people view gay men as belonging in the ambiguous position of shifting acceptability—gay men are shifting from being acceptable to unacceptable targets of prejudice. In contrast, they view politicians as belonging in the position of justified prejudice—politicians are acceptable targets of prejudice.

Second, Mendiburo-Seguel and Ford found that participants judged prejudice against gay men as more acceptable after reading gay-disparaging jokes versus gay-disparaging serious comments or no disparagement. In contrast, reading politician-disparaging jokes did not increase tolerance for prejudice against politicians compared to the other two conditions.

Third, disparagement humor targeting one 'normative ambiguity' group (gay men) fostered the greater acceptance of prejudice against other normative ambiguity groups (e.g., women, transgenders/transsexuals, foreigners and lesbians) not targeted by the humor. This finding suggests that disparagement humor targeting one normative ambiguity group could promote discrimination against, not only that group but other groups that occupy a similar social position with regard to the acceptability of prejudice.

Disparagement Humor Legitimizes Prejudice

Hodson and colleagues (Hodson & MacInnis, 2016; Hodson, Rush, & MacInnis, 2010) developed their social dominance model of humor appreciation within a larger framework of social dominance theory (Pratto, Sidanius, Stallworth, & Malle, 1994; Sidanius & Pratto, 1999). Hodson et al. (2010) proposed that disparagement humor serves the abrasive intergroup function of legitimising prejudice; it makes the targeted group seem more deserving of prejudice (see Chapter 10 of this volume).

According to social dominance theory, societies are structured hierarchically so that there exists an imbalance in power and resources among high- versus low-status groups (Pratto et al., 1994; Sidanius & Pratto, 1999). Further, individuals differ in their social dominance orientation (SDO), that is, the degree to which they support the status quo of existing hierarchies and power imbalances. People at the high end of the SDO continuum want their in-group to dominate and be superior to relevant out-groups; they more strongly agree with statements like, 'Some groups of people are simply inferior to other groups,' and disagree with statements such as 'Group equality should be our ideal' (Pratto et al., 1994).

People high in SDO rely on 'legitimising myths' to justify bias against lower status out-groups. A legitimising myth is an attitude, value, ideology or belief that validates the status quo of inequality and mistreatment (Sidanius & Pratto, 1999). Hodson et al. (2010) proposed that 'cavalier humor beliefs' (CHB) represent a legitimising myth. People high in CHB have a general attitude of levity believing jokes are inherently harmless. Thus, they believe that a disparaging joke targeting a social group merits a 'pass' or a pardon because it is 'just a joke.'

Hodson et al. (2010) hypothesised that people high in SDO would become even more prejudiced against a low-status out-group upon exposure to disparagement humor *because* of their cavalier beliefs about the humor. They first measured Canadian participants' attitudes toward Mexicans (pre-test), SDO and degree of endorsement of CHB. Then, they exposed participants to jokes that disparaged Mexicans or to non-disparaging jokes. Finally, they measured participants' reactions to the jokes and their attitudes toward Mexicans (post-test).

They found that participants higher in SDO reported more negative post-test attitudes toward Mexicans following exposure to anti-Mexican jokes. CHB mediated this effect. Because participants high CHB view disparagement humor as benign amusement they were amused and not offended by the anti-Mexican jokes and as a result assented to an implicit subtext of the jokes that Mexicans are deserving targets of disparagement and disdain.

Disparagement Humor Subverts Prejudice (Potentially)

The research we have reviewed to this point suggests that disparagement humor can have the detrimental social consequence of fostering prejudice in intergroup settings. However, researchers have argued that it can have *beneficial* intergroup consequences when people use it constructively to expose the absurdity and ugliness of prejudice (e.g., Rappoport, 2005; Saucier, O'Dea, & Strain, 2016; Strain, Martens, & Saucier, 2016). Holmes and Marra (2002) referred to disparagement humor that exposes and challenges injustice and the status quo of inequality as 'subversive humor.' Subversive humor fits into Ruch and Heintz' (2016) more general category of corrective humor, humor intended to criticise, oppose and mock societal wrongdoings. Further, subversive humor is often expressed through the comic style or genre of *satire* (Ruch, Heintz, Platt, Wagner, & Proyer, 2018).

As mentioned earlier, disparagement humor communicates two paradoxical messages. The first is an explicit message derived from the content (e.g., sexist stereotypes, disparagement of women) along with an implicit affectively positive subtext (e.g., sexism can be trivialised). Humor is meant to be derived from the explicit message of disparagement. Subversive humor is subtly different. It often communicates the same explicit message (e.g., sexist stereotypes, disparagement of women) but with a different implicit subtext (e.g., sexism is wrong, Strain et al., 2016). It is meant to derive humor from the implicit subtext (e.g., making sexism, not women, the actual butt of the humor).

Accordingly, through subversive humor, members of oppressed social groups can 'appropriate' disparagement and slurs used to target them to serve positive intergroup functions. For instance, research has shown that members of oppressed groups use subversive humor to dissociate the in-group from the derogatory content of the humor (Bianchi, 2014), affirm in-group pride or solidarity (e.g., Bianchi, 2014; Boskin & Dorinson, 1985; Hom, 2008), take a critical stance against the usual derogatory uses of stereotypes and slurs (Bianchi, 2014; Hom, 2008; Hornsby, 2001), cope with oppression (Hart, 2007; Juni & Katz, 2001), remind people of the status quo of inequality and discrimination (Hom, 2008), and encourage collective action against inequality (Riquelme, Carretero-Dios, Megías, & Romero-Sánchez, 2020).

Believing it has the potential to undermine prejudice, many comedians (e.g., Iliza Schlesinger, Stephen Colbert, Ryan Niemiller, Bo Burnham, Chris Rock, and Hannah Gadsby) have incorporated subversive humor into their routines. For example, in one episode of the sketch show *Key & Peele*, known for its satirical racial comedy, Keegan Michael Key portrays a substitute teacher from the inner city (with a majority Black student body), now assigned to a class with mostly White students (Key & Peele, 2012). As he calls names for attendance, he regularly mispronounces the students' names (e.g., pronouncing 'Blake' as 'Bah-LAH-kay', and 'Aaron' as 'Ay-AY-ron'), growing frustrated when the students try to provide the correct pronunciations and continues to mispronounce their names even after being corrected. The sketch concludes when he calls on 'Tih-MOE-thee', and the sole Black student promptly replies 'pre-sent,' to which the teacher thanks the student for not 'playing games.' The goal of this sketch is not to mock the pronunciation of Black people's names, but rather to express, through humor, the frustration Black people can feel when Whites mispronounce their names.

Iliza Shlesinger similarly uses subversive humor in her stand-up comedy to challenge gender stereotypes and perceptions of feminism. In her show *Unveiled*, she regularly tells a disparaging joke and then points out the inappropriateness of the stereotypes or prejudice underlying the joke (Shlesinger & Paley, 2019).

Although comedians often use subversive humor with good intentions, empirical research suggests that it can backfire, making it a risky means of challenging prejudice. The purpose of subversive humor is to activate an anti-prejudice norm that discourages expressions of prejudice. In practice, however, it often does the opposite; it establishes a prejudiced norm that *encourages* expressions of prejudice (Saucier et al., 2018). Across three studies, Saucier et al. (2018) found that many participants (between one-third and one half) misinterpreted jokes intended to challenge anti-Black prejudice (e.g., 'What do you call a Black guy that flies a plane? A pilot you F*%#@ racist!') as Black-disparaging jokes. Participants missed the subversive intent underlying the jokes. Accordingly, the jokes intended to discourage prejudice had the opposite effect: participants ascribed more stereotypical characteristics to Blacks upon exposure to subversive versus neutral jokes.

Saucier et al. (2018) and Saucier et al. (2016) noted that subversive humor backfires because of an inherent 'Catch-22.' Subversive humor presents a surface message of prejudice (e.g., alluding to negative stereotypes) that one easily perceives with little effort. However, it takes effortful, critical thinking to perceive the deeper meaning of its less obvious subtext (i.e., prejudice is wrong). And, because humor (subversive or otherwise) signals one to withhold such critical thinking, one is apt to miss the subversive intent.

Research has shown that people are especially likely to miss the subversive subtext when their personal biases favour the surface message (e.g., LaMarre, Landreville, & Beam, 2009; Vidmar & Rokeach, 1974). LaMarre et al. (2009), for instance, examined people's perceptions of Stephen Colbert's satirical humor on *The Colbert Report*. Colbert (a liberal) portrayed a deadpan caricature of an extreme conservative, making jokes that mocked liberals on the surface, but that was intended to implicitly challenge conservative thinking through the absurdity of the character's dialogue (e.g., when discussing global warming, Colbert asks 'What's wrong with the ice melting... maybe now Greenland will actually turn green.'). LaMarre et al. (2009) found that while conservatives and liberals rated the clip as equally funny, they perceived it differently. Conservatives processed the surface-level message as reflecting Colbert's true beliefs, while liberals processed the subversive subtext as reflecting Colbert's true beliefs. Thus, conservatives missed the implicit subtext of the humor and interpreted it as anti-liberal; they tended to think Colbert identified as conservative and that he disliked liberals.

Next Steps

We have reviewed research demonstrating that disparagement humor is more than 'just a joke'; it has the power to affect its *recipients* in intergroup contexts by releasing, legitimising and possibly even subverting prejudice against the targeted group. Comparatively less research has addressed the consequences of disparagement humor from the *target's* perspective. Thus, an important next step is to more fully consider the social and emotional consequences of disparagement humor targeting one's own group.

Initial investigations from our laboratory have shown that ingroup disparagement humor can trigger a social identity threat, making people feel at risk of being devalued and rejected because of their group membership. In one line of research, Ford, Woodzicka, Petit, Richardson, and Lappi (2015) demonstrated that sexist humor could trigger social identity threat for women in the form of self-objectification: women reported greater state self-objectification and monitored their appearance more following exposure to sexist versus neutral comedy clips.

These findings raise a number of directions for future research on the consequences of sexist humor for women. First, self-objectification has been shown to impair women's ability to engage in focused attention. The vigilant self-monitoring of one's physical appearance usurps attentional resources from the performance of other cognitive tasks (e.g., Fredrickson, Roberts, Noll, Quinn, & Twenge, 1998). Thus, by triggering self-objectification, sexist humor might impair women's performance on tasks that require focused attention. Second, objectification has been shown to affect women's *behaviour* in social interactions. Saguy, Quinn, Dovidio, and Pratto (2010) found that women disclosed less about themselves to a male partner when they felt objectified, reducing their presentation of self to their bodies. It is possible then, that sexist humor negatively affects women in social interactions with men by narrowing their presentation of self and perhaps by depleting cognitive resources available for processing interpersonal information.

In another line of research, Ford *et al.* (2019) demonstrated that disparagement humor could trigger a social identity threat that involves a diminished self-concept and feelings of social exclusion. They found that when others engaged in humor disparaging one's political in-group, participants experienced a social identity threat—they feared others would devalue and discriminate against them because of their political affiliation. As a result, they constructed more negative representations of their possible selves and felt socially excluded.

Collectively, these initial lines of investigation inspire questions for future research about other ways people might experience social identity threat in response to disparagement humor. For instance, stereotype threat is a form of social identity threat induced by an expectation that people might judge a person according to negative stereotypes about their social group (Steele & Aronson, 1995; Steele, 1997). It can be stressful enough to impair performance on tasks for which one's group is negatively stereotyped (see Schmader, Johns, & Forbes, 2008, for a review). Thus, it is possible that in-group disparagement humor could induce stereotype threat and impair people's performance on tasks for which their groups are negatively stereotyped.

In conclusion, disparagement humor targeting a social group is paradoxical. It communicates an explicit, prejudiced message of denigration with an implicit subtext that the denigration is not malicious because it is not real. The playful subtext makes the intention and meaning of the denigrating message ambiguous and gives it the appearance of social acceptability. This 'failsafe' of ambiguity makes disparagement humor a powerful means of communicating prejudice that can have complex consequences in intergroup settings. Accordingly, we have reviewed an increasingly large body of research delineating the ways disparagement humor contributes to and potentially undermines prejudice in intergroup settings. Collectively, this research reveals that disparagement humor is more than benign amusement and that investigating its role in shaping social interaction represents a critical project of social importance.

References

Apter, M. J. (1982). *The experience of motivation: The theory of psychological reversals*. London, UK: Academic.

Apter, M. J. (1991). A structural-phenomenology of play. In J. H. Kerr & M. J. Apter (Eds.), *Adult play: A reversal theory approach* (pp. 13–29). Amsterdam, NL: Swets & Zeitlinger.

Argüello Gutiérrez, C., Carretero-Dios, H., Willis, G. B., & Moya, M. (2016). Joking about ourselves: Effects of disparaging humor on ingroup stereotyping. *Group Processes & Intergroup Relations, 21*(4), 568–583.

Attardo, S. (1993). Violation of conversational maxims and cooperation: The case of jokes. *Journal of Pragmatics, 19*, 537–558.

Berger, A. A. (1993). *An anatomy of humor*. New Brunswick, NJ: Transaction.

Berlyne, D. E. (1972). Humor and its kin. In J. H. Goldstein & P. E. McGhee (Eds.), *The psychology of humor* (pp. 43–60). New York, NY: Academic.

Bianchi, C. (2014). Slurs and appropriation: An echoic account. *Journal of Pragmatics, 66*, 35–44.

Bill, B., & Naus, P. (1992). The role of humor in the interpretation of sexist incidents. *Sex Roles, 27*, 645–664.
Boskin, J., & Dorinson, J. (1985). Ethnic humor: Subversion and survival. *American Quarterly, 37*, 81–97
Crandall, C. S., & Eshleman, A. (2003). A justification-suppression model of the expression and experience of prejudice. *Psychological Bulletin, 129*, 414–446.
Crandall, C. S., Eshleman, A., & O'Brien, L. (2002). Social norms and the expression and suppression of prejudice: The struggle for internalization. *Journal of Personality and Social Psychology, 82*(3), 359–378.
Crandall, C. S., Ferguson, M. A., & Bahns, A. J. (2013). When we see prejudice: The normative window and social change. In C. Stangor & C. S. Crandall (Eds.), *Stereotyping and Prejudice* (pp. 53–70). New York: Psychology Press.
Dovidio, J. F. (2001). On the nature of contemporary prejudice: *The third wave. Journal of Social, 57*, 829–849.
Duchscherer, K. M., & Dovidio, J. F. (2016). When memes are mean: Appraisals of and objections to stereotypic memes. *Translational Issues in Psychological Science, 2*(3), 335–345.
Emerson, J. P. (1969). Negotiating the serious import of humor. *Sociometry, 32*, 169–181.
Ferguson, M. A., & Ford, T. E. (2008). Disparagement humor: A theoretical and empirical review of psychoanalytic, superiority, and social identity theories. *Humor: International Journal of Humor Research, 21*(3), 283–312.
Ford, T. E. (1997). Effects of stereotypical television portrayals of African-Americans on person perception. *Social Psychology Quarterly, 60*, 266–278.
Ford, T. E. (2000). Effects of sexist humor on tolerance of sexist events. *Personality and Social Psychology Bulletin, 26*(9), 1094–1107.
Ford, T. E., & Ferguson M. A. (2004). Social consequences of disparagement humor: A prejudiced norm theory. *Personality and Social Psychology, 8*, 79–94.
Ford, T. E., Wentzel, E. R., & Lorion, J. (2001). Effects of exposure of to sexist humor on perceptions of normative tolerance of sexism. *European Journal of Social Psychology, 31*, 677–691.
Ford, T. E., Boxer, C. F., Armstrong, J. A., & Edel, J. R. (2008). More than just a joke: The prejudice-releasing function of sexist humor. *Personality and Social Psychology Bulletin, 34*, 159–170.
Ford, T. E., Woodzicka, J. A., Triplett, S. R., & Kochersberger, A. O. (2013). Sexist humor and beliefs that justify societal sexism. *Current Research in Social Psychology, 21*(7), 64–81.
Ford, T. E., Woodzicka, J. A., Triplett, S. R., Kochersberger, A. O., & Holden, C. J. (2014). Not all groups are equal: Differential vulnerability of social groups to the prejudice-releasing effects of disparagement humor. *Group Processes & Intergroup Relations, 17*, 178–199.
Ford, T. E., Richardson, K., & Petit, W. E. (2015). Disparagement humor and prejudice: Contemporary theory and research. *Humor: International Journal of Humor Research, 28*, 171–186.
Ford, T. E., Woodzicka, J. A., Petit, W. E., Richardson, K., & Lappi, S. K. (2015). Sexist humor as a trigger of state self-objectification in women. *Humor: International Journal of Humor Research, 28*(2), 253–269.
Ford, T. E., Breeden, C. J., O'Connor, E. C., & Banos, N. (2017). Jokes and humor in intergroup relations. *The Oxford encyclopedia of intergroup communication.* doi:10.1093/acrefore/9780190228613.013.431.

Ford, T. E., Buie, H. S., Mason, S. D., Olah, A. R., Breeden, C. J., & Ferguson, M. A. (2019). Diminished self-concept and social exclusion: Disparagement humor from the target's perspective. *Self and Identity, 19*(6), 698–718.

Fredrickson, B. L., Roberts, T. A., Noll, S. M., Quinn, D. M., & Twenge, J. M. (1998). That swimsuit becomes you: Sex differences in self-objectification, restrained easting, and math performance. *Journal of Personality and Social Psychology, 75*(1), 269–284.

Glick, P., & Fiske, S. T. (1996). The ambivalent sexism inventory: Differentiating hostile and benevolent sexism. *Journal of Personality and Social Psychology, 75*, 269–284.

Greenwood, D., & Gautam, R. (2020). What's in a tweet? Gender and sexism moderate reactions to antifat sexist humor on Twitter. *Humor: International Journal of Humor Research, 33*(2), 265–290.

Greenwood, D., & Isbell, L. M. (2002). Ambivalent sexism and the dumb blonde: Men's and women's reactions to sexist jokes. *Psychology of Women Quarterly, 26*, 341–350.

Hart, M. (2007). Humour and social protest. An introduction. *International Review of Social History, 52*(S15), 1–20.

Hodson, G., & MacInnis, C. C. (2016). Derogating humor as a delegitimization strategy in intergroup contexts. *Translational Issues in Psychological Science, 2*, 63–74.

Hodson, G., Rush, J., & MacInnis, C. C. (2010). A joke is just a joke (except when it isn't): Cavalier humor beliefs facilitate the expression of group dominance motives. *Journal of Personality and Social Psychology, 99*, 660–682.

Holmes, J., & Marra, M. (2002). Over the edge? Subversive humor between colleagues and friends. *Humor: International Journal of Humor Research, 15*, 65–87.

Hom, C. (2008). The semantics of racial epithets. *Journal of Philosophy, 105*, 416–440.

Hornsby, J., (2001). Meaning and uselessness: How to think about derogatory words. *Midwest Studies in Philosophy, 25*, 128–141.

Husband, C. (1977). The mass media and the functions of ethnic humor in a racist society. In A. J. Chapman & H. C. Foot (Eds.), *It's a funny thing, humor* (pp. 267–272). Elmsford, NY: Pergamon.

Johnson, A. M. (1990). The 'only joking' defense: Attribution bias or impression management? *Psychological Reports, 67*, 1051–1056.

Juni, S., & Katz, B. (2001). Self-effacing wit as a response to oppression: Dynamics in ethnic humor. *The Journal of General Psychology, 128*, 119–142.

Kane, T. R., Suls, J., & Tedeschi, J. T. (1977). Humour as a tool of social interactions. In A. J. Chapman & H. C. Foot (Eds.), *It's a funny thing, humor* (pp. 13–16). Elmsford, NY: Pergamon.

Key, K. M., & Peele, J. (2012, October 17). Substitute teacher – Key & Peele [Video]. [Comedy Central]. Retrieved from https://www.youtube.com/watch?v=Dd7FixvoKBw.

Khoury, R. M. (1985). Norm formation, social conformity, and the confederating function of humor. *Social Behavior and Personality, 13*, 159–165.

La Fave, L., & Mannell, R. (1976). Does ethnic humor serve prejudice? *Journal of Communication, 26*, 116–123.

La Fave, L., Haddad, J., Maesen, W. A. (1976). Superiority enhanced self-esteem, and perceived incongruity humor theory. In A. J. Chapman & H. C. Foot (Eds.). *Humor and laughter: Theory, research, and applications* (pp. 63–91). New York: John Wiley.

LaFrance, M., & Woodzicka, J. A. (1998). No laughing matter: Women's verbal and nonverbal reactions to sexist humor. In J. Swim & C. Stangor (Eds.), *Prejudice: The target's perspective* (pp. 61–80). San Diego, CA: Academic.

LaMarre, H. L., Landreville, K. D., & Beam, M. A. (2009). The irony of satire: Political ideology and the motivation to see what you want to see in 'The Colbert Report.' *International Journal of Press/Politics, 14*(2), 212–231.

Lewis, C. S. (1942). *The screwtape letters*. New York, NY: HarperCollins.
Mannell, R. C. (1977). Vicarious superiority, injustice, and aggression in humor: The role of the playful judgmental set. In A. J. Chapman & H. C. Foot (Eds.), *It's a funny thing, humor* (pp. 273–276). Elmsford, NY: Pergamon.
Martin, R. A., & Ford, T. E. (2018). *The psychology of humor: An integrative approach* (2nd ed.). Amsterdam, Netherlands: Academic Press.
Martineau, W. H. (1972). A model of the social functions of humor. In J. Goldstein & P. McGhee (Eds.), *The psychology of humor* (pp. 101–125). New York, NY: Academic Press.
McGhee, P. E. (1972). On the cognitive origins of incongruity humor: Fantasy assimilation versus reality assimilation. In: J. H. Goldstein & P. E. McGhee (Eds.), *The psychology of humor* (pp. 61–79). New York: Academic Press.
Mendiburo-Seguel, A., & Ford, T. E. (2019). The effect of disparagement humor on the acceptability of prejudice. *Current Psychology*. Advance online publication. doi:10.1007/s12144-019-00354-2.
Meyer, J. C. (2001). Humor as a double-edged sword: Four functions of humor in communication. *Communication Theory, 10*, 310–331.
Montemurro, B. (2003). Not a laughing matter Sexual harassment as 'material' on workplace-based situation comedies. *Sex Roles, 48*(9-10), 443–445.
Mulkay, M. (1988). *On humor: Its nature and its place in modern society*. New York, NY: Blackwell Inc.
Pearson, A. R., Dovidio, J. F., & Gaertner, S. L. (2009). The nature of contemporary prejudice: Insights from aversive racism. *Social and Personality Psychology Compass, 3*(3), 314–338.
Pratto, F., Sidanius, J., Stallworth, L. M., & Malle, B. F. (1994). Social dominance orientation: A personality variable predicting social and political attitudes. *Journal of Personality and Social Psychology, 67*, 741–763.
Rappoport, L. (2005). *Punchlines: The case for racial, ethnic, and gender humor*. Westport, CT: Praeger.
Raskin, V. (1985). *Semantic mechanisms of humor*. Dordrecht, NL: Reidel.
Riquelme, A. R., Carretero-Dios, H., Megías, J. L., & Romero-Sánchez, M. (2020). Joking for Gender Equality: Subversive Humor Against Sexism Motivates Collective Action in Men and Women with Weaker Feminist Identity. *Sex Roles*. Advance online publication. doi:10.1007/s11199-020-01154-w.
Romero-Sánchez, M., Duran, M., Carretero-Dios, H., Megías, J. L., & Moya, M. (2010). Exposure to sexist humor and rape proclivity: The moderator effect of aversiveness ratings. *Journal of Interpersonal Violence, 25*(12), 2339–2350.
Romero-Sánchez, M., Carretero-Dios, H., Megías, J. L., Moya, M., & Ford, T. E. (2017). Sexist humor and rape proclivity: The moderating role of joke teller gender and severity of sexual assault. *Violence against women, 23*(8), 951–972.
Romero-Sánchez, M., Megías, J. L., & Carretero-Dios, H. (2019). Sexist humor and sexual aggression against women: When sexist men act according to their own values or social pressures. *Journal of Interpersonal Violence*. Advance online publication. doi:10.1177/0886260519888518.
Ruch, W., & Heintz, S. (2016). The virtue gap in humor: Exploring benevolent and corrective humor. *Translational Issues in Psychological Science, 2*(1), 35–45.
Ruch, W., Heintz, S., Platt, T., Wagner, L., & Proyer, R. T. (2018). Broadening humor: Comic styles differentially tap into temperament, character, and ability. *Frontiers in Psychology, 9*(6), 1–18.
Ryan, K. M., & Kanjorski, J. (1998). The enjoyment of sexist humor, rape attitudes, and relationship aggression in college students. *Sex Roles, 38*, 743–756.

Saguy, T., Quinn, D. M., Dovidio, J. F., & Pratto, F. (2010). Interacting like a body: Objectification can lead women to narrow their presence in social interactions. *Psychological Science, 21*(2), 178–182.

Saucier, D. A., O'Dea, C. J., & Strain, M. L. (2016). The Bad, the good, the misunderstood: The social effects of racial humor. *Translational Issues in Psychological Science, 2*(1), 75–85.

Saucier, D. A., Strain, M. L., Miller, S. S., O'Dea, C. J., & Till, D. F. (2018). 'What do you call a Black guy who flies a plane?': The effects and understanding of disparagement and confrontational racial humor. *Humor: International Journal of Humor Research, 31*(1), 105–128.

Schmader, T., Johns, M., & Forbes, C. (2008). An integrated process model of stereotype threat effects on performance. *Psychological Review, 115*(2), 336–356.

Shlesinger, I., & Paley, S. (2019). *Unveiled* [Video]. Netflix. Retrieved from https://www.netflix.com/browse.

Sidanius, J., & Pratto, F. (1999). *Social dominance: An intergroup theory of social hierarchy and oppression.* Cambridge, UK: Cambridge University Press.

Steele, C. M. (1997). A threat in the air: How stereotypes shape the intellectual identities and performance of women and African-Americans. *American Psychologist, 52*, 613–629.

Steele, C. M., & Aronson, J. (1995). Stereotype threat and the intellectual test performance of African Americans. *Journal of Personality and Social Psychology, 69*(5), 797–811.

Stephenson, R. M. (1951). Conflict and control functions of humor. *American Journal of Sociology, 56*, 569–574.

Strain, M. L., Martens, A. L., & Saucier, D. A. (2016). 'Rape is the new black': Humor's potential for reinforcing and subverting rape culture. *Translational Issues in Psychological Science, 2*(1), 86–95.

Taylor, D. G., Sheatsley, P. B., & Greeley, A. M. (1978). Attitudes toward racial integration. *Scientific American, 238*(6), 42–49.

Thomae, M., & Pina, A. (2015) Sexist humor and social identity: the role of sexist humor in men's in-group cohesion, sexual harassment, rape proclivity, and victim blame. *Humor: International Journal of Humor Research, 28*(2), 187–204.

Thomae, M., & Viki, G. T. (2013). Why did the woman cross the road? The effect of sexist humor on men's rape proclivity. *Journal of Social, Evolutionary, and Cultural Psychology, 7*(3), 250–269.

Thomas, C. A., & Esses, V. M. (2004). Individual differences in reactions to sexist humor. *Group Process & Intergroup Relations, 7*(1), 89–100.

Vidmar, N., & Rokeach, M. (1974). Archie Bunker's bigotry: A study in selective perception and exposure. *Journal of Communication, 74*, 36–48.

Viki, G. T., Thomae, M., Cullen, A., & Fernandez, H. (2007). The effect of sexist humor and type of rape on men's self-reported rape proclivity and victim blame. *Current Research in Social Psychology, 13*(10), 122–132.

West, K., & Hewstone, M. (2012). Culture and contact in the promotion and reduction of anti-gay prejudice: Evidence from Jamaica and Britain. *Journal of Homosexuality, 59*(1), 44–66.

Weston, C. M., & Thomsen, C. J. (1993, August). *No joking matter: Sex-typed comedy perpetuates traditional views of women.* Paper presented at the American Psychological Association conference, Toronto, Canada.

Wright, C. L., DeFrancesco, T., Hamilton, C., & Vashist, N. (2018). 'Boy's Club:' Examining sexist humor on types of sexism and femininity ideology using two research approaches. *Humor: International Journal of Humor Research, 31*(1), 129–150.

Zenner, W. P. (1970). Joking and ethnic stereotyping. *Anthropological Quarterly*, 2, 93–113.

Zillman, D., & Cantor, J. R., (1996/[1976]). A dispositional theory of humor and mirth. In A. J. Chapman & H. C. Foot (Eds.), *Humor and laughter: Theory, research, and applications* (pp. 93–116). New York: John Wiley.

Zillmann, D. (1983). Disparagement humor. In P. E. McGhee & J. H. Goldstein (Eds.), *Handbook of humor research* (pp. 85–107). New York, NY: Springer-Verlag.

Ziv, A., & Gadish, O. (1990). The disinhibiting effects of humor: Aggressive and affective responses. *Humor: International Journal of Humor Research*, 3(3), 247–257.

10

CAVALIER HUMOR BELIEFS

Dismissing jokes as 'just jokes' facilitates prejudice and internalizes negativity among targets

Gordon Hodson and Elvira Prusaczyk

Our capacity for humor, it can be argued, is a fundamental aspect of the human experience, presumably making us relatively distinct from other animals[1]. We value humor tremendously, both in ourselves and in others (e.g., Lippa, 2007; Martin & Ford, 2018). For instance, the creation and appreciation of humor are often considered markers of intelligence (Tisljar & Bereczkei, 2005), making these qualities socially desirable. People with a good sense of humor are also considered to be more attractive and romantically suitable (McGee & Shevlin, 2009), and partners who use more affiliative humor—humor intended to amuse others and put others at ease (Martin, Puhlik-Doris, Larsen, Gray, & Weir, 2003)—are more satisfied with their relationships (Caird & Martin, 2014). Without doubt, humor makes our lives richer, leaving many to believe that it prolongs longevity (although some empirical evidence speaks to the contrary, see Cernerud & Olsson, 2004; Martin, 2002; Stewart & Thompson, 2015). Meta-analytic data also indicates that employees who use humor at work are more productive and satisfied, more bonded with their coworkers, and less likely to experience burnout (Mesmer-Magnus, Glew, & Viswesvaran, 2012). It is little wonder that the phrase *laughter is the best medicine* has social traction among creatures who are not only hedonistic but incredibly social, linguistic, capable of symbolic thought, and cognitively sophisticated.

Given its positive connotations, it is not surprising that humor plays a key role in conveying status. Those higher (*vs.* lower) in status use more dominant laughter, and those using more dominant laugher are perceived as being higher (*vs.* lower) in status (Oveis, Spectre, Smith, Liu, & Keltner, 2016)[2]. Moreover, higher (*vs.* lower) income people tend to use aggressive humor more frequently (Navarro-Carrillo, Torres-Marín, & Carretero-Dios, 2020), likely signaling their status and (alleged) superiority over others. Unsurprisingly, therefore, humor and joke-telling can be used to denigrate, delegitimize, mock, bully, or otherwise target others. Consider a recent example from the 2020 COVID-19 pandemic, widely thought to originate in China. At the height of the crisis, a Chinese-born, American-raised CBS News Whitehouse reporter claimed that a Trump aide made a joke to her about the 'Kung Flu' virus (Mackey, 2020). This represents an explicitly intergroup 'joke' no doubt intended to belittle Chinese people and rule them in as suitable targets for bias. This comes at a time when President Trump was trying to label the virus the *Chinese* or *Wuhan* virus, against scientific protocols, and when the FBI was issuing concerns about spikes in anti-Asian hate crimes (Margolin, 2020). That this incident happened at the White House, during a deadly pandemic, illustrates the strategic importance of intergroup humor.

In the present chapter, we focus largely on the *intergroup* functions of humor, where the goal is to demean (i.e., belittle) or to attack (i.e., aggressive) the social group in question. In either case, both the purpose and the outcome concern delegitimizing and/or disempowering an outgroup. Unlike regular insults, (disparaging) humor relays insulting content with an air of fun and levity, providing the communicator with cover against anti-prejudice social norms. In broad terms, humor can be employed to attain group dominance or to maintain the status quo in ways that keep existing hierarchies intact (see Hodson & MacInnis, 2016). Below we outline some of the key findings from our research lab on the question of disparaging humor as a tool for (inter)group dominance.

Intergroup Functions of Disparaging Humor

People naturally differ from each other in terms of their humor temperaments, with some of these differences having implications for intergroup relations. Indeed, researchers have become increasingly interested in the ways that humor is used, and for what purpose(s), both positive and negative. One of the dominant contemporary approaches, proposed by Rod Martin and colleagues (Martin et al., 2003; Vernon, Martin, Schermer, & Mackie, 2008) concerns individual differences in humor styles (or what we might call 'functions' or 'uses,' because they speak to *why* humor is engaged). *Affiliative* humor involves social bonding with others and generally serves a positive function, as does *self-enhancing* humor (coping with stress; self-regulation). From the Humor Styles Questionnaire (Martin et al., 2003), an affiliative humor item reads 'I enjoy making people laugh,' whereas a self-enhancement item reads 'My humorous outlook on life keeps me from getting overly upset or depressed about things.' In these ways, humor can be employed to bring us closer to others and buffer ourselves against threats to the self. Interestingly, these authors also posit that humor can play distinctly negative roles, of the sort that are particularly relevant to this chapter. One involves *self-defeating humor*, whereby the goal is to endear oneself to others by putting oneself down; a sample item includes 'I will often get carried away in putting myself down if it makes my family or friends laugh.' The other negative function of humor style involves *aggressive* motives, characterized by hostility, apathy, and manipulation or exploitation; a sample item includes 'If I don't like someone, I often use humor or teasing to put them down.' It is this last function of humor that is the most directly relevant to intergroup dynamics.

Aggressive Functions of Humor Relevant to Prejudice

In one study, we administered the Humor Styles Questionnaire to a Canadian university sample (98% White), along with assessing four prejudice-relevant individual differences (Hodson, MacInnis, & Rush, 2010). Modern racism (McConahay, Hardee, & Batts, 1981) assesses the belief that discrimination against Black people is largely historical and no longer relevant. We also assessed a cognitive style variable, Personal Need for Structure (Neuberg & Newsom, 1993), that taps basic epistemic needs for routine and cognitive simplicity, a factor in predicting prejudicial responses (Dhont & Hodson, 2014; Jost, Glaser, Kruglanski, & Sulloway, 2003). We also assessed two ideological variables that carry much of the weight in predicting prejudice (Altemeyer, 1998; Hodson, MacInnis, & Busseri, 2017): Right-wing authoritarianism (RWA; Altemeyer, 1996) reflects the desire for conformity, tradition, and punishment of and aggression against deviants, whereas social dominance orientation (SDO; Sidanius & Pratto, 1999) reflects beliefs that hierarchies and intergroup dominance are preferable means for structuring society.

Overall, our participants endorsed the positive (affiliative; self-enhancing) relative to negative humor functions. But we found that using humor for aggressive purposes was significantly correlated with SDO ($r = .34$), Modern Racism ($r = .24$), and Personal Need for Structure ($r = -.18$), but not with RWA ($r = -.02$). Especially noteworthy is that SDO uniquely predicted aggressive humor use after accounting for the other variables, whereas RWA did not. Thus, aggressive humor use is related to *dominance* motives, but not necessarily to motives relevant to conformity or tradition. Also noteworthy is the finding that these prejudice-relevant variables were largely unrelated to the other humor functions. Prejudice-prone people, it seems, use aggressive humor to attack others, but do not use humor to make themselves feel positive or to bond with others. Such people particularly draw on the negative functions of humor, highlighting the importance of considering humor communications to understand intergroup bias better.

Group-Based Dominance Model of Humor Appreciation

In the intergroup relations literature, theorists have become increasingly interested not only in documenting the existence of dominance and prejudice but in better understanding the mechanisms through which such processes operate. Key in this development has been Social Dominance Theory (Sidanius & Pratto, 1999), a theoretical approach arguing that human societies are overwhelmingly organized hierarchically and that people have a vested interest in attaining or maintaining existing hierarchies in the service of (among other interests) dominance motives. These unequal and hierarchical social structures promote differential and unequal access to power, in terms of finances but also symbolic and cultural power. As such, those in dominant positions (e.g., men in the case of sex-based hierarchies; White people in the case of many race-based hierarchies) endorse ideologies that justify the ranked or ordered intergroup positions.

One key tool in the study of Social Dominance Theory is SDO (discussed above), an individual difference measure of the degree to which people view hierarchy and dominance as a favorable way to structure society. SDO is most strongly associated with the 'dark' personality traits of Machiavellianism, psychopathy, and to some degree, narcissism (Hodson, Hogg, & MacInnis, 2009). With the common core of this so-called Dark Triad correlating almost perfectly with (low) Honesty-Humility (see Hodson et al., 2018), this means that SDO corresponds to being low in sincerity, greed avoidance, fairness, and modesty (see Lee & Ashton, 2004). Moreover, as characterized by Duckitt (2006, p. 685), SDO characterizes 'motivational goals of group power, dominance, and superiority over others.' Not surprisingly, therefore, SDO is a strong predictor of prejudices (Altemeyer, 1998; Hodson et al., 2017; Pratto, Sidanius, Stallworth, & Malle, 1994; Sidanius & Pratto, 1999).

Yet those higher in SDO do not operate in a social vacuum. Rather, in contemporary society, they rely on *legitimizing myths* that release or facilitate the release of social dominance motives. That is, 'group-based hierarchy is ... affected by ... legitimizing myths ... [the] attitudes, values, beliefs, stereotypes that provide moral and intellectual justification for the social practices that distribute social value' (Sidanius & Pratto, 1999, p. 45). Legitimizing myths are considered potent to the extent that they can mediate (or explain the relation) between dominance motives (as reflected in SDO) and intergroup outcomes such as discrimination or other means to maintain or exacerbate hierarchies. Within the Social Dominance framework, such ideologies tend to be rather broad and general. For instance, the Protestant Work Ethic (belief that hard work will be rewarded) can function as a legitimizing myth to justify restricting resources to privileged groups and not, equitably distributing them to ethnic minorities. But legitimizing myths can also be more specific and targeted. In humor contexts, we posited that beliefs that 'jokes are just jokes,' and by implication amusing and harmless, can operate as legitimizing myths to facilitate the release of prejudice toward lower status outgroups. This line of thought became central to our development of the Group Dominance Model of Humor Appreciation (Hodson, Rush, & MacInnis, 2010; Hodson & MacInnis, 2016).

Cavalier Humor Beliefs (CHBs)

As noted by Ford and colleagues, humor contexts prime the expectation of levity, setting the stage for relaxed social norms (Ford, 2000; Ford, Boxer, Armstrong, & Edel, 2008; see Chapter 9 of this volume). We reasoned that people presumably differ in the degree to which they, in general, hold the belief that humor should be treated with levity, as 'just a joke.' Specifically, we argued that:

> ... CHBs capture a lighthearted, less serious, uncritical, and nonchalant mindset toward humor generally. Theoretically, those higher in CHB are unconcerned about the social consequences of joke telling, believing instead that people should lighten up and avoid reading meaning into jokes. By stressing the positive value of humor and casually disregarding negative outcomes from jokes, CHBs may serve as legitimizing myths releasing dominance motives.
>
> (Hodson, Rush et al., 2010, p. 663)

Some of this conceptualization is worth unpacking here. First, people will differ along a continuum, with some people very uptight and rigid around humor (and thus easily offended), and others at the other extreme feeling that people take comical communications too seriously (and thus are not easily offended). Most people, of course, would fall somewhere in the middle of these extremes. Theoretically this distinction this should apply to most jokes, not simply sensitive or disparaging jokes. One consequence is that those higher (*vs.* lower) in CHB should view most jokes as relatively more amusing and less offensive, including rather bland and neutral jokes, but also including biting, racy, provocative, and outwardly disparaging jokes. Expressing the mindset that virtually all types of jokes are amusing and inoffensive provides the 'grease' to facilitate the expression of dominance motives, stressing the importance of 'letting go,' relaxing, and allowing the joke to be 'just a joke' and nothing more. That is, deeming both neutral and outgroup disparaging jokes to have positive social value offers psychological cover for truly prejudicial expressions (Hodson, Rush et al., 2010), much in the same way that ambiguous situations (i.e., those also offering non-prejudicial explanations for behaviors), allow people to express intergroup negativity (Dovidio & Gaertner, 2004; Hodson, Dovidio, & Gaertner, 2002; Hodson, Dovidio, & Gaertner, 2004). In an attributional sense, attention can be drawn away from potential accusations of bias and aggression, and instead toward the socially approved norms of relaxation, light-heartedness, and affiliative norms characterizing humor contexts. Dismissing one's laughter to an off-color joke because it is 'just a joke' could be interpreted as either bias or frivolity, making CHB a strong contender to serve as a legitimizing myth.

An initial project (Hodson, Rush et al., 2010, Study 1) set about developing the CHB scale with a sample from a Canadian university. The six items (see Table 10.1) formed a single factor with strong internal consistency. Important for the theoretical angle, CHB correlated positively and significantly with most of the Humor Styles Questionnaire, most notably with affiliative humor ($r = .32$), self-enhancing humor ($r = .17$), and aggressive humor ($r = .49$), but not with self-defeating humor ($r = .05$). That is, CHB captures both positive (affiliative; self-enhancing) and negative (aggressive) functions of humor. In our thinking, this makes CHB an ideal candidate to serve as a legitimizing myth in humor contexts. On the one hand, the cheerfulness and lightheartedness expressed by CHB enhances one's likeability and cues openness for social bonding; on the other hand, it functions to act out aggression on others. One can pass jokes off as just jokes for

TABLE 10.1 Item Wording for the Cavalier Humor Beliefs (CHBs) Scale

Sometimes people need to relax and realize that a joke is just a joke.
Society needs to lighten up about jokes and humor generally.
People get too easily offended by jokes.
It is okay to laugh at the differences between people.
Jokes are simply fun.
People should try to tell jokes that don't put others down (reverse scored).

Note: From Hodson et al. (2010).

'good' reasons, but also 'bad' ones, allowing its use to have some ambiguity that can fuel bias.' This dual nature can allow one to pass a joke off as 'just a joke' without necessarily incurring social costs. Although CHB was related to low seriousness as expected, it was not related to being cheerful or in a positive/negative mood. Again, it is well poised to serve as a levity-inducing construct that encourages and promotes relaxed social norms. Consistent with this notion, CHB was positively (and significantly) correlated with SDO (but not RWA) and with modern racism toward Black people, but was negatively (and significantly) correlated with universal orientation (endorsement of tolerant and inclusive ideologies) and internal motivations to control prejudice. At the very least it appears that holding a cavalier attitude toward humor is not related to simply regarding jokes as mere jokes, but rather is linked systematically to prejudice-relevant constructs, levity, and lack of personal restraint on biases.

In Study 1 of Hodson, Rush et al. (2010), participants were also exposed to several jokes and asked to rate the degree to which the jokes were *amusing* (i.e., pleasurable) and *inoffensive* (i.e., harmless). All jokes used in that paper can be found in its Appendix B. One of the jokes was neutral in terms of human intergroup relations (A man went for a meal at a chicken restaurant. He asked the manager, 'How do you prepare the chickens?' The manager said, 'We just tell them straight out that they're going to die'), and the other three disparaged Mexicans, a lower-status group (e.g., 'What's the first thing a Mexican girl does when she wakes up? Walks home'). Inclusion of such jokes was critical for testing the Group-Dominance Model of Humor Appreciation, specifically, that (a) for anti-Mexican jokes, the effects of SDO on increased ratings of joke amusement and inoffensiveness would be mediated by CHB (see Figure 10.1); but (b) SDO would not predict favorability ratings of neutral jokes, although CHB would. The Group-Dominance model predicts that this would be expected even after controlling for disliking of the outgroup in question (i.e., attitudes), that is, not simply being a matter of laughing at a group we dislike (an interesting finding, but one already well documented in the field). The results supported the model, such that the effect of SDO on anti-Mexican joke reactions was fully indirect via CHB, supporting the notion that CHB serves as a potent legitimizing myth.

The subsequent study (Hodson, Rush et al., 2010, Study 2) sought not only to evaluate the replicability of this finding but to introduce some methodological

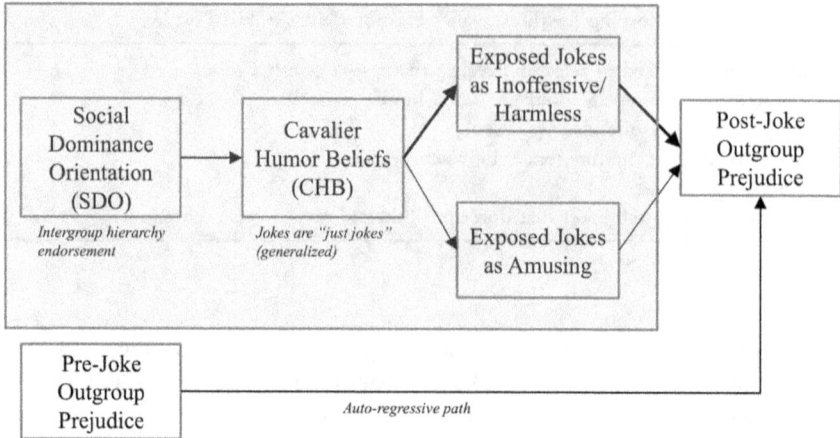

FIGURE 10.1 The Group-Dominance Model of Humor Appreciation, depicting how Cavalier Humor Beliefs facilitate 'favorable' reactions to outgroup-disparaging humor, which in turn exacerbate outgroup prejudice. Thicker paths through inoffensiveness/ harmlessness indicate primary theoretical mechanism. Reproduced with permission from Hodson and MacInnis (2016)

refinements. Each participant in this study read four neutral jokes, plus 18 outgroup disparaging jokes, providing a more complete and fulsome analysis. Specifically, we tested a key aspect of the Group-Dominance model we had proposed, namely that CHB should serve as a legitimizing myth (explaining the relation between SDO and favorable joke reactions) with regard to jokes targeting a *lower* status outgroup (e.g., Mexicans), but not with regard to a higher status outgroup (e.g., Americans), or toward the ingroup (Canadians). That is, a cavalier approach to humor was posited to grease the wheels of dominance toward a lower status outgroup specifically. This reasoning is predicated on theorizing and findings that SDO (but not RWA) is particularly focused on bias toward 'socially subordinate groups low in power and status' (Duckitt, 2006, p. 684). Thus, in this study, participants read and responded to the same neutral jokes and the same disparaging jokes, but we systemically altered whether the target of any particular joke was the lower status outgroup, higher status outgroup, or the ingroup. This method experimentally controls for joke content, ensuring that any appreciation of disparaging jokes is a direct function of whom the joke targets, not properties of the joke itself. Controlling for pre-existing attitudes toward the group in question (as per Study 1), we found support for the Group-Dominance model. That is, CHB facilitated the expression of social dominance motives on favorable joke reactions, but only for jokes disparaging the lower-status outgroup (i.e., not for jokes disparaging the higher-status group, one's ingroup, or for the neutral jokes).

The findings reviewed thus far show support for CHB serving as a legitimizing myth in humor contexts. But our attention has been focused on reactions toward the jokes in question, in terms of their amusement levels and inoffensiveness, while controlling for pre-test attitudes toward the joke target. Yet presumably one of the reasons researchers would care about positive reactions toward outgroup disparaging jokes is that these reactions in themselves might, in turn, foster greater prejudice. Hodson, Rush, et al. (2010, Study 3) tested this assumption , but this time also assessing attitudes toward Mexicans *following* joke exposure and the expressed joke reactions, in a test of the 'extended' Group-Dominance Model of Humor Appreciation (see the full model in Figure 10.1). In the non-disparagement condition, participants read and reacted to four neutral jokes, whereas in the disparagement condition participants read and evaluated a neutral joke followed by three anti-Mexican jokes. Any between-group differences in such a design would be attributable to exposure to jokes targeting Mexicans. As expected, within the neutral condition, CHB did not facilitate SDO-based joke reactions or subsequent outgroup attitudes. However, in the disparagement condition, CHB not only facilitated SDO-based joke reactions but predicted greater prejudice toward Mexicans. Moreover, it did so through expressions that the jokes were inoffensive (i.e., harmless), even after statistically controlling for pre-existing prejudice toward Mexicans. Particularly compelling is the finding that this extended model effect occurred through ratings of joke inoffensiveness, rather than through joke amusement. Apparently dismissing a joke as harmless is better suited to rationalizing or legitimizing an expressed bias than is finding the joke pleasurable.

Being Targeted by Disparaging Humor: Internalizing or Rejecting Negativity

To this point, our review has focused on a dominant or advantaged group (e.g., Canadians) reacting to disparaging humor targeting a less dominant, disadvantaged group (e.g., Mexicans). In keeping with the Group-Dominance Model of Humor Appreciation, we see that we do not simply laugh at outgroups we dislike. Rather, humor contexts can play a key role in fostering negativity toward lower-status groups in ways that can keep outgroups in a disadvantaged social position. Social dominance motives play a role, impacting both joke reactions and post-exposure outgroup prejudices, through the greater endorsement of CHB, a legitimizing myth that helps link dominance motives with outgroup derision.

We have focused considerably on the *perpetration* of outgroup bias (see also Ford et al., 2008). But an equally important and valid question concerns how people, particularly from *disadvantaged or lower status groups*, react to disparaging humor that targets their ingroup. For instance, do women simply reject sexist jokes[3]? Or do they internalize the negativity? Moreover, what factors predict whether any specific woman rejects or internalizes a joke? Past research informs us that women higher in hostile sexism, an antipathy toward women coupled with perceived inferiority of women relative to men, show greater favorability toward sexist jokes (Greenwood & Isbell, 2002; LaFrance & Woodzicka, 1998; Thomas & Esses, 2004; Woodzicka & Ford, 2010). Antagonistic attitudes toward women, it appears, makes women more open to sexist jokes. Although the impact of SDO among women on predicting sexist jokes reactions has been previously unexplored, among men, SDO predicts favorable reactions (Thomas & Esses, 2004), leading us to speculate that SDO might again play a role in predicting humor reactions, but here among the disadvantaged group (women).

Before launching our investigation, we recognized that reactions to sexist jokes among women would not be uniform. Ingroup-disparaging humor, for instance, is more palatable when originating from one's ingroup than outgroup (see Thai, Borgella, & Sanchez, 2019). This nicely illustrates that humor does not take place in a vacuum, with stimuli being funny or unfunny, or offensive or inoffensive, solely on the basis of their own properties. Rather, humor and jokes are evaluated and employed as a function of social and intergroup factors. What is funny when originating from Group X might be deemed offensive when originating from Group Y. Mainstream theories in social psychology, such as Social Identity Theory (Tajfel & Turner, 1979), Self-Categorization Theory (Turner, Hogg, Oakes, Reicher, & Wetherell, 1987), and Integrated Threat Theory (Stephan & Stephan, 2000) would predict a general resistance to negativity from the outgroup, in the interest of bolstering the ingroup. Pro-ingroup bias is, after all, a strong player in intergroup relations (Brewer, 1979; Greenwald & Pettigrew, 2014). But we also recognized that members of disadvantaged groups could express views that run contrary to their group's interest, perhaps best captured by System Justification Theory (Jost & Hunyady, 2002), whereby people can prioritize stability and epistemic certainty over resistance (see also Ford, Woodzicka, Triplett, & Kochersberger, 2013).

Specifically, we reasoned that female university students would, overall, react unfavorably toward sexist jokes targeting their group. In our context, this would involve rating jokes about domestic violence against women (for example) as unamusing and offensive. But we also anticipated that women higher in CHB, hostile sexism or SDO might demonstrate *less resistance* and hence *more acceptance or internalization* of such jokes. Like men, women endorsing hierarchy-enhancing ideologies such as hostile sexism or SDO should consider sexist (but not neutral) jokes to be more amusing and less offensive, despite the fact that such favorable reactions go against their group's self-interest. In contrast, CHB (but not hostile sexism or SDO) was expected to predict favorability toward sexist and neutral jokes (as in Hodson, Rush et al., 2010). Given that prejudice-prone people are more likely to adopt CHB, likely as a cover for their prejudice, we expected CHB to be more relevant for predicting amusement and lower offensiveness for *sexist* than neutral jokes. In responding relatively more positively to sexist jokes, women might express their biases in a socially approved way.

In our first study (Prusaczyk & Hodson, 2020, Study 1) we adopted a within-subjects design, randomly exposing female undergraduates at a Canadian university to 30 written jokes, asking them to rate each for amusement and offensiveness. Ten of these jokes were *aggressive* (e.g., 'I like my violence like I like my beer: domestic'; 'What do you tell a woman with two black eyes? Nothing, you already told her twice'), 10 were *belittling* (e.g., 'What do women and beer bottles have in common? They're both empty from the neck up'; 'What do UFOs and smart women have in common? You keep hearing about them, but never see any'), and 10 were *neutral* (e.g., 'How do you make an Octopus laugh? With ten-tickles'). The first two can both be considered 'sexist' but of a distinct nature. The aggressive jokes advocated or condoned violence against women, whereas belittling jokes were non-violent yet demeaned women in terms of their intelligence and abilities. Participants also filled out CHB, hostile sexism, and SDO individual difference measures.

In this study, CHB correlated positively with favorability toward all joke types, but hostile sexism and SDO only correlated with approval of sexist (not neutral) jokes, as expected. For each joke type, we specified a model whereby these individual difference measures simultaneously predicted both joke amusement and offensiveness. As expected, CHB uniquely predicted greater amusement and lower offensiveness regarding all joke types (aggressive, belittling, neutral), even after controlling for SDO and hostile sexism. In contrast, greater hostile sexism predicted greater joke appreciation for both types of sexist jokes (aggressive; belittling) but not neutral jokes; SDO played little to no unique role in predicting joke reactions.

Interestingly, the relation between CHB and lower joke offensiveness ratings was significantly stronger when predicting aggressive or belittling jokes than when predicting neutral jokes. This is in keeping with our proposition that CHB is more than simply benign but rather promotes bias. If CHB were simply and purely about treating a 'joke as just a joke,' encouraging levity around humor, such differential patterns along intergroup lines would not be evidenced.

In Prusaczyk and Hodson (2020, Study 1), we had used a within-subjects design which allowed us to compare reactions across joke types controlling for the respondent. That is, every participant read and rated all jokes. This design helped us to recognize CHB and hostile sexism (but not SDO) as independent players in this ingroup-derogation space. For Study 2, we introduced a between-subjects design, with female university participants randomly assigned to read the aggressive or neutral jokes from Study 1.[4] Across conditions, participants were informed: 'Imagine you are sitting in a train. You overhear two men telling each other the following jokes and they laugh.' Our goal was to encourage participants in the aggressive condition to frame the jokes as originating from the advantaged outgroup, not from the ingroup (see Thai et al., 2019). Pre-exposure, participants completed measures of CHB and hostile sexism, and post-exposure they completed various dependent measures: discrimination against women, sexism, and support for women's rights. We expected that women exposed to aggressive sexist (*vs.* neutral) jokes would, overall, react unfavorably toward the jokes, based in part on the results of Study 1. But we also expected CHB and hostile sexism to moderate or modulate the reactions to the manipulation, such that those higher (*vs.* lower) in CHB or hostile sexism (measured pre-manipulation) would attenuate their pro-ingroup responses. Put another way, we expected that women who treat jokes as 'just jokes,' along with those who feel antipathy toward women, would be more likely to internalize the negativity from the aggressively sexist jokes[5].

The results of Prusaczyk and Hodson (2020, Study 2) revealed several key findings of note. As expected, when exposed to aggressive (*vs.* neutral) jokes, women reacted unfavorably, rating such jokes as unamusing and offensive[6]. But these effects were significantly moderated by pre-existing levels of CHB and hostile sexism. That is, women higher (*vs.* lower) in CHB (or hostile sexism) pushed back significantly less against the aggressive (*vs.* neutral) jokes, finding these jokes relatively funny and inoffensive. Impressively, CHB exerted this attenuation effect even after statistically controlling for hostile sexism, meaning that it is not simply a case of women-hating women finding sexist jokes more acceptable. Independent of one's sexism, CHB attenuates the pushback reaction against in-group harming jokes. Interestingly, we found evidence that CHB (and to a lesser degree, hostile sexism) also moderated the effect of jokes on post-exposure discrimination toward women and modern sexism, such that women higher (*vs.* lower) in CHB became relatively more discriminatory and sexist following the joke exposure.

Such findings are consistent with Prejudiced Norm Theory (Ford & Ferguson, 2004), whereby sexist jokes promote more sexism, especially among men and women higher in hostile sexism. Importantly, our findings extend Prejudiced Norm Theory by isolating the role of CHB and showing that regardless of pre-existing sexist beliefs, CHB perpetuates biases against women following exposure to sexist joke. Unlike hostile sexism, the lightheartedness afforded by CHB can mask women's prejudiced intentions. That is, people can more easily hide behind outwardly benign beliefs about humor than hostile views about women, making CHB an equally important variable to target in interventions.

Of note, neither CHB nor hostile sexism moderated the impact of aggressive jokes on women's rights, highlighting a boundary effect on its influence. Holding a cavalier approach to humor might make women more open to sexist humor, and may exacerbate bias (discrimination, sexism) against women in society, but even high endorsement of CHB does not inhibit pushback against basic rights for one's group.

Humor as a Tool in the Delegitimization Toolkit

At a Democrat Primary event on February 19, 2020, Elizabeth Warren challenged fellow contender Mike Bloomberg on his track record with women, directly asking him to disclose the number of women under his employ who had signed Non-Disclosure Agreements (a tool often used to silence women, particularly around claims of sexual harassment or sexism). His retort plays straight from the CHB playbook we have outlined: 'None of them accused me of doing anything other than maybe they didn't like the joke I told' (Phillips, 2020). Roughly translated, Bloomberg was arguing that his actions were *just* humor-based, that there is nothing of importance to see or consider there, that some women simply did not 'get' his jokes as *mere* jokes. In an age where open displays of prejudice and discrimination are increasingly disapproved of, and where the #MeToo movement has drawn a sharp focus on bullies, harassers, and assaulters, we (unfortunately) expect CHBs to become more (not less) relevant as a means to fuel prejudice and direct attributions of bias away from perpetrators.

As evident in this review, humor is a powerful form of communication, and humor can be a powerful conduit to promote intergroup bias. We have seen how CHBs might appear relatively value-free, and non-intergroup in nature, and indeed those higher (*vs.* lower) in CHB express favorability toward all types of humor, including neutral jokes (Hodson, Rush et al., 2010; Prusaczyk & Hodson, 2020). But we have also seen but that CHB is positively associated with prejudices (racism, sexism) and ideologies such as SDO that emphasize group-based dominance. Clearly, CHBs have the power to do more than simply release the appreciation of comical communications and foster levity. In particular, we have evidenced how higher-status groups employ CHBs to facilitate the expression of social dominance motives on lower status outgroups in ways that can then exacerbate prejudice toward the joke-targeted group (Hodson, Rush et al., 2010, Studies 1–3). The influence of these dominance motives operates above and beyond mere prejudice toward that lower status outgroup, that is, taking pleasure in humor that targets disliked groups (although we find evidence for that process also). We have also seen how CHBs can operate among lower-status groups (e.g., women) when faced with jokes communicated by a more advantaged outgroup (e.g., men) targeting the ingroup (Prusaczyk & Hodson, 2020). Although women overall rejected the sexist jokes, CHB played a role in modulating these reactions. Even controlling for hostile sexism, CHB not only predicted greater joke amusement ratings and lower offensiveness ratings, but it did so significantly more for aggressive and belittling jokes than for neutral jokes, affording us a peek at the subtle intergroup relevance of CHB. Moreover, women higher (*vs.* lower) in CHB, and to some extent higher (*vs.* lower) in hostile sexism, were less likely to pushback against the sexist jokes, and more likely to endorse subsequent anti-woman sexism and discrimination (but with no effect on women's rights). Thus, passing jokes off as 'just jokes,' in a derogatory humor context, effectively inhibits reactance against an attack toward the ingroup, and instead promotes anti-ingroup sentiments. Whether CHBs operate among dominant groups toward lower status groups, or among lower-status groups dealing with humor-based attacks from advantaged outgroups, they function to maintain a status quo that favors dominant groups.

As such, humor and CHBs in particular play key roles in the delegitimization process. According to Bar-Tal and Hammack (2012), the goal of delegitimization is to slot people into low-value groups to remove them from moral consideration afforded to most people (or at least to higher status people). According to Hodson and MacInnis (2016), there are three key 'legs' to the delegitimization toolkit, any of which can be at play when attempting to marginalize and depower other social groups (see Figure 10.2). One strategy is to endorse the status quo, that is, to justify existing power structures and group positions in the hierarchy. Prioritizing the system ahead of people delegitimizes concerns about those at the bottom of the social structure: *It's just the way things are*. Another strategy is to dehumanize the specific target in question, either as being animal-like or machine-like (see Haslam, 2006; Hodson, MacInnis, & Costello, 2014). Psychologically distancing a social target from the human category, removes protections for the target, given the primacy afforded to humans over other animals. Of interest to our present discussion, dehumanization rules the target OUT for concern, compassion, and care: *We need to prioritize people first, and unfortunately you are relatively less human than we are*. The third leg in the delegitimization toolkit is disparaging humor, the ridicule of others through jokes and other communications passed off as comical. As we have seen in this chapter, these can be aggressive or belittling in nature, both with strong effects. Unlike dehumanization, where the function is to rule targets out (from considerations and protections), the function of disparaging humor is to rule targets IN as socially acceptable targets at the receiving end of a socially palatable form of communication: *You are well-suited to, and ideal for, ridicule and belittlement at the expense of others*. In this way, '… jokes about Republicans/Democrats or blondes represent socially shared means of targeting social groups for putdowns, that are cloaked in humor, valuing a sense of humor, or otherwise being cavalier and fun-loving and nonserious' (Hodson & MacInnis, 2016, p. 69). Therefore, cavalier humor beliefs play an important role in affording humor-based ridicule and marginalization the social cover deemed necessary in contemporary society.

A demonstration of the three legs of the delegitimization toolkit was played out craftily by Donald Trump after being famously caught on a live microphone saying extremely lewd and offensive comments about women, including:

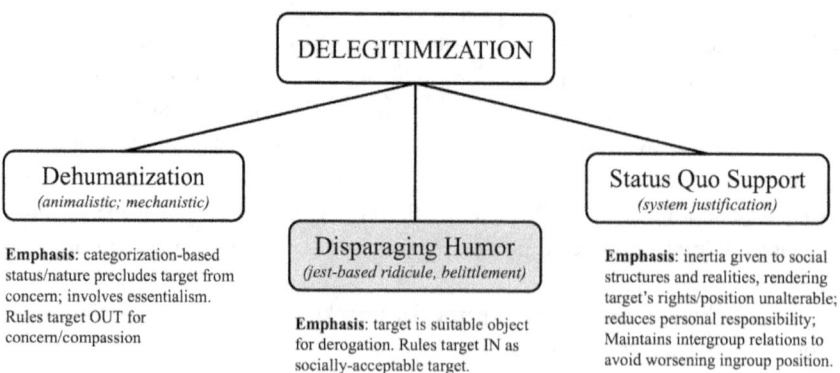

FIGURE 10.2 A visual depiction several strategies to delegitimize others. Reproduced with permission from Hodson and MacInnis (2016)

- 'I moved on her like a bitch' (dehumanization)
- 'Your girl's hot as shit' (sexual objectification)
- 'Then all of a sudden I see her, she's now got the big phony tits and everything' (sexual objectification)
- 'Grab them by the pussy... You can do anything' (sexual objectification; removal from concern; status quo maintenance)
- 'I just start kissing them. It's like a magnet. Just kiss. I don't even wait' (removal from concern; status quo maintenance).

As icing on the cake, Trump's defensive reaction to being caught also plays from the CHB playbook: 'This was locker room banter' (Fahrenthold, 2016). Of note, this defence clearly worked—weeks later Donald Trump was elected President of the United States. This is consistent with experimental research showing that framing otherwise inappropriate behavior (e.g., bullying) as 'boys just being boys' lowers collective guilt for holding a privileged or powerful position, in turn lowering opposition to bullying (Hoffarth & Hodson, 2014, Study 2). Framing situations or communications as '*just* X' is a critical step in minimizing perceived harm, culpability, or need to take restorative action.

Next Steps

Flowing most directly from our research reviewed, it is clear that we need to better understand the psychological nature of CHBs, including their origins and cultural molding. At present, we know little about changes in CHB over time, either across people or cultures nor how age relates to CHB or its development over the lifespan. Although cavalier humor beliefs might have a biological basis, we suspect that much of the variance between people originates from social contexts, both the local (e.g., within families) and at a higher level (e.g., national culture). For instance, cultures that are more 'loose' (characterized by relaxed social norms, acceptance of deviance) presumably promote CHBs more than those that are socially 'tight' (characterized by strict social rules and laws concerning acceptable thoughts and behavior; see Harrington & Gelfand, 2014). Each of these questions can be followed up in future research.

To date we know that CHBs have been shown to operate both as a mediator, facilitating group dominance motives, and as a moderator, quelling pushback against derogatory humor targeting one's group, so better understanding CHBs will be critical in implementing interventions. It is possible that merely educating people on the harmful effects of CHBs will suffice, but here we urge caution—critics and opponents will view such a strategy as 'political correctness run amok.' To be clear, we do not believe that humor or CHBs are entirely negative in nature. To the contrary, it is precisely their positive functions and appearance that permit them to serve as releasors of bias in otherwise socially sensitive contexts. Here, the negative is piggybacking off of the positive aspects. We suspect that interventions that provide information, solutions, and positive social norms will be the most effective in curbing the defensive deployment of CHBs.

In addition to focusing on individual differences such as CHBs, we see tremendous value in focusing on social aspects. Humor, and certainly disparaging humor, is inherently social in nature. This insight informs interventions and future direction for researchers. Recent research by Thomas et al. (2020) shows that, in disparaging humor contexts, the role of *bystanders* is key to determining whether a communication is considered prejudiced or not. People are very much influenced by others in determining the nature of humor communication, and we suspect that CHBs will play a key role in shaping these perceptions, cognitions, and emerging emotions. Interventions that draw on others (including bystanders), and our growing understanding of CHB functions, will be well poised to remedy intergroup tensions.

Relatedly, we see great potential for using humor to combat prejudice (see Allport, 1954; Hodson, Rush et al., 2010; Hodson & MacInnis, 2016). For example, online activists already use humor to fight the terrorist organization ISIS, superimposing rubber duck heads on their photographs (Gunter, 2015). In the U.K. protesters used mocking humor and giant blimps of 'baby' President Trump to communicate powerful messages of resistance (Jackson, 2019). Likewise, humor was a key strategy used to deflate Milosevic's grip on power in Serbia in the 1990s, leading Sorensen (2008) to argue that humor is a meaningful tactic for engaging in non-violent protests. Being cavalier about humor can therefore become a powerful tool to delegitimize not only the disadvantaged but also against those seeking to undo social progress and to suppress human rights.

Notes

1 We increasingly learn, however, that other animals are capable of higher-order cognitions (see De Waal, 2016), meaning that this perceived uniqueness might be illusory.
2 Meta-analytic syntheses suggest, however, that laughter is associated with greater perceived verticality (i.e., high-status position), but not necessarily with actual verticality (Hall, Coats, & LeBeau, 2005).
3 We recognize the existence of sexist anti-men jokes, but for our purposes 'sexist' jokes refer to those targeting women.
4 The joke stimuli can be found in the appendix for that paper.
5 In this study, we treat CHB as a potential moderator, not a mediator. This project, unlike the Hodson and colleagues (2010) study on Canadians' reactions to humor disparaging less advantaged Mexicans, examines reactions to *ingroup* disparaging humor. SDO did not predict reactions to ingroup humor in Hodson and colleagues (Study 2) nor in Prusaczyk and Hodson (Study 1). The Group-Dominance Model of Humor Appreciation is thus more appropriate for studying humor-based reactions to a lower status outgroup, where CHB might mediate the effects of SDO on humor reactions. In studying women's reactions to ingroup-targeting sexist humor we were interested in CHB as a moderator, helping us identify it as a buffering agent which can deter the rejection of harmful jokes. We pre-registered this conceptual role in advance of data collection given the deviation from our previous theoretical direction focusing on outgroup disparagement (e.g., Hodson, Rush et al., 2010).
6 As noted in the supplemental analyses of that paper, exposure to aggressive (*vs.* neutral) jokes also significantly increased body shame and self-objectification.

References

Allport, G. W. (1954). *The nature of prejudice*. Cambridge, MA: Addison-Wesley.
Altemeyer, B. (1996). *The authoritarian specter*. Cambridge, MA: Harvard University Press.
Altemeyer, B. (1998). The other 'authoritarian personality.' In M. P. Zanna (Ed.), *Advances in experimental social psychology* (Vol. 30, pp. 47–92). New York, NY: Academic Press.
Bar-Tal, D., & Hammack, P. L. (2012). Conflict, delegitimization, and violence. In L. R. Tropp (Ed.), *The Oxford handbook of intergroup conflict* (pp. 29 –52). New York, NY: Oxford University Press.
Brewer, M. B. (1979). Ingroup bias in the minimal group situation: A cognitive motivational analysis. *Psychological Bulletin, 86*, 307–324.
Caird, S., & Martin, R. A. (2014). Relationship-focused humor styles and relationship satisfaction in dating couples: A repeated-measures design. *Humor, 27*, 227–247.
Cernerud, L., & Olsson, H. (2004). Humour seen from a public health perspective. *Scandinavian Journal of Public Health, 32*, 396–398.
De Waal, F. (2016). *Are we smart enough to know how smart animals are?* New York, US: Norton.
Dhont, K., & Hodson, G. (2014). Does lower cognitive ability predict greater prejudice? *Current Directions in Psychological Science, 23*, 454–459.
Dovidio, J. F., & Gaertner, S. L. (2004). Aversive racism. In M. P. Zanna (Ed.), *Advances in experimental social psychology* (Vol. 36, pp. 1–51). San Diego, CA: Academic Press.
Duckitt, J. (2006). Differential effects of right-wing authoritarianism and social dominance orientation on outgroup attitudes and their mediation by threat from and competitiveness to outgroups. *Personality and Social Psychology Bulletin, 32*, 684–696.
Fahrenthold, D. A. (2016, October 8). Trump recorded having extremely lewd conversation about women in 2005. The Washington Post. Retrieved from https://www.washingtonpost.com/politics/trump-recorded-having-extremely-lewd-conversation-about-women-in-2005/2016/10/07/3b9ce776-8cb4-11e6-bf8a-3d26847eeed4_story.html.
Ford, T. E. (2000). Effects of sexist humor on tolerance of sexist events. *Personality and Social Psychology Bulletin, 26*, 1094–1107.
Ford, T. E., Boxer, C. F., Armstrong, J., & Edel, J. R.(2008). More than "just a joke": The prejudice-releasing function of sexist humor. *Personality and Social Psychology Bulletin, 34*, 159–170.
Ford, T. E., & Ferguson M. A. (2004). Social consequences of disparagement humor: A prejudiced norm theory. *Personality and Social Psychology, 8*, 79–94.
Ford, T. E., Boxer, C. F., Armstrong, J., & Edel, J. R. (2008). More than 'just a joke': The prejudice-releasing function of sexist humor. *Personality and Social Psychology Bulletin, 34*, 159–170.
Ford, T. E., Woodzicka, J. A., Triplett, S. R., & Kochersberger, A. O. (2013). Sexist humor and beliefs that justify societal sexism. *Current Research in Social Psychology, 21*, 64–81.
Greenwald, A. G., & Pettigrew, T. F. (2014). With malice toward none and charity for some: Ingroup favoritism enables discrimination. *American Psychologist, 69*, 669–684.
Greenwood, D., & Isbell, L. M. (2002). Ambivalent sexism and the dumb blonde: Men's and women's reactions to sexist jokes. *Psychology of Women Quarterly, 26*, 341–350.
Gunter, J. (2015, November 28). Isis mocked with rubber ducks as internet fights terror with humour. The Guardian. Retrieved from https://www.theguardian.com/world/2015/nov/28/isis-fighters-rubber-ducks-reddit-4chan.
Hall, J. A., Coats, E. J., & Lebeau, L. S. (2005). Nonverbal behavior and the vertical dimension of social relations: A meta-analysis. *Psychological Bulletin, 131*, 898–924.

Harrington, J. R., & Gelfand, M. J. (2014). Tightness-looseness across the 50 United States. *Proceedings of the National Academy of Sciences USA, 111*, 7990–7995. doi:10.1073/pnas.1317937111.

Haslam, N. (2006). Dehumanization: An integrative review. *Personality and Social Psychology Review, 10*, 252–264.

Hodson, G., & MacInnis, C. C. (2016). Derogating humor as a delegitimization strategy in intergroup contexts. *Translational Issues in Psychological Science, 2*, 63–74.

Hodson, G., Dovidio, J. F., & Gaertner, S. L. (2002). Processes in racial discrimination: Differential weighting of conflicting information. *Personality and Social Psychology Bulletin, 28*, 460–471.

Hodson, G., Dovidio, J. F., & Gaertner, S. L. (2004). The aversive form of racism. In J. L. Lau (Ed.), *The psychology of prejudice and discrimination* (Vol 1., pp. 119–135). Westport, CT: Praeger Press.

Hodson, G., Hogg, S. M., & MacInnis, C. C. (2009). The role of 'dark personalities' (narcissism, Machiavellianism, psychopathy), Big Five personality factors, and ideology in explaining prejudice. *Journal of Research in Personality, 43*, 686–690.

Hodson, G., MacInnis, C. C., & Rush, J. (2010). Prejudice-relevant correlates of humor temperaments and humor styles. *Personality and Individual Differences, 49*, 546–549.

Hodson, G., Rush, J., & MacInnis, C. C. (2010). A 'joke is just a joke' (except when it isn't): Cavalier humor beliefs facilitate the expression of group dominance motives. *Journal of Personality and Social Psychology, 99*, 660–682.

Hodson, G., MacInnis, C. C., & Costello, K. (2014). (Over)Valuing 'humanness' as an aggravator of intergroup prejudices and discrimination. In P. G. Bain, J. Vaes, & J.-Ph. Leyens (Eds.), *Humanness and dehumanization* (pp. 86–110). London, UK: Psychology Press.

Hodson, G., MacInnis, C. C., & Busseri, M. A. (2017). Bowing and kicking: Rediscovering the fundamental link between generalized authoritarianism and generalized prejudice. *Personality and Individual Differences, 104*, 243–251.

Hodson, G., Book, A., Visser, B. A., Volk, A. A., Ashton, M. C., & Lee, K. (2018). Is the Dark Triad common factor distinct from low Honesty-Humility? *Journal of Research in Personality, 73*, 123–129.

Hoffarth, M. R., & Hodson, G. (2014). Is subjective ambivalence toward gays a modern form of bias? *Personality and Individual Differences, 69*, 75–80.

Jackson, M. (2019, June 4). Trump UK visit: Protesters mix humour and expletives to make their point. *BBCNews*. Retrieved from https://www.bbc.com/news/uk-48517606

Jost, J. T., & Hunyady, O. (2002). The psychology of system justification and the palliative function of ideology. *European Review of Social Psychology, 13*, 111–153.

Jost, J. T., Glaser, J., Kruglanski, A. W., & Sulloway, F. J. (2003). Political conservatism as motivated social cognition. *Psychological Bulletin, 129*, 339–375.

Kessler, G. (2016, August 2). Donald Trump's revisionist history of mocking a disabled reporter. The Washington Post. Retrieved from https://www.washingtonpost.com/news/fact-checker/wp/2016/08/02/donald-trumps-revisionist-history-of-mocking-a-disabled-reporter.

LaFrance, M., & Woodzicka, J. A. (1998). No laughing matter: Women's verbal and nonverbal reactions to sexist humor. In J. K. Swim & C. Stangor (Eds.), *Prejudice: The target's perspective* (pp. 61–80). Cambridge, MA: Academic Press.

Lee, K., & Ashton, M. C. (2004). Psychometric properties of the HEXACO personality inventory. *Multivariate Behavioral Research, 39*, 329–358.

Lippa, R. A. (2007). The preferred traits of mates in a cross-national study of heterosexual and homosexual men and women: An examination of biological and cultural influences. *Archives of Sexual Behavior, 36*, 193–208.

Mackey, R. (2020, March 17). Trump shrugs off spike in anti-Chinese racism, even in his White House. *The Intercept*. Retrieved from https://theintercept.com/2020/03/17/trump-blames-china-virus-white-house-aide-makes-racist-joke-asian-reporter/

Margolin, J. (2020, March 27). FBI warns of potential surge in hate crimes against Asian Americans amid coronavirus. *ABC News*. Retrieved from https://abcnews.go.com/US/fbi-warns-potential-surge-hate-crimes-asian-americans/story?id=69831920

Martin, R. A. (2002). Is laughter the best medicine? Humor, laughter, and physical health. *Current Directions in Psychological Science*, *11*, 216–220.

Martin, R. A., & Ford, T. (2018). *The psychology of humor: An integrative approach*. Burlington, MA: Academic Press.

Martin, R. A., Puhlik-Doris, P., Larsen, G., Gray, J., & Weir, K. (2003). Individual differences in uses of humor and their relation to psychological well-being: Development of the Humor Styles Questionnaire. *Journal of Research in Personality*, *37*, 48–75.

McConahay, J. G., Hardee, B. B., & Batts, V. (1981). Has racism declined? It depends on who's asking and what is asked. *Journal of Conflict Resolution*, *25*, 563–579.

McGee, E., & Shevlin, M. (2009). Effect of humor on interpersonal attraction and mate selection. *The Journal of Psychology*, *143*, 67–77.

Mesmer-Magnus, J., Glew, D. J., & Viswesvaran, C. (2012). A meta-analysis of positive humor in the workplace. *Journal of Managerial Psychology*, *27*, 155–190.

Navarro-Carrillo, G., Torres-Marín, J., & Carretero-Dios, H. (2020). Class-based differences in the use of (aggressive) humor: The mediating role of empathic concern. *Personality and Individual Differences*, *159*, 109868.

Neuberg, S. L., & Newsom, J. T. (1993). Personal need for structure: Individual differences in the desire for simpler structure. *Journal of Personality and Social Psychology*, *65*, 113–131.

Oveis, C., Spectre, A., Smith, P. K., Liu, M. Y., & Keltner, D. (2016). Laughter conveys status. *Journal of Experimental Social Psychology*, *65*, 109–115.

Phillips, A. (2020, February 20). A guide to the most biting brawls of the contentious Las Vegas presidential debate. The Washington Post. Retrieved from https://www.washingtonpost.com/politics/2020/02/20/candidate-fights-nevada-debate/.

Pratto, F., Sidanius, J., Stallworth, L. M., & Malle, B. F. (1994). Social dominance orientation: A personality variable predicting social and political attitudes. *Journal of Personality and Social Psychology*, *67*, 741–763.

Prusaczyk, E., & Hodson, G. (2020). 'To the moon, Alice': Cavalier humor beliefs and women's reactions to aggressive and belittling sexist jokes. *Journal of Experimental Social Psychology*, *88*, 103973.

Sidanius, J., & Pratto, F. (1999). *Social dominance: An intergroup theory of social hierarchy and oppression*. Cambridge, UK: Cambridge University Press.

Sorensen, M. J. (2008), Humour as a serious strategy of nonviolent resistance to oppression. *Peace & Change*, *33*, 167–190.

Stephan, W. S., & Stephan. C. W. (2000). An integrated threat theory of prejudice. In S. Oskamp (Ed.), *Reducing prejudice and discrimination* (pp. 23–46). Mahwah, NJ: Lawrence Erlbaum.

Stewart, S., & Thompson, D. R. (2015). Does comedy kill? A retrospective, longitudinal cohort, nested case–control study of humour and longevity in 53 British comedians. *International Journal of Cardiology*, *180*, 258–261.

Tajfel, H., & Turner, J. C. (1979). An integrative theory of intergroup conflict. In W. G. Austin and S. Worchel (Eds.), *The social psychology of intergroup relations* (pp. 33–47). Monterey, CA: Brooks/Cole Publishing Company.

Thai, M., Borgella, A. M., & Sanchez, M. S. (2019). Its only funny if we say it: Disparagement humor is better received if it originates from a member of the group being disparaged. *Journal of Experimental Social Psychology, 85,* 1–10.

Thomas, C., & Esses, V. M. (2004). Individual differences in reactions to sexist humor. *Group Processes and Intergroup Relations, 7,* 89–100.

Thomas, E. F., Mcgarty, C., Spears, R., Livingstone, A. G., Platow, M. J., Lala, G., & Mavor, K. (2020). 'That's not funny!' Standing up against disparaging humor. *Journal of Experimental Social Psychology, 86,* 1–17.

Tisljar, R., & Bereczkei, T. (2005). An evolutionary interpretation of humor and laughter. *Journal of Cultural and Evolutionary Psychology, 3,* 301–309.

Turner, J. C., Hogg, M. A., Oakes, P. J., Reicher, S. D., & Wetherell, M. S. (1987). *Rediscovering the social group: A self-categorization theory.* Oxford, UK: Blackwell.

Vernon, P. A., Martin, R. A., Schermer, J. A., & Mackie, A. (2008). A behavioral genetic investigation of humor styles and their correlations with the Big-5 personality dimensions. *Personality and Individual Differences, 44,* 1116–1125.

Woodzicka, J. A., & Ford, T. E. (2010). A framework for thinking about the (not-so-funny) effects of sexist humor. *Europe's Journal of Psychology, 3,* 174–195.

11
ADDRESSING THE CHALLENGES OF CONFRONTING DISPARAGEMENT HUMOR

Julie A. Woodzicka and Robyn K. Mallett

Although humor is correlated with positive intra- and interpersonal experiences, not all humor has positive consequences. Group-based disparagement humor demeans, insults, stereotypes, victimises, or objectifies a person based on their group membership (LaFrance & Woodzicka, 1998). This unique type of humor is associated with a host of negative effects (Ford, Triplett, Woodzicka, Kochersberger, & Holden, 2014; Woodzicka & Ford, 2010). For example, sexist humor can create distressing, hostile work environments for women (Duncan, Smeltzer, & Leap, 1990; Hemmasi, Graf, & Russ, 1994; Woodzicka & LaFrance, 2005). Sexist humor also affects the ways that men think about women and perceive sexism (Ford, 2000; Ford, Wentzel, & Lorion, 2001) and increases men's willingness to engage in subtle sexist behaviour (Ford, Boxer, Armstrong, & Edel, 2008). Moreover, sexist humor can increase self-objectification of women (Ford, Woodzicka, Petit, Richardson, & Lappi, 2015) and acceptance of societal sexism (Ford, Woodzicka, Triplett, & Kochersberger, 2013). Likewise, racist humor may reinforce every day and systematic White supremacy (Pérez, 2017). Despite causing myriad negative outcomes, disparagement humor can be easily disregarded as 'just a joke' and not worthy of attention (Pérez, 2017).

Interpersonal confrontation provides one promising avenue for decreasing the occurrence of group-based disparagement humor. Confronting prejudice and discrimination can reduce prejudicial attitudes and curb future biased behaviour (Czopp, Monteith, & Mark, 2006; Mallett & Wagner, 2011). However, interpersonal confrontation comes with well-documented costs (Kaiser & Miller, 2004; Swim & Hyers, 1999) and confronting disparagement humor may carry increased costs for the confronter (Woodzicka, Mallett, Hendricks, & Pruitt, 2015). In this chapter, we review research that examines the challenges of confronting disparagement humor, along with confrontation strategies that may reduce costs for the confronter. We suggest future research to test lower-cost confrontation strategies that combat group-based disparagement humor. Before turning to the challenges of confronting humor, we review the benefits and costs of confronting bias for both the confronter (i.e., the person who does the confronting), and the confrontee (i.e., the person who is confronted for bias).

The Benefits of Confronting Bias

Confronting bias provides benefits for the confronter, the confrontee, and society. At a basic level, confrontation is a powerful tool in combatting interpersonal bias. When White people are confronted for expressing racism, they feel negative self-directed affect and are more likely to reduce their biased attitudes and control their stereotypic responses in the future than when they are not confronted (Czopp et al., 2006). Similarly, if men who are confronted for sexism attempt to make up for their biased behaviour and experience mutual liking with the confronter, then they control their future use of sexist language (Mallett & Wagner, 2011). We may measure the effectiveness of a confrontation by its likelihood to reduce discriminatory behaviour—either immediately or in the future. Confrontations are most effective at generating concern for controlling future bias when they present clear evidence of bias and its negative consequences. For example, when people learn that their evaluations of a female job applicant showed bias, they report negative self-directed affect, which increases concern about regulating gender bias (Parker, Monteith, Moss-Racusin, & Van Camp, 2018).

When confronted, it may be difficult for confrontees to see any intrapersonal benefits. Many people fear being accused of bias (Tatum, 1999). Although confrontation makes confrontees uncomfortable, it may benefit the confrontee by educating them about the impact of their behaviour (Sue, 2015). At times, people are simply unaware that what they have said or done is offensive, or they may not realise that their behaviour diverges from their egalitarian values (Goodman, 2011). Defining a behaviour as biased helps the confrontee understand more about the experience of the target group (Sue et al., 2019). Labelling an event as bias is the first step in attitude change. People must become aware of their bias and feel bad about it to change their attitudes and behaviour (Monteith, Ashburn-Nardo, Voils, & Czopp, 2002). When the confronter draws attention to the discrepancy between a person's behaviour and their egalitarian ideals, that person may experience dissatisfaction with the self and be motivated to reduce future discriminatory responses (Devine, Monteith, Zuwerink, & Elliot, 1991; Monteith & Voils, 1998). As such, confronting someone for bias has the potential to increase awareness of bias, trigger negative self-directed affect, and motivate regulation of one's attitudes and behaviour.

Confronters may experience both interpersonal and intrapersonal benefits from speaking up against bias. First, confronters may receive positive regard from others who witness their behaviour. Ingroup members who confronted (versus ignored) racism were evaluated more positively by Black Americans and Asian Americans who strongly identified with their racial group (Kaiser, Hagiwara, Malahy, & Wilkins, 2009). Similarly, women who confronted (versus ignored) sexism were both liked and respected by women who strongly identified with their gender group (Dodd, Giuiliano, Boutell, & Moran, 2001). Confronters are also seen as more authentic (e.g., honest, intelligent, independent) than people who do not confront (Saunders & Senn, 2009). Second, confronters experience intrapersonal benefits from standing up to bias. Targets of prejudice who confront report greater feelings of empowerment and less regret and anger than targets who remain silent (Haslett & Lipman, 1997; Hyers, 2007). Similarly, women who confront sexism report feeling more competent and report higher self-esteem than women who remain silent (Gervais, Hillard, & Vescio, 2010). Confronting might also provide a release valve for expressing anger and frustration associated with experiencing or observing bias (Hyers, 2007).

When people confront bias, society also benefits because confrontation communicates societal expectations for appropriate behaviour. Confrontations often occur in front of a wider audience than the confronter and the confrontee; they may happen at family gatherings, at work, in the classroom, or social settings (Swim, Hyers, Cohen, Fitzgerald, & Bylsma, 2003). Regardless of whether the confrontee changes their attitudes and behaviour, they receive the message that their peers do not approve. Simply witnessing another person publicly (versus privately) label a remark as sexist increases the likelihood that female and male witnesses rate the remark as sexist (Gervais & Hillard, 2014). Similarly, when women read about a teacher who confronted sexism in the classroom, they report fewer sexist attitudes than when the sexism was ignored (Boysen, 2013). Confrontation may be especially helpful when it labels ambiguous behaviour as unacceptable. Czopp (2007) showed participants a video where a racist joke was either ignored, confronted, and the confrontee apologised or confronted, and the confrontee lashed out. The racist joke was liked less, rated as less funny, and participants said they would be less likely to retell it when it was confronted, and the confrontee apologised for telling it compared to the other conditions. This underscores the power of confrontation to shape shared expectations for behaviour.

Public confrontation, whether in person or online, establishes injunctive norms for behaviour—that is, how people should behave. When confrontation reinforces egalitarian norms, it helps to reduce prejudice (Blanchard, Crandall, Brigham, & Vaughn, 1994). Paluck (2011) trained high school students to confront their peers' bias. She found that the effects of the intervention spread to the friends of students who were trained. Although they had not personally been trained to confront bias, friends of the trained students were better able to recognise bias and were more likely to support collective action in support of lesbian, gay, and bisexual rights than friends of students in the control group. In contrast, ignoring bias reinforces the idea that bias is acceptable (Blanchard et al., 1994) and unintentionally reinforces discrimination (Czopp, 2019).

The Costs of Confronting

Despite the benefits of confrontation, people may choose not to confront if they fear social or economic backlash for doing so (Kaiser & Miller, 2001, 2004; Swim &

Hyers, 1999). The more women fear being disliked for confronting, the more they recall remaining silent following discrimination (Good, Moss-Racusin, & Sanchez, 2012). Similarly, women report fewer confrontational responses as perceived interpersonal costs and anxiety increase, and as perceived interpersonal benefits decrease (Kaiser & Miller, 2004). For example, Shelton and Stewart (2004) manipulated the costs of confronting by having women imagine that they were interviewing for their dream job in a tough job market against highly competitive applicants (high cost) or that they were just doing the interview to gain experience and they had another job (low cost). When facing high costs for confronting a sexist job interviewer, few women (22%) confronted (Shelton & Stewart, 2004). In comparison, when facing low costs for confronting, most (92%) women called out the biased interviewer, using surprised exclamations or assertively questioning the interviewer.

Fears of backlash are often well-founded. Confronters tend to be evaluated more harshly with regards to liking, social distance, and approach-related behaviours than if they remain silent (Czopp et al., 2006). Reports from confrontees and third-party evaluators consistently show that confronters are labelled as oversensitive and as whiners or complainers (Czopp & Monteith, 2003; Dodd et al., 2001; Parker et al., 2018). Yet, when people remain silent, they may experience intrapersonal costs, including rumination and guilt. People who want to confront but choose not to do so may also experience distraction and performance decrements (Shelton, Richeson, Salvatore, & Hill, 2006). As such, there are costs, even if one chooses not to speak up.

Choosing not to confront bias also has unintended consequences for one's own attitudes towards the perpetrator and towards bias more generally. Ignoring bias may create dissonance for people who value social justice. To minimise the extent to which one's behaviour diverges from personal standards of morality, people may bring their attitudes in line with their actions. For example, when women ignore a man's sexist remark, they later minimise the importance of confronting sexism relative to women who do not have a chance to confront (Rasinski, Geers, & Czopp, 2013). The women who ignore sexism also report liking the man who made the sexist remark more than the women who had no chance to confront him. Women's attitudes towards sexual harassment are also affected by the decision to confront sexism. Mallett, Ford, and Woodzicka (2019) gave women the opportunity to confront or ignore either a sexist or non-sexist offensive remark that was delivered in a humorous or non-humorous manner. The more women ignored the sexist remark, the more they endorsed sexually harassing attitudes; this was true regardless of whether the remark was delivered in a humorous or serious manner. In a second study, women who imagined ignoring sexism aligned their attitudes with their behaviour. Women who imagined ignoring (versus confronting) sexism reported more dissonance and the more dissonance they reported, the more they tolerated sexual harassment. Ignoring sexism in any form creates dissonance, but women were less supportive of survivors of sexual harassment when they imagined ignoring sexist jokes compared to sexist statements.

The Challenges of Confronting Disparagement Humor

Everyday prejudice is communicated in many ways, including via statements, jokes, memes, and humorous stories (Duchscherer & Dovidio, 2016; Swim, Cohen, & Hyers, 1998). Although disparaging jokes and comments share the underlying message that the disparaged group is lesser, the mode of communication changes the perceived meaning of the biased remark. Compared to non-humorous messages, a humorous message is open to various interpretations. Humor encourages a paratelic state, or a playful state of mind (Apter, 1991), communicating that one need not consider the message seriously (Ford & Ferguson, 2004). While in a paratelic state, the main goal is to enjoy the interaction by refraining from thinking too hard about the message and instead enjoying the humorous context. Humorous messages, including prejudicial ones, signal that the message should not be scrutinised (Bill & Naus, 1992) and are beyond reproach (Attardo, 1993; Gray & Ford, 2013). In support of this, Ford et al. (2008) found that a biased incident was viewed as less severe when the bias was framed in a humorous (versus non-humorous) manner.

The justification-suppression model (Crandall & Eshleman, 2003) of prejudice helps explain why humorous messages are perceived as less damaging than non-humorous messages. The model contends that because egalitarian social norms are valued in society, high prejudice individuals learn to suppress their bias to maintain self-esteem. However, they may use humor as a justification to express prejudice under the guise that they are 'just joking.' Humor changes the social context, permitting the expression of prejudice without fear of negative consequence because people may claim that they were enjoying an entertaining joke rather than the prejudicial message. Duchscherer and Dovidio (2016) found that pre-existing support of stereotyping facilitated a noncritical mindset toward disparagement humor. That is, people who strongly endorsed stereotype-supporting beliefs rated a meme depicting disparagement humor to be more socially acceptable than a non-humorous disparaging meme.

Although they may be perceived as less severe, a message couched in humor can be just as, or even more, harmful than a non-humorous message. For example, Ford et al. (2008) found that for men high in hostile sexism, exposure to sexist humor (versus a non-humorous sexist comment) increased discrimination against women. These effects are not limited to sexist humor. Rather, other historically disadvantaged groups for whom egalitarian norms have begun to emerge (e.g., Muslims; lesbian, gay, and bisexual people are susceptible to the prejudice-releasing effects of disparagement humor (Ford et al., 2014). Specifically, among participants who were highly prejudiced against Muslim people and people who are gay, exposure to anti-Muslim and anti-gay jokes resulted in a release of prejudice against those groups (Ford et al., 2014).

Below, we elaborate on research that highlights the way that humor complicates the process of confronting prejudice. Ashburn-Nardo et al. (2008) proposed a five-step Confronting Prejudiced Responses (CPR) model to predict when individuals will confront discrimination. Their model asserts that an individual must first detect discrimination (Step 1) and then deem the incident as needing intervention (Step 2). Next, the individual must take responsibility to confront the discrimination (Step 3) and decide how they will confront (Step 4). Despite progressing through the first four steps, several factors may prevent people from actually confronting the perpetrator (Step 5). Framing confronting as five steps instead of one helps explain why confrontation rates are relatively low and why people frequently anticipate confronting more than they actually confront (Woodzicka & LaFrance, 2001). We, like others (Ashburn-Nardo & Karim, 2019), contend that the five steps are more challenging to navigate when humor is involved.

Steps 1 and 2

Subtle or ambiguous bias is difficult to recognise (Swim, Mallett, Russo-Devosa, & Stangor, 2005). Humor creates ambiguity, producing a situation in which a biased message may go unnoticed, creating a barrier to detecting bias (Step 1). Even when a racist or sexist joke is viewed as an act of bias, humor may mitigate the perceived harm and decrease perceptions that the act is confrontation-worthy (Step 2). We tested the first two steps of the CPR model with a scenario study in which participants were randomly assigned to read one of four scenarios that varied in the type of prejudice (racism or sexism) and mode of communication (humorous or non-humorous) (Woodzicka et al., 2015). In the humorous conditions, participants imagined that they were hanging out with a small group of people in the break room at work and one of them told the following joke, 'What do you call a woman [Black] with half a brain? Gifted.' Another joke followed this, 'What's the difference between a woman [Black] and a battery? A battery has a positive side.' The non-humorous conditions contained the same biased sentiments as humorous conditions but did not use humor. They read, 'It doesn't seem like women [Blacks] as a group are very smart' followed by, 'Yeah, overall women [Blacks] don't have that many positive qualities.' Participants rated how offensive and confrontation-worthy the remarks were. As expected, participants rated non-humorous remarks as more offensive and confrontation-worthy than humorous remarks that expressed the same sentiment. Further, ratings of offensiveness and confrontation-worthiness were positively correlated (Woodzicka et al., 2015).

Supporting the idea that humor allows bias to go undetected, in a different study we examined whether delivering a sexist remark in a humorous versus non-humorous manner tempered perceptions that the speaker was sexist (Mallett, Ford, & Woodzicka, 2016). Women interacted through Instant Messaging with an alleged male partner who made a humorous or a non-humorous sexist remark that expressed the same sentiment. After the interaction, participants rated the extent to which their partner was sexist. As expected, humor changed perceptions of the perpetrator—women were less likely to perceive their male partner as sexist if he expressed sexism in humorous versus non-humorous manner. That is, women were more likely to give their alleged partner the benefit of the doubt and refrain from labelling him as sexist if the sexism was couched in humor. Importantly, as perceptions of his sexism decreased, so did confronting (Mallett et al., 2016).

Step 3

After deciding that an act of bias is worthy of confrontation, one must decide if they will take responsibility to confront (Step 3). As reviewed earlier, people both perceive and actually face costs for confronting discrimination. Confronters are perceived by some perpetrators and bystanders as oversensitive and as less likeable than those who stay silent (Czopp et al., 2006; Czopp & Monteith, 2003; Dodd et al., 2001; Parker et al., 2018). A confronter is especially likely to receive backlash for confronting ambiguous bias because the confrontation may be seen as an over-reaction. For example, a Black confronter was rated more negatively for confronting an ambiguously racist comment compared to confronting a blatantly racist comment (Zou & Dickter, 2013). A woman who refused patronising help from a man was rated less favourably than a woman who accepted the help (Becker, Glick, Ilic, & Bohner, 2011). And a blind person was rated less favourably for confronting patronising help than for confronting blatantly offensive behaviour (Wang, Silverman, Gwinn, & Dovidio, 2015). Although we are not aware of research that has specifically examined how humor impacts feelings of responsibility for confronting, the ambiguous nature of humor is likely to increase the perceived and actual risks for confronting. The more costs that people anticipate receiving for confrontation, the less likely they may be to accept responsibility for confronting.

Steps 4 and 5

If people successfully navigate the first three steps, then they must decide how to confront (Step 4) and actually engage in confronting behaviour (Step 5). Because of the costs associated with confronting disparagement humor, we expect that individuals may prefer confronting in ways that minimise costs. Confronters might prefer strategies that are both effective (i.e., stop the disparagement) and protective (i.e., reduce costs and increase liking). We found variability in the extent to which confrontation strategies are associated with social costs for the confronter (Woodzicka et al., 2015). Participants read one of six scenarios that contained either a racist or a sexist joke. They learned that a co-worker responded to the joke in one of three ways: ignoring it, declaring that the joke was not funny, or labelling the joke as biased (i.e., racist or sexist). Labelling the joke as bias is the most blatant way to confront, followed by saying that it is not funny and ignoring the joke. For racist jokes, we found that labelling the joke as racist and saying that the joke was not funny were both rated as more appropriate than ignoring it. For sexist jokes, saying that the joke was not funny was rated as more appropriate than labelling it as sexist or doing nothing. Further, the confronter was viewed as less likeable when confronting a sexist versus a racist joke. The costs of confronting were steepest in terms of likeability when the confronter labelled the sexist joke as sexist.

People value others who have a sense of humor (Mesmer-Magnus, Glew, & Viswesvaran, 2012). Those who blatantly confront group-based disparagement humor risk being labelled humorless or overly sensitive, especially when confronting types of bias that are considered less serious. For example, taboos against racist behaviour are stronger than taboos against sexist behaviour (Czopp & Monteith, 2003). Hate speech against Black people is seen as more offensive than hate speech against women (Cowan & Hodge, 1996). Anti-Black racism is seen as more prejudiced than sexism (Rodin, Price, Bryson, & Sanchez, 1990). Thus, blatantly confronting racism, even racist humor, is deemed more appropriate than blatantly confronting sexism—especially sexist humor (Woodzicka et al., 2015).

Perhaps because of the unique costs associated with confronting disparagement humor, the ways in which participants actually confront humor (Step 5) appear to be somewhat different than how they confront non-humorous statements. In two studies, we found that women were less likely to assertively confront a humorous (versus non-humorous) sexist remark (Mallett et al., 2016). In addition, when confronting a sexist joke, women challenged the confronter less and expressed a desire to be liked more than when confronting a sexist statement (Mallett et al., 2016). In sum, humor creates a normative context in which confronting is more difficult because of increased ambiguity and costs. Given that disparagement humor has the power to release prejudice (Ford et al., 2014) and interpersonal confrontation is effective in combating prejudice (Czopp et al., 2006), low-cost confrontation strategies deserve more attention.

Using Humor to Confront Discrimination

From studies of real-world confronting, we know that people often choose not to confront sexism (Woodzicka & LaFrance, 2001). When they do confront, they frequently use subtle strategies rather than directly labelling the person or behaviour as sexist (Hyers, 2007). For example, in response to sexism, women often question the sexist confederate, ask him to repeat himself, or ask a rhetorical question (Swim & Hyers, 1999). The assumption is that more subtle confrontations, such as saying 'What did you say?' or 'Can you repeat that?' signals disagreement and prompts perpetrators to recognise their bias without the confronter directly labelling the transgression. Participants report that questioning the perpetrator is less risky than directly commenting on his inappropriateness (Swim & Hyers, 1999). Thus, people may use subtle confrontations to minimise interpersonal costs.

Little research has tested the frequency, effectiveness, and protective benefits of confronting with humor. Humor generally diffuses threat (Kuiper, Martin, & Olinger, 1993) and non-threatening forms of confrontation are viewed more favourably. For example, Czopp et al. (2006) confronted participants about a stereotypic response using a threatening or non-threatening confrontation style.

In the threatening condition, the confronter was called 'some kind of racist' whereas in the non-threatening condition, the confronter was asked to think about how 'Blacks don't get equal treatment in our society.' Consistent with the research outlined above, participants liked the non-threatening confronter more than the threatening confronter. Monteith, Burns, and Hildebrand (2019) advise would-be confronters who are concerned with social costs to avoid hostility, aggression, and threat when selecting a specific confrontation style.

Most of us can think of a time we witnessed a discriminatory joke or comment and thought of a fitting response as we walked away. At times, those imagined responses are witty or clever (i.e., humorous). Indeed, online articles with titles such as 'The Best Comebacks to Sexist Comments' (Bates, 2013) and '44 of the Best Internet Clapbacks to Racists' (Bar, 2019) advocate the use of humor in confrontation. We have recently begun to test how often individuals use witty comebacks, whether a humorous confrontation is seen as effective and whether it minimizes social costs, and whether witty confronting is better suited for humorous versus non-humorous comments.

Society values people who have a sense of humor (Cann & Calhoun, 2001). A confronter who uses humor may be more likeable than a confronter who addresses bias in a non-humorous way. Although witty confronters may be likeable, humorous confrontations may be less effective than non-humorous confrontations (Monteith et al., 2019). Drawing from the persuasion literature, Swim, Gervais, Pearson, and Stangor (2009) argue that people must attend to the message at the heart of a confrontation for it to be effective. If a humorous confrontation is subtle or includes qualifying statements, then the confrontee may not understand that it is intended to challenge biased behaviour. As a result, witty confrontations may be less effective than non-humorous confrontations in reducing biased attitudes and behaviour. One aim of our research program has been to test how the use of humor in confrontations impacts confronter likeability and perceived effectiveness of the confrontation (Woodzicka, Mallett, & Melchiori, 2020).

To explore the frequency with which individuals spontaneously use witty confrontations and how such confrontations are perceived, we asked participants to imagine how they would respond to a scenario where a co-worker told a sexist joke (Woodzicka et al., 2020). All participants imagined the following: '*You are in the break room at work. You are talking to a male co-worker about the recent internet search that you did. He says, "That reminds me of a joke…Is Google male or female? Female, because it doesn't let you finish a sentence before making a suggestion."*' We asked participants, 'How would you respond to your co-worker?' Using an open-ended format, most respondents (51%) reported that they would laugh or smile in response to the joke. Only 35% of respondents stated that they would verbally confront the joke, and 25% imagined responding with a serious confrontation (e.g., 'That's a bit offensive'). Ten per cent of respondents spontaneously generated a witty confrontation, and more women (16%) wrote a witty confrontation than did men (4.5%). For instance, some participants wrote, 'Don't quit your day job' and 'Wow, so original!' Although overall confrontation rates were low, a substantial percentage of women imagined using a humorous confrontation upon hearing a sexist joke.

To further test whether women and men prefer humorous versus non-humorous confrontations, we asked the same participants to rate the likelihood that they would use two specific witty confrontations ('What? I couldn't hear you over my eyes rolling' and 'I'm pretty sure that sounded funnier in your head') and two specific serious confrontations ('That's sexist' and 'That's not funny!'). Women were more likely than men to say they would use the witty, but not serious, confrontations. Humor smooths conflict in interpersonal relationships (Collison, 1988; Coser, 1959; Mulkay, 1988). A witty comeback may allow the confronter to send a message that the sexism is unwelcome, but in a way that minimises social backlash. Although it may not be a conscious choice, women may favour witty confrontations to circumvent the social costs associated with serious confrontation (Czopp & Monteith, 2003; Gulker, Mark, & Monteith, 2013; Shelton & Stewart, 2004; Swim & Hyers, 1999).

At the end of this same study (Woodzicka et al., 2020), participants read about an interaction during which a male friend told a sexist joke, and another friend confronted using a witty ('Still single aren't you?') or a non-humorous ('You're not funny') remark. Participants rated how much they liked and wanted to be friends with the confronter, along with how effective the confrontation would be immediately and in the future in terms of stopping sexism. As expected, witty confronters were rated as more likeable than non-humorous confronters. Overall, witty confrontations were rated as moderately effective, receiving a 3.70 on a 5-point scale where 5 indicated extremely effective. Although non-humorous confrontations were rated as more effective in-the-moment than were witty confrontations, they were rated as equally effective in decreasing future acts of sexism. In sum, although witty confrontations protect confronters from the social costs that come with non-humorous confrontations, they are perceived to be slightly less effective.

In an unpublished study, we tested a matching hypothesis whereby participants would prefer a witty response to a humorous versus non-humorous sexist remark (Woodzicka, Mallett, & Melchiori, 2018). Participants evaluated a scenario in which a person made a humorous or non-humorous sexist remark that was either not confronted, received a witty confrontation, or received a non-humorous confrontation. As expected, the witty confrontation was rated as more effective in response to a humorous versus non-humorous sexist remark; non-humorous confrontations were rated as equally effective for humorous and non-humorous sexist remarks. Replicating our work (Woodzicka et al., 2020), the non-humorous confrontation was viewed as more effective than the witty confrontation or no confrontation. However, even though witty confrontation was rated as significantly less effective than non-humorous confrontation, mean effectiveness ratings for witty confrontations fell above the mid-point of the scale, suggesting at least moderate effectiveness. Replicating our results for likeability, the witty confronter was viewed as significantly more likeable and less of a 'complainer' than the non-humorous confronter.

People may confront sexist remarks in many ways, and each type of confrontation has its own costs and benefits (Czopp, 2019). We provide initial evidence that witty confrontation may reduce bias while providing some protection from the social costs of confrontation. Using humor to confront sends the message that the sexist remark is not welcome and may be less socially risky for confronters. Our research program is in the early stages, and many additional questions need to be addressed. In the next section, we highlight future directions for research on confronting disparagement humor and more specifically, the use of witty or humorous confrontation.

Next Steps

Confronting disparagement humor poses unique challenges. Discrimination couched in humor is seen as less harmful (Ford, 2000; Ford et al., 2008) and as less confrontation-worthy than discrimination conveyed via non-humorous remarks (Woodzicka et al., 2015). As such, confronters may be more effective and experience fewer costs if they broaden their repertoire to include witty strategies for confronting disparagement humor. Our research has focused on using humor to confront disparagement humor, but future work should continue to explore the utility of this strategy and identify additional ways to stop bias and reduce costs to the confronter. Most of our research has tested humorous confrontation in the context of sexism. It is essential to see whether the utility of humorous confrontations generalises to many forms of bias or whether humor works best for confronting bias that society takes less seriously.

Future research should test whether intersectional stereotypes affect reactions to confronters who use humor. Witty confrontation is generally perceived as effective and, importantly, confronters who use humor are viewed as more likeable than confronters who do not. However, the protective nature of humorous confrontation may only extend to confronters with specific social identities. Although we have varied the names of the confronters in our scenarios, most names have been stereotypically White, and we have not explicitly manipulated the ethnicity of the confronter. We know little about whether humor offers the same protection to confronters of various ethnicities, genders, sexual orientations, and so on. For example, the 'angry Black woman' stereotype portrays Black women as aggressive, overbearing, and hostile (Childs, 2005; Harrison, Pegoraro, Romney, & Hull, 2019). When the angry Black woman stereotype is evoked, a Black woman's witty confrontation may be discredited, and she may be viewed more negatively than White women who confront in the same manner. This may be especially likely if a Black woman's witty confrontation is seen as driven by her perceived anger, rather than the perpetrator's actions. Currently, we are testing whether the same witty confrontations employed by a Black woman versus a White woman are perceived as motivated by anger and seen as subsequently less effective. It may be useful to examine how stereotypes concerning warmth and competence affect perceived anger and the likeability of the confronter, along with the effectiveness of the confrontation.

It will also be important to test whether sharing a group membership with the confronter shapes the effectiveness and protectiveness of humorous confrontations. We know that ingroup confronters are typically better received than outgroup confronters (Czopp, 2019), but research has yet to test the limits of this effect. For instance, if men are more receptive to being confronted for sexism by a man versus a woman, would a White male confronter be more effective and receive less backlash than a Black male or Asian male confronter? The nature of bias (e.g., sexism, racism, heterosexism) and the perceived threat posed by the target group may be key to understanding the outcomes, with more threatening outgroup identities eliciting more backlash for the confronter and less attitude change from the perpetrator.

Future research should also test the cognitive demands required to generate humorous confrontations and the effect of cognitive load on one's willingness and ability to use humorous confrontation. Most people can vividly remember a time when they could not think of how to confront bias in the moment but later thought of the perfect (often witty) confrontation. Ability to produce humor is variable and strongly related to creativity (Clabby, 1980). For some, humor production is easy; for others, it is extremely difficult. Generating a witty confrontation may be more difficult than producing a non-humorous confrontation. Further, the stress of experiencing bias taxes one's cognitive capacity (Shelton et al., 2006), likely making humorous confrontation difficult even for those who are easily able to produce humor.

One way to make it easier for people to use humorous confrontations is to provide people with witty confrontations that can be used on-demand. We are beginning to examine whether providing participants with witty confrontations increases the likelihood of confrontation, especially if the response can apply to many biased remarks. For example, humorous confrontations such as 'Still single, huh?' 'Can you repeat that—I didn't hear you over my eyes rolling' and 'You're a real charmer' are general enough to be used as a response to most disparagement humor. Research on training people to confront using more general tactics suggests that this is a promising avenue to pursue. Lawson, McDonough, and Bodle (2010) found that when students practised using specific responses, they were more likely to confront compared to a control group that did not practice. Perhaps witty confrontation training would likewise increase rates of confronting.

We must also determine whether there are differences in the effectiveness and protectiveness of using humor to confront bias in imagined versus actual interactions. Our initial research has relied heavily on analogue studies, which typically ask participants to read a scenario that contains a person making a biased comment in a humorous or non-humorous manner, followed by the person responding with humorous or non-humorous confrontation. Participants then rate the effectiveness of the confrontation and the likeability of the confronter. Sometimes we ask participants how they think they would respond to sexist or racist jokes, with an eye toward capturing spontaneous, humorous confrontations. Although these first steps using analogue studies are typical, how people think they will respond rarely mirrors how they actually respond (Swim & Hyers, 1999; Woodzicka & LaFrance, 2001). We have recently begun to test the effects of witty confrontation during a dyadic interaction where a man or woman confronts male participants for sexism using a humorous or non-humorous confrontation.

Confronting group-based disparagement humor is especially challenging given the ambiguity inherent in humor. Biased messages that contain humor are perceived as less harmful and confrontation-worthy than those that are non-humorous. Thus, the decision to confront disparagement humor is more complex, and those who do confront may incur more social costs than those who confront non-humorous remarks. The most successful confrontations will stop the discrimination, let bystanders know that such behaviour is not acceptable, and mitigate the interpersonal costs associated with confronting. We focused on one strategy, witty confrontation, which shows initial promise in terms of both effectiveness and protection. Given that interpersonal confrontation may decrease bias, continued research on low-cost and effective confrontation strategies is justified.

References

Apter, M. J. (1991). A structural-phenomenology of play. In J. H. Kerr & M. Apter (Eds.), *Adult play: A reversal theory approach* (pp. 13–19). Amsterdam, NL: Swets & Zeitlinger.

Ashburn-Nardo, L., & Karim, M. F. (2019). The CPR model: Decisions involved in confronting prejudiced responses. In R. K. Mallett & M. J. Monteith (Eds.) *Confronting prejudice and discrimination: The science of changing minds and behaviors*. Philadelphia, PA: Elsevier.

Ashburn-Nardo, L., Morris, K. A., & Goodwin, S. A. (2008). The confronting prejudiced responses (CPR) model: Applying CPR in organizations. *Academy of Management Learning & Education*, 7(3), 332–342.

Attardo, S. (1993). Violation of conversational maxims and cooperation: The case of jokes. *Journal of Pragmatics*, 19, 537–558.

Bar, S. (2019). 44 of the best internet clapbacks to racists. Retrieved from https://www.boredpanda.com/comebacks-to-racist-comments/?utm_source=google&utm_medium=organic&utm_campaign=organic.

Bates, L. (2013). The best comebacks to sexist comments. Retrieved from https://www.theguardian.com/lifeandstyle/womens-blog/2013/dec/06/best-comebacks-sexist-comments-everyday-sexism.

Becker, J. C., Glick, P., Ilic, M., & Bohner, G. (2011). Damned if she does, damned if she doesn't: Consequences of accepting versus confronting patronizing help for the female target and male actor. *European Journal of Social Psychology*, 41(6), 761–773.

Bill, B., & Naus, P. (1992). The role of humor in the interpretation of sexist incidents. *Sex Roles: A Journal of Research*, 27(11-12), 645–664.

Blanchard, F. A., Crandall, C. S., Brigham, J. C., & Vaughn, L. A. (1994). Condemning and condoning racism: A social context approach to interracial settings. *Journal of Applied Psychology*, 79, 993–997.

Boysen, G. A. (2013). Confronting math stereotypes in the classroom: Its effect on female college students' sexism and perceptions of confronters. *Sex Roles*, 69, 297–307.

Cann, A., & Calhoun, L. G. (2001). Perceived personality associations with differences in sense of humor: Stereotypes of hypothetical others with high or low senses of humor. *Humor: International Journal of Humor Research, 14*(2), 117–130.

Childs, E. C. (2005). Looking behind the stereotypes of the "angry Black woman": An exploration of Black women's responses to interracial relationships. *Gender & Society, 19*(4), 544–561.

Clabby, J. F. Jr. (1980) The wit: A personality analysis. *Journal of Personality Assessment, 44*(3), 307–310.

Collison, D. L. (1988). Engineering humor: Masculinity, joking, and conflict in shopfloor relations. *Journal of Organizational Studies, 9*, 181–199.

Coser, R. L. (1959). Some social functions of laughter: A study of humor in a hospital setting. *Human Relations, 12*, 171–182.

Cowan, G., & Hodge, C. (1996). Judgments of hate speech: The effects of target group, publicness, and behavioral responses of the target. *Journal of Applied Social Psychology, 26*, 355–374.

Crandall, C. S., & Eshleman, A. (2003). A justification-suppression model of the expression and experience of prejudice. *Psychological Bulletin, 129*(3), 414–446.

Czopp, A. M. (2007, January). *Ramifications of confrontation observation: Does witnessing others' prejudice-related confrontations influence subsequent behavior?* Poster presented at the annual meeting of the Society for Personality and Social Psychology, Memphis, TN.

Czopp, A. M. (2019). The consequences of confronting prejudice. In R. K. Mallett, & M. J. Monteith (Eds.), *Confronting prejudice and discrimination: The science of changing minds and behaviors*. Philadelphia, PA: Elsevier.

Czopp, A. M., & Monteith, M. J. (2003). Confronting prejudice (literally): Reactions to confrontations of racial and gender bias. *Personality and Social Psychology Bulletin, 29*(4), 532–544.

Czopp, A. M., Monteith, M. J., & Mark, A. Y. (2006). Standing up for a change: Reducing bias through interpersonal confrontation. *Journal of Personality and Social Psychology, 90*, 784–803.

Devine, P. G., Monteith, M. J., Zuwerink, J. R., & Elliot, A. J. (1991). Prejudice with and without compunction. *Journal of Personality and Social Psychology, 60*, 817–830.

Dodd, E. H., Giuiliano, T. A., Boutell, J. M., & Moran, B. E. (2001). Respected or rejected: Perceptions of women who confront sexist remarks. *Sex Roles, 45*, 567–577.

Duchscherer, K. M., & Dovidio, J. F. (2016). When memes are mean: Appraisals of and objections to stereotypic memes. *Translational Issues in Psychological Science, 2*(3), 335–345.

Duncan, W. J., Smeltzer, L. R., & Leap, T. L. (1990). Humor and work: Applications of joking behavior to management. *Journal of Management, 16*(2), 255–278.

Ford, T. E. (2000). Effects of sexist humor on tolerance of sexist events. *Personality and Social Psychology Bulletin, 26*(9), 1094–1107.

Ford, T. E., & Ferguson, M. A. (2004). Social consequences of disparagement humor: A prejudiced norm theory. *Personality and Social Psychology Review, 8*(1), 79–94.

Ford, T. E., Wentzel, E. R., & Lorion, J. (2001). Effects of exposure to sexist humor on perceptions of normative tolerance of sexism. *European Journal of Social Psychology, 31*(6), 677–691.

Ford, T. E., Boxer, C. F., Armstrong, J., & Edel, J. R. (2008). More than "just a joke": The prejudice-releasing function of sexist humor. *Personality and Social Psychology Bulletin, 34*(2), 159–170.

Ford, T. E., Woodzicka, J. A., Triplett, S. R., & Kochersberger, A. O. (2013). Sexist humor and beliefs that justify societal sexism. *Current Research in Social Psychology, 21*, 64–81.

Ford, T. E., Triplett, S. R., Woodzicka, J. A., Kochersberger, A. O., & Holden, C. (2014). Not all groups are equal: Differential vulnerability of social groups to the prejudice-releasing effects of disparagement humor. *Group Processes and Intergroup Relations, 17,* 178–199.

Ford, T. E., Woodzicka, J. A., Petit, W. E., Richardson, K., & Lappi, S. (2015). Sexist humor as a trigger of self-objectification in women. *Humor: International Journal of Humor Research. 28,* 253–269.

Gervais, S. J., & Hillard, A. L. (2014). Confronting sexism as persuasion: Effects of a confrontation's recipient, source, message, and context. *Journal of Social Issues, 70,* 653–667.

Gervais, S. J., Hillard, A. L., & Vescio, T. K. (2010). Confronting sexism: The role of relationship orientation and gender. *Sex Roles, 63*(7-8), 463–474.

Good, J. J., Moss-Racusin, C. A., & Sanchez, D. T. (2012). When do we confront? Perceptions of costs and benefits predict confronting discrimination on behalf of the self and others. *Psychology of Women Quarterly, 36,* 210–226.

Goodman, D. (2011). *Promoting diversity and social justice: Educating people from privileged groups.* New York, NY: Routledge.

Gray, J. A., & Ford, T. E. (2013). The role of social context in the interpretation of sexist humor. *Humor: International Journal of Humor Research, 26*(2), 277–293.

Gulker, J. E., Mark, A. Y., & Monteith, M. J. (2013). Confronting prejudice: The who, what, and why of confrontation effectiveness. *Social Influence, 8*(4), 280–293.

Harrison, G., Pegoraro, A., Romney, M., & Hull, K. (2019). The "angry Black woman": How race, gender, and American politics influenced user discourse surrounding the Jemele Hill controversy. *Howard Journal of Communications Howard Journal of Communications, 31*(2), 137–149.

Haslett, B. B., & Lipman, S. (1997). Micro inequities: Up close and personal. In N. V. Benokraitis (Ed.), *Subtle sexism: Current practice and prospects for change* (pp. 34–53). Thousand Oaks, CA: Sage.

Hemmasi, M., Graf, L. A., & Russ, G. S. (1994). Gender-related jokes in the workplace: Sexual humor or sexual harassment? *Journal of Applied Social Psychology, 24*(12), 1114–1128.

Hyers, L. L. (2007). Resisting prejudice every day: Exploring women's assertive responses to anti-Black racism, anti-Semitism, heterosexism, and sexism. *Sex Roles, 56,* 1–12.

Kaiser, C., & Miller, C. T. (2004). A stress and coping perspective on confronting sexism. *Psychology of Women Quarterly, 28*(2), 168–178.

Kaiser, C. R., & Miller, C. T. (2001). Stop complaining! The social costs of making attributions to discrimination. *Personality and Social Psychology Bulletin, 27*(2), 254–263.

Kaiser, C. R., Hagiwara, N., Malahy, L. W., & Wilkins, C. L. (2009). Group identification moderates attitudes toward ingroup members who confront discrimination. *Journal of Experimental Social Psychology, 45*(4), 770–777.

Kuiper, N. A., Martin, R. A., & Olinger, L. J. (1993). Coping humour, stress, and cognitive appraisals. *Canadian Journal of Humor Science, 25,* 81–96.

LaFrance, M., & Woodzicka, J. A. (1998). No laughing matter: Women's verbal and nonverbal reactions to sexist humor. In J. Swim & C. Stangor (Eds.), *Prejudice: The target's perspective* (pp. 61–80). San Diego, CA: Academic Press.

Lawson, T. J., McDonough, T. A., & Bodle, J. H. (2010). Confronting prejudiced comments: Effectiveness of a role-playing exercise. *Teaching of Psychology, 37,* 257–261

Mallett, R. K., Ford, T. E., & Woodzicka, J. A. (2019). Ignoring sexism increases women's tolerance of sexual harassment. *Self and Identity.* Advance online publication. https://doi.org/10.1080/15298868.2019.1678519.

Mallett, R. K., & Wagner, D. E. (2011). The unexpectedly positive consequences of confronting sexism. *Journal of Experimental Social Psychology, 47*(1), 215–220.

Mallett, R. K., Ford, T. E., & Woodzicka, J. A. (2016). What did he mean by that? Humor decreases attributions of sexism and confrontation of sexist jokes. *Sex Roles, 75*(5-6), 272–284.

Mesmer-Magnus, J., Glew, D. J., & Viswesvaran, C. (2012). A meta-analysis of positive humor in the workplace. *Journal of Managerial Psychology, 27*(2), 155–190.

Monteith, M. J., & Voils, C. I. (1998). Proneness to prejudiced responses: Toward understanding the authenticity of self-reported discrepancies. *Journal of Personality and Social Psychology, 75*(4), 901–916.

Monteith, M. J., Ashburn-Nardo, L., Voils, C. I., & Czopp, A. M. (2002). Putting the brakes on prejudice: On the development and operation of cues for control. *Journal of Personality and Social Psychology, 83*(5), 1029–1050.

Monteith, M. J., Burns, M. D., & Hildebrand, L. L. (2019). Navigating successful confrontations: What should I say and how should I say it? In R. K. Mallett & M. J. Monteith (Eds.), *Confronting prejudice and discrimination: The science of changing minds and behaviors* (pp. 225–248). London, UK: Academic Press: Elsevier.

Mulkay, M. (1988). *On humor: Its nature and its place in modern society*. New York, NY: Basil Blackwell.

Paluck, E. L. (2011). Peer pressure against prejudice: A high school field experiment examining social network change. *Journal of Experimental Social Psychology, 47*, 350–358.

Parker, L. R., Monteith, M. J., Moss-Racusin, C. A., & Van Camp, A. R. (2018). Promoting concern about gender bias with evidence-based confrontation. *Journal of Experimental Social Psychology, 74*, 8–23.

Pérez, R. (2017). Racism without hatred? Racist humor and the myth of 'color blindness.' *Sociological Perspectives, 60*(5), 956–974.

Rasinski, H. M., Geers, A. L., & Czopp, A. M. (2013). 'I guess what he said wasn't that bad': Dissonance in nonconfronting targets of prejudice. *Personality and Social Psychology Bulletin, 39*(7), 856–869.

Rodin, M. J., Price, J. M., Bryson, J. B., & Sanchez, F. J. (1990). Asymmetry in prejudice attribution. *Journal of Experimental Social Psychology, 26*(6), 481–504.

Saunders, K. A., & Senn, C. Y. (2009). Should I confront him? Men's reactions to hypothetical confrontations of peer sexual harassment. *Sex Roles: A Journal of Research, 61*(5-6), 399–415. doi:10.1007/s11199-009-9638-0.

Shelton, J. N., & Stewart, R. E. (2004). Confronting perpetrators of prejudice: The inhibitory effects of social costs. *Psychology of Women Quarterly, 28*(3), 215–223.

Shelton, J. N., Richeson, J. A., Salvatore, J., & Hill, D. M. (2006). Silence is not golden: The intrapersonal consequences of not confronting prejudice. In S. Levin & C. van Laar (Eds.), *The Claremont symposium on Applied Social Psychology. Stigma and group inequality: Social psychological perspectives* (pp. 65–81). Lawrence Erlbaum Associates Publishers.

Sue, D. W. (2015). *Race talk and the conspiracy of silence*. Hoboken, NJ: Wiley.

Sue, D. W., Alsaidi, S., Awad, M., Glaeser, E., Calle, C. Z., & Mendez, N. (2019). Disarming racial microaggressions: Microintervention strategies for targets, White allies, and bystanders. *The American Psychologist, 74*(1), 128–142.

Swim, J. K., & Hyers, L. L. (1999). Excuse me—What did you just say?!: Women's public and private reactions to sexist remarks. *Journal of Experimental Social Psychology, 35*(1), 68–88.

Swim, J. K., Cohen, L. L., & Hyers, L. L. (1998). Experiencing everyday prejudice and discrimination. In J. K. Swim & C. Stangor (Eds.), *Prejudice: The target's perspective* (pp. 37–60). Cambridge, MA: Academic Press.

Swim, J. K., Hyers, L. L., Cohen, L. L., Fitzgerald, D. F., & Bylsma, W. B. (2003). African American college students' experiences with everyday anti-Black racism: Characteristics of and responses to these incidents. *Journal of Black Psychology, 29*, 38–67.

Swim, J. K., Gervais, S. J., Pearson, N., & Stangor, C. (2009). Managing the message: Using social influence and attitude change strategies to confront interpersonal discrimination. In F. Butera & J. M. Levine (Eds.), *Coping with minority status: Responses to exclusion and inclusion* (pp. 55–81). Cambridge, UK: Cambridge University Press.

Swim, J. K., Mallett, R., Russo-Devosa, Y., & Stangor, C. (2005). Judgments of sexism: A comparison of the subtlety of sexism measures and sources of variability in judgments of sexism. *Psychology of Women Quarterly, 29*(4), 406–411. doi:10.1111/j.1471-6402.2005.00240.x.

Tatum, B. D. (1999). When you're called a racist. *The Education Digest, 65*(1), 29–32.

Wang, K., Silverman, A., Gwinn, J. D., & Dovidio, J. F. (2015). Independent or ungrateful? Consequences of confronting patronizing help for people with disabilities. *Group Processes & Intergroup Relations, 18*(4), 489–503.

Woodzicka, J. A., & Ford, T. E. (2010). A framework for thinking about the (not-so-funny) effects of sexist humor. *Europe's Journal of Psychology, 6*(3), 174–195.

Woodzicka, J. A., & LaFrance, M. (2001). Real versus imagined gender harassment. *Journal of Social Issues, 57*(1), 15–30.

Woodzicka, J. A., & LaFrance, M. (2005). Working on a smile: Responding to sexual provocation in the workplace. In R. E. Riggio & R. S. Feldman (Eds.) *Applications of nonverbal communication* (pp. 139–155). Mahwah, NJ: Erlbaum.

Woodzicka, J. A., Mallett, R. K., & Melchiori, K. (2020). Gender differences in using humor to respond to sexist jokes. *Humor: International Journal of Humor Research, 33*, 219–238.

Woodzicka, J. A., Mallett, R. K., Hendricks, S., & Pruitt, A. V. (2015). It's just a (sexist) joke: Comparing reactions to sexist versus racist communications. *Humor: International Journal of Humor Research, 28*, 289–309.

Woodzicka, J. A., Mallett, R. K., & Melchiori, K. (2018, April). Fighting fire with fire: Using humor to confront sexist jokes. Paper presented at the Midwestern Psychology Association Annual Meeting in Chicago, IL.

Zou, L. X., & Dickter, C. L. (2013). Perceptions of racial confrontation: The role of color blindness and comment ambiguity. *Cultural Diversity and Ethnic Minority Psychology, 19*(1), 92–96.

INDEX

absurdity 16, 41, 42, 44, 46–8, 51, 54, 74, 76, 161, 163
advertising 4–11, 17–9, 21, 23, 32–8, 68, 72
ambiguity 42, 50, 57, 68, 114, 115, 121
ambivalence 3, 4, 11–9, 129, 186
ambivalence theory of humor 12
appraisal theory of emotions 11, 16

backlash 49, 191, 192, 195, 198, 200
benign violation theory of humor 12, 18, 57, 58, 72
bona-fide versus non-bona-fide information processing 69–71, 154
bonding 70, 74, 75, 77, 78, 82, 86, 171, 174

cavalier humor beliefs 161, 166, 170–87
clarification function 61, 63–5, 69, 70, 71
communication competence 130–8, 140
confronting: bias 191, 192; disparagement humor 189, 193–9; discrimination 195; public 191; prejudiced responses model 193; humorous/witty vs. non-humorous 197–200
coping 76, 83, 85, 114, 171; humor 72, 77, 84
counterargument disruption 22, 48, 51
creativity: humor and 62, 65, 70, 75, 115, 200

delegitimization toolkit 180–2
differentiation function 61, 67–9, 70, 71
discounting: message 22, 30, 30, 49, 50
disparagement/putdown humor 68, 133, 151–64, 177, 189–90, 193–201
disparagement theory of humor, *see* superiority theory of humor
disposition theory 134, 135, 137, 138, 139
dissonance 44, 102, 192
distraction: by humor 4, 5, 6, 22, 76, 138, 139, 144

divisive humor 60, 61

explicit versus implicit: communication 131; message 20, 25–6, 151, 154
elaboration likelihood model 4, 5, 22, 29, 49, 137, 138
emotion regulation: model 76, 83; extrinsic interpersonal 77
enforcement function 61, 65–7, 69, 70, 71
ethnography 111, 114, 117–9, 120, 123

gateway theory 30
gender/sex differences 87, 115
gender functions 115–6
group-dominance model of humor appreciation 173, 175, 176, 177, 184

heteronormativity 86
hierarchy 113, 114, 115, 124, 173, 178, 182
honesty-humility 173
humor mindset 12, 154–5, 159
humor orientation scale 141, 142
humor styles: model 61; questionnaire 78, 171, 172, 174

identification function 61–3, 64, 65, 69, 70, 71
identity threat 44, 45, 46, 50, 51, 163, 164
incongruity theory of humor 70, 112, 133–4, 143
incongruity resolution 11, 16, 135, 137, 139, 141
in-group versus out-group: stereotyping 176, 178, 179, 181, 184, 200
instructional humor processing theory/ IHPT 137–45
integrated threat theory 178
intractable conflict 39, 40, 42, 43, 51

irony 65, 94–6, 103, 104

justification-suppression model of humor 193

leadership 62, 68, 114–5
learning: affective 140, 142, 143; cognitive 140, 141, 142
legitimising myths 160, 173–7
lifespan: changes across the 87, 183

machiavellianism 173
memory: recall 21, 23, 130; recognition 21, 23; retention 21, 23, 131, 138, 139
mirth 57, 77, 83, 94, 133, 143
modern racism 172, 175
mood: humor effects on 5, 29, 77, 113, 175

narcissism 173
natural selection theories 75–6
need for cognition 25, 30
need for structure 172
neuroscience 93, 98
norms/social norms/group norms: 5, 58, 59, 60, 62, 64, 65, 66, 67, 68, 115, 118, 120, 131, 132, 137, 143, 152–4, 158, 171, 173, 174, 175, 183, 184, 191, 193

offensive humor 136, 140, 143
organisational citizenship behaviour 114

persuasion, humor effects on: attention 4, 5, 21, 23, 44, 48, 49, 63, 64, 131, 138, 141, 163, 174; attitudes 4, 7–11, 13, 14, 21–3, 24–7, 29–31, 47–51, 151, 153, 157, 160, 161, 177, 189, 190–1, 197, 200; purchase behavior 21; source credibility 21, 63, 134, 142
playfulness 82–3
political correctness 122, 124, 183
political: comedy 20, 24, 25, 27, 29, 30; efficacy 25, 28, 30; engagement/participation 25, 28, 29, 30; interest 25; knowledge 25, 27, 28, 29
pragmatic effect 96, 97, 101, 102, 105
prejudice: legitimisation of 160; normative window model of 153;
release of 173, 193 subversion of 161–3
prejudiced norm theory 152–3, 159, 180
psychopathy 173

racist humor/joke 12, 132, 151, 158, 189, 191, 195, 196, 200
rape proclivity 159
related versus unrelated humor 5, 135, 136, 140, 144, 145
relational humor 77, 80–1, 88; inventory 78, 81
relational process model 113
relational-functional models 77–8
relationship success 75, 78
relief theory/release theory/arousal relief theory 133, 134–5, 143
rhetorical question 94, 95, 103, 196
right-wing authoritarianism 172

safety valve theory of humor 117
satire 4, 6, 9, 10, 20, 21, 22, 23, 24–6; Horatian versus Juvenalian 30, 48; simple 20, 24; complex 20, 21, 23, 25, 26, 29, 30
self-categorization theory 178
self-deprecating humor: political 24–6
self-expansion theory 76
self-objectification 163, 184, 189
sexism: #metoo 111, 123, 124, 181; institutional 156; hostile 156, 157, 159, 177, 178, 179, 180, 181, 193
sexist humor/joke 26, 115, 152, 156, 157, 158, 159, 163, 180, 184, 189, 193, 194, 195, 196, 197, 198
sexual violence 158, 159
shared identity 63
sleeper effect 49
social identity theory 178
social dominance theory 160, 172, 173
social dominance model of humor appreciation 160
social dominance orientation 160, 172
social identity threat 163, 164
stereotypes 121, 136, 151, 155, 157, 158, 161, 162, 164, 173, 189, 193, 199
stress relief 113–4
subversive humor 161–3
superiority theory of humor 133, 134, 135, 143

task goal versus relational goal 131
teasing 67, 83, 94, 118, 122, 136, 172
three dimensional model of humor in
 romantic relationships 79

unfreezing 41–7

unifying humor 60, 61
unlaughter 117

wheel model of humor 115
work performance 113, 114–5,
 116, 123